WE ARE
PUGET SOUND

DISCOVERING & RECOVERING THE SALISH SEA

DAVID L. WORKMAN | LEONARD FORSMAN | MINDY ROBERTS | BRIAN J. CANTWELL

PHOTOGRAPHY BY BRIAN WALSH AND OTHER CONTRIBUTORS

FOREWORD BY MARTHA KONGSGAARD

IN PARTNERSHIP WITH WASHINGTON ENVIRONMENTAL COUNCIL

BRAIDED RIVER

Contents

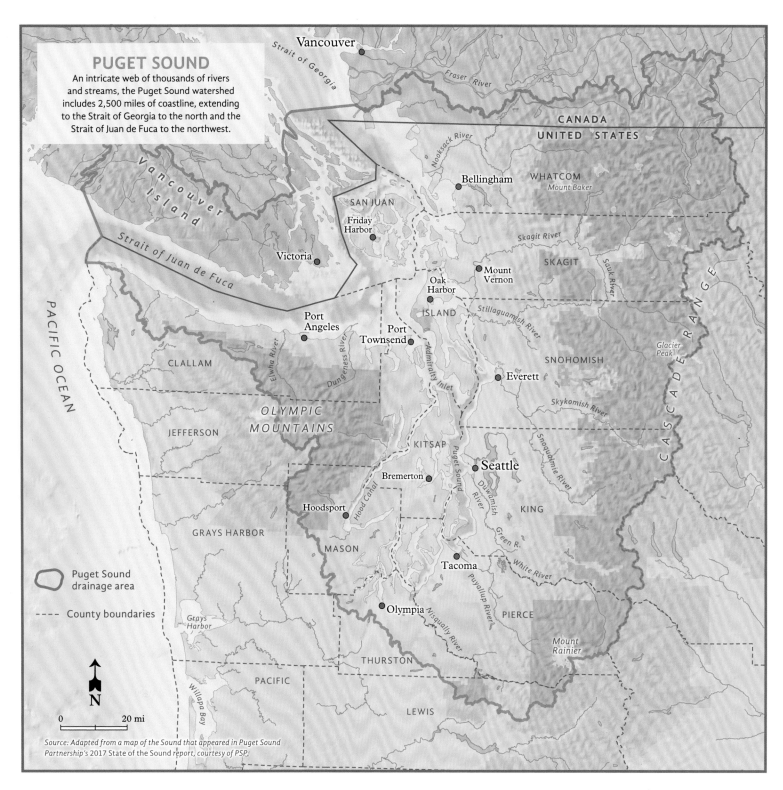

PUGET SOUND

An intricate web of thousands of rivers and streams, the Puget Sound watershed includes 2,500 miles of coastline, extending to the Strait of Georgia to the north and the Strait of Juan de Fuca to the northwest.

Vancouver

Strait of Georgia

Fraser River

CANADA
UNITED STATES

Nooksack River

Bellingham

WHATCOM

Mount Baker

Vancouver Island

SAN JUAN

Friday Harbor

Skagit River

Mount Vernon

SKAGIT

Sauk River

Victoria

Strait of Juan de Fuca

Oak Harbor

ISLAND

Stillaguamish River

Port Angeles

Port Townsend

Admiralty Inlet

SNOHOMISH

Glacier Peak

CLALLAM

Elwha River

Dungeness River

Everett

Skykomish River

PACIFIC OCEAN

OLYMPIC MOUNTAINS

JEFFERSON

KITSAP

Puget Sound

Snoqualmie River

C
A
S
C
A
D
E

R
A
N
G
E

Bremerton

Seattle

Duwamish River

KING

Hoodsport

Hood Canal

Green R.

MASON

White River

GRAYS HARBOR

Tacoma

Puyallup River

Puget Sound drainage area

County boundaries

Grays Harbor

Olympia

Nisqually River

PIERCE

Mount Rainier

Willapa Bay

PACIFIC

THURSTON

N

0   20 mi

LEWIS

Source: Adapted from a map of the Sound that appeared in Puget Sound Partnership's 2017 State of the Sound report, courtesy of PSP.

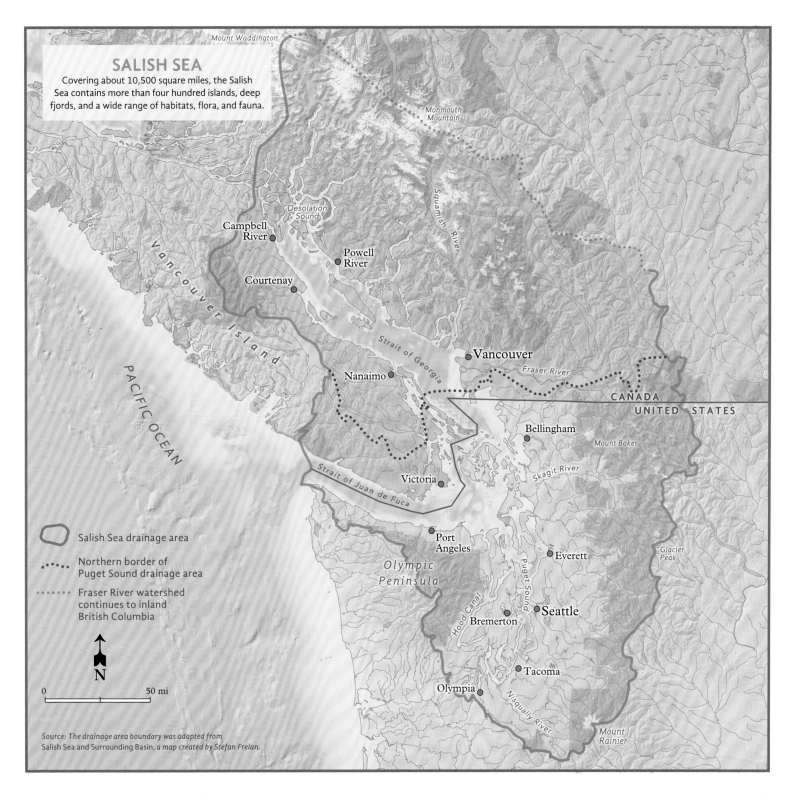

SALISH SEA

Covering about 10,500 square miles, the Salish Sea contains more than four hundred islands, deep fjords, and a wide range of habitats, flora, and fauna.

Mount Waddington

Monmouth Mountain

Squamish River

Desolation Sound

Campbell River

Powell River

Courtenay

Vancouver Island

Strait of Georgia

Vancouver

Fraser River

CANADA

UNITED STATES

Nanaimo

Bellingham

Mount Baker

Victoria

Skagit River

Strait of Juan de Fuca

PACIFIC OCEAN

Port Angeles

Olympic Peninsula

Everett

Glacier Peak

Puget Sound

◯ Salish Sea drainage area

•••• Northern border of Puget Sound drainage area

•••••• Fraser River watershed continues to inland British Columbia

Bremerton

Seattle

Hood Canal

↑
N

Tacoma

0   50 mi

Olympia

Nisqually River

Mount Rainier

Source: The drainage area boundary was adapted from Salish Sea and Surrounding Basin, a map created by Stefan Frelan.

Great egrets like this one searching for food in Billy Frank Jr. Nisqually National Wildlife Refuge were hunted nearly to extinction in the late nineteenth century. Their feathers were used in fashionable attire, particularly hats. Concern about the plight of the great egret and similar birds with striking plumage led to the passage of laws to protect birds from such plunder. These egrets have since recovered and their population is now stable—a testament to the resilience of nature.

THE TRIBES OF THE SALISH SEA

For thousands of years, indigenous peoples have lived throughout the greater Salish Sea region. Their numerous tribes have developed a rich culture and established hundreds of seasonal camps and permanent villages. The arrival of tall ships from Europe in the late 1700s led to profound change in their lives.

Monmouth Mountain

Homalco

MAINLAND COMOX

Klahoose

ISLAND COMOX

SLIAMMON

Sliammon

SQUAMISH

Squamish River

Comox

SECHELT

Tait

Shíshálh (Sechelt)

HALKOMELEM

Fraser River

PENTLATCH

Qualicum

Squamish   Tsleil-Waututh

Vancouver

CANADA
UNITED STATES

Nanoose

Kwikwetlem (Coquitlam)   Katzie   Chehalis

Musqueam

Nanaimo

Kwantlen   Stó:lō

Pilalt

Snuneymuxw

Chilliwack

Strait of Georgia

Tsawwassen

Sumas

Chemainus

Semiahmoo   Nooksack

Penelekut

Lummi   NOOKSACK

Quw'utsun' (Cowichan)

Bellingham

Nuu-Chah-Nulth

Malahat

STRAITS SALISH

Nuwhaha

Mount Baker

Skagit River

Saanich   Samish

Saanich/ Esquimalt   Songhees

Upper Skagit

Strait of Juan de Fuca

T-Sou-ke

Victoria

Swinomish

Sauk-Suiattle

NORTHERN LUSHOOTSEED

PACIFIC OCEAN

Skagit

Port Angeles

Stillaguamish River

Stillaguamish

Glacier Peak

Makah

Lower Elwha Klallam

Jamestown S'Klallam

Tulalip

Snohomish

Port Gamble S'Klallam

Skykomish

S'KLALLAM

Quilleute

Suquamish

Snoqualmie

Puget Sound

Seattle

TWANA

SOUTHERN LUSHOOTSEED

QUINAULT

Hood Canal

Duwamish

Quinault

Skokomish

Muckleshoot

Puyallup

Squaxin Island

Tacoma

White River

Steilacoom

Olympia

Nisqually

UPPER CHEHALIS

Chehalis

Nisqually River

Mount Rainier

LOWER CHEHALIS

COWLITZ

Cowlitz

TWANA Language Territory

Skokomish Culture

N

0   50 mi

Source: S'abadeb, the Gifts: Pacific Coast Salish Art and Artists, edited by Barbara Brotherton, published by Seattle Art Museum and University of Washington Press, 2008.

Looking toward Mount Rainier from Oro Bay on Anderson Island, Puget Sound's southernmost island, accessible via ferry from Steilacoom

Foreword

Summarizing what modern physics has understood about time, theoretical physicist Carlo Rovelli explains that it is the measure of change, not of permanence and not of being, but of becoming. Although the modern tenancy of the great Puget Sound basin has been a mere century and a half, its impact has been enormous enough to fundamentally alter its pre-European grandeur, majesty, and functionality. In this part of the twenty-first century, her inhabitants, her constituents, here in what we wistfully call "Salmon Nation," struggle to find the best language to describe our world, both natural and man-made, which continues its ceaseless flux, ubiquitous impermanence, continual transformation.

And so we ask ourselves as we look both backward and toward an unknowable future, what is the value or collective meaning of this unusual part of our country, this northeastern shore of the Pacific? We recognize that we are all People of the Salish Sea and the uplands that feed this enormous estuary, which bisects the 49th parallel, where more than eight million of us live. Surely, it is a place, an idea, an ideal, a future, the sum of its historic parts. It is our shared vernacular. It's a chemical and biological system that churns on with or without our inputs or protections. It is the economic engine of the region, a source of communal pride.

It's a superhighway, shipping apples and wheat and crude oil along the mighty Strait of Juan de Fuca, a 100-kilometer gouge that cuts across the continental shelf sending an Amazon River–size flow of nutrient-rich, deep-ocean water into the Salish Sea. It's what attracts and keeps the right-brain economy here and our left brain sane. It is a rallying cry, and a spiritual hallowed ground, from the snowcaps to the white caps, from the Campbell and Powell Rivers in the north and west to the Makah tribal lands, from the western flanks of Mount Shuksan in the North Cascades to the Olympic Sculpture Park in Seattle.

It has been said to be one of only a few places that is so lovely, so temperate, so varied, so well watered, so civil, so wealthy, so educated, and so new. Mount Baker has been known to bank up to seventy-two feet of snow in a season while the easterly rain shadow of the Olympic Range reduces the precipitation in Sequim to a miserly Los Angeles equivalent of sixteen inches per year. It's remote in part: Gettysburg gets more visitors in a busy weekend than the half-million-acre North Cascades National Park gets in a year. The major port city of Seattle is the fastest growing city in the United States while the lesser known British Columbian city of Surrey is on track to grow at double the rate of Vancouver and surpass it in size by 2030. In terms of its future, its population is only going to grow, a lot. We are forecasted to receive an extra dose of folks from drought-stricken regions that we are already referring to as Water Refugees.

It is the quantifiable—the stats on the pH, the dissolved oxygen, the length of the coastline, the yearly snowpack. And it's the ineffable—the value of sharing these waters with the totemic and endangered orca and the chinook they depend on; the value of a softened waterfront bulkhead, reengineered for the sake of salmon and those bottom-of-the-food-chain herring;

the undeniable majesty of an old-growth cedar; of learning (over and over) how to better share these lands with and respect the treaty rights of the first peoples, our tribal brothers and sisters. It is about the value of seeing the sun rise on the flanks of Mount Kulshan and set over the Brothers through clear skies increasingly compromised by wildfire smoke in summer.

But it is also in fact a dumping ground, the background, the place we take for granted, a backdrop for short-term thinking. The great Salish Sea receives all of the waters brought by gravity through the basin, from your house in Sequim or Tacoma or our house in Burnaby, creating the toxic soup that comes from simply waking up on a modern North American morning and getting to work.

It's complex, it's complicated, and it's difficult to figure out a solution, what will get it done. There are lists, top 10s—do this, don't do that, vote for her, buy that product, don't buy stuff, get kids outside, get out of your car, fund transit, enforce regulations.

It's science, it's policy, it's the primacy of cheap energy, it's equity, and our obligation to the yet arrived. It's the underlying philosophies upon which we build our lives and which we therefore want to see reflected in our government (or maybe we just want to see the dismemberment of same). It's demographics and pernicious incentives, it's treaty rights, it's property rights, it's facts that the citizenry don't buy when their values trump the best available science. How do we think about "recovery" of a deeply altered ecosystem in a world where the population is growing but the geography isn't (barring "the big one"!)— and then manage out twenty years, another twenty, and on, out seven generations?

You don't have to be John Muir to understand this notion: that when you pull on a single thing in nature, you find it is attached to everything else. To this nearly perfect aphorism, I add: you'll find that it is attached to *everyone* else as well. The answer is in fact *all of the above* as we move toward what Jane Jacobsen called a durable prosperity, managing the ecosystem with people at the center, toward, as she championed, a resiliency that expresses equally our rights and responsibilities to each other in a world with a reduced carrying capacity.

We all struggle to avoid feeling overwhelmed by the complexity of it all. The United Nations estimates that the world's population has reached beyond seven billion. Understanding that in the past fifty years, the global population has more than doubled, we ask ourselves: What are the implications for the eight million people living around the Salish Sea today? By 2040, the equivalent of another Portland is projected to nestle its way into the four counties around Seattle alone—whether we plan for them or not.

How will the Möbius strip of science and policy help us understand our choices as we grapple with our need to conform the economy to the limits of nature? To this need we add the twin peril devilishly linked to population growth—climate change. This seminal challenge will take a planetary collective response whose success will be measured in geologic time. In the debate between transition and transformation, as my friend K. C. Golden would say, we have no time for the former and hopefully it is not too late for the latter.

AND SO WHAT TO DO WITH THESE FACTS, THIS ALARM? Data without a constituency is a simple report. "Tell your story," urged the legendary Nisqually tribal elder and moral lodestar of this region, Billy Frank Jr. This is a story worth telling over and over from multiple perspectives as we take our turn at stewarding this "universe in a mountain cradle," as William Dietrich calls it, these troubled but treasured waters and the people who call this place home. Let's ask ourselves as we absorb this history and stories, what we would attempt, what we would safeguard and with what vigor, how we would live if we thought we couldn't fail, if we thought this would be our last year on this implausibly beautiful blue-and-green planet.

There exists in this region a vast citizenry of neighbors, immigrants, citizen scientists, students, agitators, developers, multiple generations of recreational anglers, and barefoot little clamming kids who make up a virtual army of the committed, selfless, and often impatient. These are people whose experiences in the outdoors establish a fresh baseline every time a fish is caught or isn't, every time a whale plies the water or doesn't, every time the snowpack accumulates sufficiently to feed the rivers on time in the spring or doesn't. This loose affiliation of witnesses and actors is strung across the landscape like a shield, protecting and advocating for this singular place on earth. It will take them all caring deeply and armed with facts to join in a collective

The former chair of the Puget Sound Partnership Leadership Council, Martha Kongsgaard participates in a roundtable discussion about restoration efforts.

effort to understand what is at stake as the earth warms and the seas sour.

Make no mistake—this is how we will be remembered: by how well we managed this sacred obligation, what we left behind.

—Martha Kongsgaard, September 2019

OPPOSITE Pablo and Maura Silva harvest certified organic strawberries from their farm in the Skagit Valley. A sustainable approach to farming, such as that practiced by the Silvas, helps preserve the health of agricultural land while also protecting Puget Sound from harmful runoff from fertilizers and pesticides.

ABOVE The Puget Sound region supports an abundance of farmers markets, including Seattle's iconic Pike Place Market, which offer locally grown and seasonal fruits, vegetables, fish and shellfish, meat, poultry, eggs, and flowers. The region's farmers markets provide a variety of jobs and strengthen connections between farmers, consumers, and the land.

ABOVE Seward Park Audubon Center director Joey Manson advances nature-based education programs that facilitate positive experiences in Seattle's wild spaces.
OPPOSITE Magnificent birds of prey, snowy owls occasionally venture as far south as the Puget Sound region from the Arctic in winter. These two owls are confronting each other after one arrived on the other's perch.

OPPOSITE Snow geese blanket a field in the Skagit Valley near Mount Vernon. The Skagit River delta, Skagit Bay, and surrounding farm fields provide habitat for thousands of wintering waterfowl, among other creatures.

ABOVE A flock of snow geese

Puget Sound serves as habitat for both transient and resident orcas.

Introduction

"I think I heard a whale blow!"

The young woman standing next to the rail on the Washington State Ferry *Kennewick* looked out across Admiralty Inlet to scan for the telltale signs of orcas, or killer whales. On this rare clear January day in 2018, sunshine bathed the labyrinthine patterns in the surface currents with light. In this turbulent passage, nearly all of the water within Puget Sound is exchanged with that of the Straits of Juan de Fuca and Georgia, an area that altogether is collectively known as the Salish Sea.

"There they are! Next to the sailboat! Orcas!"

The passengers on the upper deck all dashed to the port side to watch four orcas, including one juvenile, surface and blow—one even spy-hopped. The *ooh*s and *aah*s sounded like people watching fireworks. For a nominal fee to ride the ferry, passengers were treated to a spectacular whale-watching outing, albeit one that did not slow down for a long look. Snippets of conversation revealed that a few passengers were tourists but most were people who lived in the Puget Sound region. Another woman remarked to her companion, "I feel honored to witness this." The squeals, animated talking, and rapid snaps of photos indicated that the feeling was shared.

Moments like this are what tie many of us to this wondrous place. Yet they also bring into sharp relief the struggle of the Southern Resident killer whales, orcas that subsist almost entirely on chinook, not only to thrive but survive in the Salish Sea, raising questions about the future of our region, and the orcas. Here in Washington, we have a strong foundation for action at the state and local levels—hopefully at the federal level, too—and we have the technology we need to do so. Yet we are not making progress fast enough, and the Southern Resident orca population has continued to decline, to seventy-four individuals at the time of this writing. For us at Braided River and Washington Environmental Council, the question is not "Can we?" but "Will we?"

Will we reverse the stunning decline of chinook salmon, on which people and orcas feed? Will we implement modern controls on stormwater that collects toxic substances which in turn drains into the Sound where those substances accumulate in the fatty tissue of orcas? Will we address the disruption that vessels, including ferries, pose to orcas? Will we discuss with our friends and neighbors why we value the Sound? Will we stand up and demand that our elected officials prioritize and champion the health of the Salish Sea? Will we fund the programs needed for Puget Sound protection and recovery?

Over ten years ago, then governor Chris Gregoire established 2020 as the target date to achieve recovery of Puget Sound. Yet political will and public engagement have lagged.

For the Salish peoples who have called our region home for millennia, this place is known simply as Whulge, a Lushootseed word that means "saltwater." Native American and First Nations communities were, and still are, connected by canoes that ply the near and far waters of Puget Sound, the entire Salish Sea, and the Pacific Ocean. These journeys forge deep connections, strengthen relationships, serve as shared spiritual events, and fuel trade.

Construction at Seattle's West Point wastewater treatment plant in 1994 revealed stones carved more than three thousand years ago. Unique to the central British Columbia coast, these artifacts remind us of the longevity of the relationships between the peoples and communities around us.

Today's residents include Native Americans and First Nations peoples, as well as later transplants from faraway lands. In the 1850s, settlers of European descent lived alongside native peoples, but also battled over land and resources. This struggle over the resources of the region continues to this day. The population now exceeds eight million people—millions of individuals seeking economic opportunities and a sense of well-being—and we expect the US portion of the population to double over the next fifty years. Future residents will want clean water and clean air, safe and affordable homes, and diverse and sustainable economic opportunities. How do we grow while preserving shared cultural values, abundant natural resources, and wildlife?

We are honored to bring you this book. Our goal is to strengthen public engagement and build the political will necessary to make the recovery effort a success through an exploration of the people and places of our Sound. The actions needed to support orca recovery will, in turn, address pollution and habitat problems that threaten our future. This book reminds us of the inspiring people, places, and natural creatures that define our region, and what is at risk if we do not succeed. Now is the time for a renewed focus on Puget Sound and, by extension, the Salish Sea.

The orcas are our canary in the coal mine—an indicator of the overall health of our region. The 1989 *Exxon Valdez* oil spill in Alaska seriously affected two pods, one of them resident and the other transient, in Prince William Sound. The following year, the affected resident group declined by 33 percent while the transients declined by 41 percent. The affected transient pod no longer has any reproductive-age females, so it is on track to become extinct. The 10.8 million gallons of oil that coated Prince William Sound for months now seem a distant memory, as do the widespread calls to action that emerged following the spill, as people fought for safety protections and asked why, as a nation, we were not transitioning to clean energy faster. Yet the reality is that oil remains in the sediment of Prince William Sound, fisheries have declined, and the resident orca population has declined significantly.

We protect what we love, we love what we know, and we know what we see. The hard-to-see threats of habitat destruction, pollution, and fragmented communities make pinpointing a single villain difficult. Puget Sound lies downstream of all of us, its lovely surface hiding the impacts of our individual and collective decisions. How do we as a society recognize the slower moving, less obvious human actions that are causing the decline of orcas in the Salish Sea region today?

Washington Environmental Council has partnered with The Mountaineers and Braided River, an imprint of Mountaineers Books, to bring you this book because we are deeply committed to the protection and recovery of Puget Sound. WEC's mission is to protect, restore, and sustain Washington's natural environment for all: too often people of color and tribes are disproportionately impacted by pollution, yet their voices are not heard by decision-makers.

In these pages, you'll meet some of the exceptional people of Puget Sound and visit some of the notable places that make up our region as well as our shared history. You will hear the voices of individuals who did not consider themselves conservationists until they witnessed devastation firsthand, triggering them to act. People whose lives and livelihoods are intricately

After traveling thousands of miles across the Pacific Ocean, this male sockeye is headed upstream to its spawning grounds.

interwoven with the health of the Sound share their stories and remind us all of the rich tapestry that defines the region.

We also provide a glimpse into the future of Puget Sound recovery. That future will depend on people like Laura James, who spotlights the underwater reality of stormwater pollution, people like Jeromy Sullivan and Ron Charles, who are leading their tribe into economies of the future. It will depend on people like you, who recognize your connections to our people and places. Each of us can rewrite the future of our Sound.

Beyond the pages of this book, we invite you to explore our companion website, www.wearepugetsound.org, and share what "My Puget Sound" means to you, because every viewpoint is fundamentally different, from a new technology worker from India joining the Seattle workforce, to a farmer in the Skagit Valley whose parents and grandparents tilled the same soil, to a tribal member harvesting shellfish when the tide goes out.

We cannot accept the notion that further damage is inevitable, and we need your help to reverse existing damage. Habitat degradation, pollution, and overharvesting are not solely modern phenomena. An 1892 publication described "sewage from unclean sewers pouring down contagion and filth" to the Duwamish River—a pollution pattern that continues today. Lake Union supported a trout population that was wiped out by 1905 from residential and industrial development. And an 1874 poem laments the damage logging did to commercial clam harvests.

Change takes public pressure to happen and it moves slowly. The good news is that as we recognize the negative impacts past practices have had on natural resources—and on people—we are making progress. We stopped dumping industrial waste directly into places like Commencement Bay in Tacoma, and life is returning even to Superfund sites like the Thea Foss Waterway, the inlet connecting the bay to the Tacoma tideflats. Shellfish beds that were closed because of bacterial pollution are being reopened with the help of community-based support and solutions. Changing habits will ensure that working forests and farms continue to support rural economies. By adopting new practices, our community can continue to grow while maintaining the natural resource web that defines our region and us.

Anthropologist Margaret Mead once wrote: "Never doubt that a small group of thoughtful, committed citizens can change the world; indeed, it's the only thing that ever has." In this book and in the companion website, we share with you the remarkable people and places that define us. Our hope is to grow the chorus of voices who actively value and protect this wonderful place.

We *are* Puget Sound. We need your help to accelerate Puget Sound's recovery. That's the only way we will succeed in preserving the people, places, and orcas for future generations to enjoy.

—Helen Cherullo, Publisher,
Braided River, an imprint of
Mountaineers Books

—Mindy Roberts, Puget Sound Director,
Washington Environmental Council

Found west of the Cascade Range from southern British Columbia to Northern California, the Pacific rhododendron can reach heights of up to thirty feet. Native plants like this flowering bush depend on healthy soil and clean water.

A kayaker navigates a turbulent area of the Snoqualmie River. Descending from the west side of the Cascade Range near North Bend, the Snoqualmie meets the Skykomish River near Monroe to form the Snohomish River, which in turn empties into Puget Sound at Everett. The health of our region's rivers directly affects the Sound.

A family gathers around a bonfire at Golden Gardens in Seattle as the sun sets behind the Olympic Mountains across the Sound—the sort of shared experience that connects people to each other and to the natural world.

Kelp beds, such as this one near Lime Kiln Point on San Juan Island, support myriad fish, including salmon and rockfish, as well as river otters, crustaceans, and sea urchins.

Looking northeast from Friday Harbor, on San Juan Island, toward Shaw and Orcas Islands: only four of the numerous islands in this archipelago between Vancouver Island and the mainland US are accessible via state ferry.

LEFT A black bear rests on a downed tree on the Olympic Peninsula, home to protected old-growth forests of Sitka spruce, western hemlock, coastal Douglas-fir, and western redcedar. Black bears on the Peninsula feed on huckleberries and spawning salmon, as well as the bark of young trees and insect mounds.

OPPOSITE The Dungeness River on the Olympic Peninsula supports a variety of wildlife, including salmon. The combination of deciduous and coniferous trees in the riparian forest and the varying ages and sizes that result when the forest recovers from flooding makes for excellent habitat. Bigleaf maple, cottonwood, willow, alder, Douglas-fir, and western redcedar are all common in this habitat.

Looking toward the Olympic Mountains at sunset from the Nisqually Reach in South Sound: protecting critical habitat, including eelgrass beds, pocket estuaries, and sandy beaches, the aquatic reserve named after the reach extends from the Nisqually River delta north to McNeil Island.

OUR PUGET SOUND

DAVID L. WORKMAN

CANADA AND THE UNITED STATES SHARE MORE THAN A national border where they meet on the verdant Pacific coast. They also share a spectacular gathering place. It is the Puget Sound and Salish Sea watershed—an intricate web of thousands of rivers and streams. It is also an ecosystem, a multitude of living things and their habitat. At the heart of this basin is an inland sea. The US waters are often collectively referred to as Puget Sound, although some definitions do not include the San Juans. Once you have seen and experienced this place, you will not forget it.

Here, the salty Pacific Ocean surges in and out of a dramatic, glacier-carved, geologically active coastline. In the Salish Sea, saltwater mixes with the freshwater from gentle uplands and the soaring peaks of the Olympic Mountains and Cascade Range of Washington and from the Coast Range and Vancouver Island Ranges of British Columbia.

The ocean enters this landscape from the outer coast, between Washington's Olympic Peninsula and British Colum-

bia's Vancouver Island, by way of the Strait of Juan de Fuca, a wide, deep, and often storm-tossed channel. Continuing inland, the strait meets Admiralty Inlet, south of which lies what is sometimes more strictly defined as Puget Sound. To the north, the strait meets Whidbey Island and the waters surrounding the San Juan Islands, part of the more broadly outlined Puget Sound. Farther north, the waters surround British Columbia's Gulf Islands and become the Strait of Georgia in the Inside Passage between the Canadian mainland and massive Vancouver Island.

In 2009 and 2010, the boards of geographic names for Washington State and British Columbia designated these shared waters, as far north as Desolation Sound, as the Salish Sea. The name recognizes the Coast Salish Indian tribes and First Nations peoples who have lived here for thousands of years. But the true boundaries of this region are wider still—branching upward along the rivers and creeks of the Cascade Range and the Olympic Mountains.

Raindrops on Douglas-fir needles: the ecosystem of Puget Sound is driven by water.

The Salish Sea in both nations includes about 10,500 square miles of sea surface area (the equivalent of three Yellowstone National Parks) and hits a maximum depth of more than 2,100 feet in the Georgia Basin of Canada. Its 4,600 miles of shoreline includes 419 islands. Reaching up to the crests of the surrounding hills and peaks, its total area is more than 68,000 square miles on both sides of the international border. The entire Salish Sea watershed is nearly as large as Oklahoma or Missouri.

The American waters include numerous straits, passages, smaller sounds, inlets, and bays. Among them are Hood Canal, Rosario Strait, Possession Sound, Saratoga Passage, Elliott Bay, Commencement Bay, Sinclair Inlet, Dyes Inlet, Carr Inlet, the Nisqually Reach, Case Inlet, Dana Passage, and a series of finger inlets at the southern end of the Sound, including Henderson, Budd, Eld, Totten, and Hammersley Inlets and Skookum and Oakland Bays. The name "Puget Sound" was originally given to the American waters in 1792 by British Naval Captain George Vancouver during an exploration of the area, in honor of his loyal lieutenant, Peter Puget. Some Coast Salish tribes called it Whulge, or "saltwater."

This fantastic maze of sea and land is the product of a restless planet. Along with tectonic and volcanic convulsions, earth-shaping glaciers advanced and retreated repeatedly over millions of years, carving out the basin that became the inland waters of Washington and British Columbia. The result is a dazzling collection of islands, peninsulas, bays, beaches, bluffs, and tidewater flats. In the southern lowlands of the Sound, the glaciers also left behind vast amounts of rocks, glacial sediments, numerous lakes, and deep depressions, as well as hundreds of aligned north-to-south hills.

This landscape is both epic in scale and intensely intimate. Whether you are standing on its shore or sailing on the waters, everywhere you look, your eyes behold both land and sea. Nowhere on the Sound are you out of sight of a shore or headland, backed by towering mountain summits beyond.

Twice daily, tides come and go, inundating and laying bare the coastal sea beds along shorelines of gravel, cobblestones, random glacial boulders, mudflats, and bluffs topped with towering evergreen trees, madronas, maples, and giant ferns. The beaches are rimmed with tangles of driftwood brought to shore by Puget Sound's big tides—typically ten to fourteen feet, compared to a few feet on the US Gulf coast and the mid-Atlantic coast. The tides and currents of the Sound demonstrate their power every day.

Parker MacCready, professor of oceanography at the University of Washington, observed in the *Puget Sound Fact Book* that "the tides are what cause the strongest currents," notably in Admiralty Inlet, at the Tacoma Narrows, and strongest of all at Deception Pass, the forbidding narrow passage between

Whidbey and Fidalgo Islands. Professor MacCready says that "because of its glacial origins, the Sound is deep"—averaging about 230 feet, compared to about 20 feet in expansive Chesapeake Bay on the mid-Atlantic coast. He says the deepest place in Washington's Puget Sound basin is off the northern tip of Bainbridge Island—nearly 940 feet.

Despite the overall depth of Puget Sound, it is the shallower waters, particularly at low tide, that challenge boats with motors or those with deep drafts, like keeled sailboats. Many a boater has run aground while motoring or sailing past underwater obstructions like shoals, spits, gravel bars, or rock outcrops, making nautical charts and depth-finding gear standard equipment. You'll also see an array of different markers for navigation that serious boaters watch for and understand. And all around, natural and man-made landmarks can be visual guides—towering peaks in every direction, Hood Canal's and Lake Washington's floating highway bridges, the soaring double span of the Tacoma Narrows Bridge, Seattle's Space Needle and skyscrapers, the monumental state capitol buildings in Olympia, and the load-lifting cranes at the Seattle waterfront.

Puget Sound lovers instantly recognize (and may be able to name) the ferries, large and small, plying their routes, carrying passengers and vehicles to and from mainland ports and island landings. Washington's state ferry system, the nation's largest, operates numerous runs from twenty terminals serving Seattle, Tacoma, Mukilteo, Bremerton, Port Townsend, Whidbey Island,

Usually made from large trees, particularly western redcedar, totem poles fulfill several cultural purposes, from commemorating ancestors and recounting legends to welcoming visitors, for the tribes of the Pacific Northwest coast. *Why the Sun Always Shines*, a totem pole carved by Dale Faulstich, was donated to the City of Sequim by the Jamestown S'Klallam Tribe.

State ferries, like the *Elwha* docked here at Orcas Island, enable locals and visitors to travel to and among several of the San Juan Islands, as well as to Whidbey, Bainbridge, and Vashon Islands and the Kitsap and Olympic Peninsulas. Washington operates the nation's largest ferry system with twenty terminals and numerous vessels crossing the Sound every day.

Bainbridge Island, Vashon Island, and the San Juan Islands. These routes, officially part of the state highway system, are complemented by private or county-operated ferries serving several smaller islands in Washington waters, up and down the Sound and the Salish Sea. Farther north, BC Ferries connects the province's mainland with Vancouver Island and numerous smaller islands in the Salish Sea. Private ferry services also transport travelers between the British Columbia capital, Victoria, and the Washington cities of Port Angeles and Seattle.

OUTSIDE THE CITIES ALONG THE SOUND, THE VIEW FROM the water is dominated by two colors: snow-white and green. The white is the permanent snowpack and ice on the peaks of the Cascades and the Olympics, especially the massive Cascade volcanoes. On a clear day (yes, there are clear days), these "mountains of fire and ice" are jaw-droppingly beautiful from great distances. Mount Baker, also known by its Nooksack and Lummi Indian Nation names of Koma Kulshan or Kulshan, hovers 10,781 feet above the inland sea to the far northeast. It is cloaked year-round with snow and ice, including fifteen named glaciers. In 1999, the nearby Mount Baker Ski Area set a world record for measured snowfall in a single season, at ninety-five feet. From the Sound, on the right day and from the right location, you can see the aptly named Glacier Peak, reaching 10,541 feet but partially hidden behind other majestic peaks in the Cascade Range.

Ninety miles farther south, Rainier commands attention at 14,410 feet. The fifth highest mountain in the Lower 48 (Mount Whitney in California is the highest), it is the most prominent from top to bottom and in girth. Known as Tahoma by the local native peoples, it has twenty-six major glaciers and thirty-six square miles of permanent snowfields and ice.

These high places are the upper margins of the Puget Sound watershed and ecosystem. The snow and ice that gather on the peaks melt as temperatures warm, combining with rain on the west-facing slopes to follow gravity's pull into rivulets and streams. Along the way, they pick up minerals, nutrients, and sediments, and transport them into the Sound, where they contribute to its richness and biological abundance.

The Salish Sea's largest source of freshwater is Canada's Fraser River, which drains a huge area of British Columbia. Other important sources include Canada's Squamish River, plus Washington's Cedar, Duwamish-Green, Elwha, Nisqually, Nooksack, Puyallup, Skagit, Skokomish, Snohomish, and Stillaguamish Rivers, many with local native names. These freshwater streams make Puget Sound an estuary, or transition zone, for thousands of species of fish, mammals, and birds, invertebrates, and plants—and for an estimated eight million people living on both sides of the international border.

From the water, a vast cloak of intense green dominates the shoreline outside the cities. Historically, the Puget Sound lowland forests were a mix of western redcedar, western hemlock, and Douglas-fir. Drier sites produced mixed forests of Douglas-fir, Garry oak, Pacific dogwood, and madrona (notable for its boa-like curling branches and reddish bark) along water's edge. Another common tree in the coastal zone is the bigleaf maple, which is commonly adorned with fuzzy moss, lichens, and ferns. These maples can reach heights of 160 feet, with broad crowns and leaves that can measure a foot across.

In a 2007 report for the Washington Department of Natural Resources (DNR), Robert Van Pelt said, "The dominance of evergreen conifers in the Pacific Northwest makes it unique among the temperate regions of the world." Western

OPPOSITE The region's snowpack and glacial meltwater feeds the rivers and ultimately the Sound. Meltwater from Winthrop Glacier on the northeastern side of Mount Rainier flows into the White River, which joins the Puyallup River and in turn flows into Commencement Bay in Tacoma.

ABOVE The Puget Sound region offers seemingly endless opportunities to get outside year-round.

Known as Tahoma by local tribes, Mount Rainier is the southernmost Cascade volcano in the Puget Sound watershed. Its slopes harbor twenty-six major glaciers, some of which are visible from Burroughs Mountain, northeast of the summit, as shown here.

Volcanic peaks, like Mount Baker east of the coastal city of Bellingham near the Canadian border, dominate the landscape around Puget Sound.

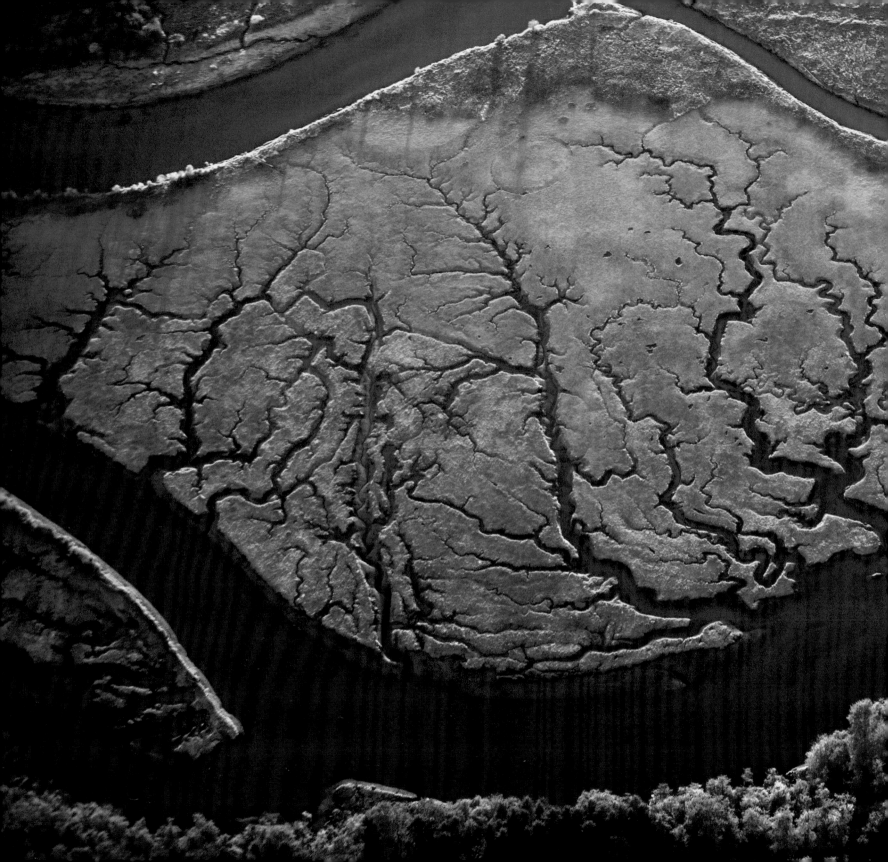

Washington, he says, "is part of the most heavily forested portion of the United States." Van Pelt went on to say, "Prior to Euro-American settlement, more than 96 percent of the forests of Western Washington were coniferous." Even today, with all the changes that humans have brought to the Puget Sound region, the preponderance of conifers shouts "green" to those afloat on the Sound's waters.

The Puget Sound watershed has a high-latitude Mediterranean climate, with cool, wet winters and warm, dry summers. The weather makers for the region are the vast Pacific Ocean, the prevailing southwesterly winds in winter and westerly-northwesterly winds in the summer, and the high peaks of the Olympic Mountains and the Cascade Range. The mountain ranges wring moisture from the air and clouds, but how much falls varies by location. Seattle's average annual precipitation is near thirty-eight inches. Olympia's average is fifty inches. Anacortes on Fidalgo Island in the Salish Sea receives about twenty-eight inches. Port Townsend on the northeastern Olympic Peninsula gets nineteen inches.

Ocean temperature and the region's weather are cyclically affected by El Niño, which tends to bring warmer and drier conditions to the Pacific Northwest in the fall and winter, and La Niña, which brings cooler-than-normal weather. Climate change in the region, and globally, is also affecting temperatures. In 2013, the Intergovernmental Panel on Climate Change reported that 1983 to 2012 was likely the warmest thirty-year period in 1,400 years in the Northern Hemisphere. In 2019,

Restoring tidal marshes, such as this one at the mouth of the Nisqually River, increases habitat for salmon and other wildlife and reestablishes Puget Sound floodplains that have been altered by humans. This tidal marsh restoration project is the largest of its kind to date in the Pacific Northwest.

Boats are docked in a marina in Budd Inlet, the southernmost arm of Puget Sound. From kayaks to ferries, boats let people experience the Sound up-close.

US government agencies declared 2014–2018 to be collectively the warmest years on record globally.

The annual average temperature for the Puget Sound area is about 60°F. As for the water, be prepared to shiver, but you won't have to ice fish. In July or August, the average water temperature is 57°F. In shallow bays of the southern Sound, you may find water around 70°F on a hot summer day. In January, the average water temperature in the Sound is 46°F. This means Puget Sound doesn't freeze over, although a thin layer of slush or ice may sometimes form in the small inlets or bays in the southern Sound, like Budd Inlet.

Oceanographer MacCready explains that the shallow waters of the South Sound "tend to be fresher (referring to less salty) and warmer, and hence less dense, than the deep waters." This, he says, creates layers, or stratification, in the water column. As a whole, Puget Sound's waters are 83 percent ocean water, but Budd Inlet near Olympia is only about 66 percent ocean and 33 percent freshwater.

According to MacCready, the ocean water mixes with less dense river water at "hot spots" of tidal turbulence, like the Tacoma Narrows. The mixing forces the heavier ocean water to the surface. "This provides the energy to keep the exchange flow going throughout the year, pulling ocean water into the deep Sound and expelling slightly fresher surface water back to the Pacific."

He says the ocean water remains in the Sound an average of about two months before being pushed back out to the Pacific. But near Whidbey Island, and in the South Sound, ocean water lingers only about a month, and in Hood Canal, where tidal currents and mixing are relatively weak, it typically remains as long as four months. However, in some locations, he explains, Hood Canal circulation can be even more stagnant, leaving some water to remain longer, possibly even years.

AS ANALYTICAL BEINGS, HUMANS SEEK TO BREAK THINGS down into their component parts. Over time and in different contexts, the name Puget Sound has referred to different parts of the inland sea. Increasingly, it has come to be understood by many Puget Sounders, including public policy makers and government agencies, as referring to all the inland marine waters in Washington State. This is the meaning that is intended by the contributors to this book.

One way of looking at the components of our sea is to define geographic basins or sub-basins. Eight regions constitute the Salish Sea:

- **STRAIT OF JUAN DE FUCA:** Southern and primary entrance to the Salish Sea, where water exchanges with the Pacific Ocean, shared by the US and Canada. Rivers enter from the Olympic Mountains of Washington and Vancouver Island in Canada.

- **STRAIT OF GEORGIA:** Northernmost part of the Salish Sea with a small entrance from the Inside Passage of Canada. Also called the Georgia Strait or Georgia Basin, this basin receives the largest freshwater source to the Salish Sea, the Fraser River, which drains much of the province of British Columbia.

- **SAN JUAN:** Includes the island group of the same name, plus Washington's Nooksack and Samish watersheds, and areas influenced by the Fraser River, which flows out of the British Columbia Coast Range past metropolitan

Letting Nature Heal a Shore

BABE (DOROTHY) KEHRES and her three brothers—the children of Ann and John Powel—grew up sharing their piece of paradise with the otters, seals, eagles, herons, ducks, and other Puget Sound creatures that their father loved.

Since 1954, Powel family members have enjoyed life on an idyllic point of land at Port Madison, on north Bainbridge Island—nearly twelve acres of low-bank waterfront and tidelands. They are the most recent occupants of this sheltered homestead. Ancient shell piles there date back at least seven centuries, bearing testimony to countless generations of inhabitants who processed shellfish for food and trade.

Sitting on the stone patio outside the 1920s vintage sandstone house where her mother lives at ninety-seven years of age, Babe gazes out at the arc of water, seashore, and ancient Douglas-fir trees. The Powel place is the site of the largest shoreline restoration project on private property in the Puget Sound basin. In 2012, the family and the Bainbridge Island Land Trust, with many partners, removed more than 1,500 feet of shoreline "armoring"—a mix of concrete bulkhead, riprap, and creosote wood retaining walls. Then they put in more than 2,600 native plants to improve nearshore vegetation. Within a few years after the new planting, a healthy ribbon of vegetation is apparent along the shore, and the native saltmarsh vegetation has expanded—supporting insects that are food for fish. Babe often sees herring jumping, and watches bubbles surfacing from little water creatures "getting their nightly feed."

Herring and other nearshore fish are vital food for salmon, which have declined throughout Puget Sound and the region. Brenda Padgham, conservation director for the Land Trust, explains that all of Bainbridge's fifty-three miles of shoreline is classified as critical habitat for different kinds of Pacific salmon throughout many of their life stages.

Designing the project, acquiring government permits, removing the armor, restoring the tidelands and beach, and putting in native vegetation has so far cost about $479,000. It was made possible by Salmon Recovery Funding Board "Puget Sound Acquisition and Restoration" grants, plus the family, volunteer efforts, and the Land Trust (the project sponsor). By reestablishing a naturally resilient shoreline, Babe's family no longer needs to maintain, repair, or replace bulkhead and other armoring on their waterfront property.

A Land Trust conservation easement protects the restoration efforts permanently and includes provisions prohibiting future shore armoring at the site, while also stipulating that trees toppling onto the beach must remain there. Brenda Padgham explains: "In nature, a messy beach is a good beach. It provides food and shelter for sea life."

"We could never have done it on our own," says Babe. "None of us in the family had the scientific or legal knowledge to deal with it." The Land Trust has documented the process, challenges, and results so other conservation partnerships with private landowners can benefit from what has occurred here.

Looking out over the native shrubs and across the beach at low tide, Babe says: "I just think in my conscience that what we've done is the right thing for the environment."

Vancouver into the sea. The greater San Juan basin includes San Juan and Whatcom Counties, and part of Island and Skagit Counties.

- **WHIDBEY:** Spans the area from Deception Pass to the Snohomish River delta, including the Skagit, Stillaguamish, and Snohomish watersheds. It includes Skagit, Snohomish, and Island Counties.

- **NORTH CENTRAL:** A sea-bottom sill generally marks the boundary between the central basin and Strait of Juan de Fuca, at Admiralty Inlet. This basin has no large watersheds and is bordered by Jefferson and Island Counties and the northern tip of Kitsap County.

- **SOUTH CENTRAL:** Includes the metropolitan eastern Sound and the suburbanizing western Sound. The urban and suburban shoreline includes south Snohomish County, King County, parts of Kitsap and Pierce Counties, and Vashon-Maury Island.

- **HOOD CANAL:** Long, narrow, hook-shaped Hood Canal is really a glacier-gouged channel rather than a man-made canal. As the *Encyclopedia of Puget Sound* explains: "Water circulation in the Canal is a serious issue. The average depth is only 177 feet, but it reaches a maximum depth of 600 feet, and circulation is poor, especially in the southern portion. Water from the Strait of Juan de Fuca mixes poorly due to an underwater sill south of the Hood Canal Bridge, and freshwater entering the canal often forms a layer at the surface." This sub-basin is the least urbanized of the Sound, and is bounded by Jefferson, Mason, and Kitsap Counties.

- **SOUTH SOUND:** The Tacoma Narrows clearly defines the transition to the South Sound and its many inlets, passages, and shallow bays and coves.

THE COMINGS AND GOINGS OF OCEAN WATER AND OCEAN creatures are the heartbeat of the Salish Sea. The SeaDoc Society, which conducts and sponsors scientific research in the inland waters of the Pacific Northwest, sums it up this way: "Oceanographic processes such as freshwater inflows and wind-driven surface currents exchange biota [animal and plant life], sediments, and nutrients throughout the larger ecosystem." The Pacific Ocean has been making the rules for the inland sea since long before humans arrived on the scene.

In a political sense, the Salish Sea is governed by the United States and Canada, by tribes and First Nations, and by state, province, and local governments. Partnerships among these entities and their respective research institutions have improved information sharing and protection and restoration efforts.

But there is a larger—and deeper—reality. "The [international] border is invisible to marine fish and wildlife," the society notes. Species, including those listed as threatened or endangered under the US Endangered Species Act or the Canadian Species at Risk Act, "traverse the boundary daily." It's a case of species without borders. It's how the ecosystem operates. Welcome to Puget Sound and the Salish Sea.

Sharing Her Love of Puget Sound

There was no large body of water for EMMA RODRIGUEZ to experience where she grew up in north central Mexico in the 1970s. But that changed in a big way when she came to the Seattle area, first Ballard and then Edmonds, and created her family of Puget Sounders. It was there that she fell in love with the salt air. "It gives me energy to see and smell the ocean. It gives me motivation to keep going," she says.

In 2015, Emma learned about, and eagerly signed up for, Washington State University Snohomish County Extension Beach Watchers, a group of more than one hundred Beach Watchers and thirty-five or so Beach Naturalists who donate more than eight thousand hours in community education and research about the Salish Sea in Snohomish County. Similar programs exist in Skagit, Island, Kitsap, and Jefferson Counties.

Emma spends most of her beach volunteer time at Mukilteo Lighthouse Park and at Brackett's Landing in Edmonds, a city-owned shoreline sanctuary next to the state's busy Edmonds-Kingston ferry terminal. Brackett's is famous for what lies under the water just off the beach—Edmonds Underwater Park, a magnet for scuba divers who explore a series of man-made reef structures and sunken vessels that form an extensive artificial habitat for a wide variety of marine life. On her beach visits, Emma sees a diverse array of people of all ages enjoying the urban coastline.

She is inspired by the act of helping people understand "how we can take care of the creatures." She says, "If I can help even a tiny amount, I am happy to do it. What concerns me most is the garbage. I like to walk on the beach, and I find straws, socks, cans, plastic bags, bottle caps, all kinds of trash."

Emma is encouraged by bans on plastic shopping bags in Seattle and in Thurston County at the south end of the Sound. She applauds Seattle's ban on the use of plastic straws—and the decision by Starbucks to quit using plastic straws in the company's network of coffee shops.

"Since I am Hispanic, I would like to see more education about the sea," she says. "I would like to see bilingual workshops for people speaking Spanish and other languages. We are part of this, and it is important that we learn how to take care of it." Emma has invited Spanish-speaking moms with young kids to the beach to learn about the ecosystem here and how to protect it. For example, she teaches them to avoid crushing the beach creatures by being careful where they walk.

When a friend's mother visited from Mexico, Emma invited her to the beach, where she walked in the water and got her photo taken with divers. On a subsequent trip, Emma took her to the Seattle Aquarium. "She touched the sea stars. She saw so many creatures," Emma relates. "She had never seen anything like that before, and now she encourages her daughter and the family to visit the beach and the aquarium."

And so it goes in Emma's life, creating friends and advocates for Puget Sound, one visitor at a time.

Ochre sea stars are slowly recovering after a mysterious wasting disease wiped out millions along the West Coast. Researchers hypothesize that the virus may have been exacerbated by warming ocean and air temperature. Scientists believe that sea stars, a keystone species of intertidal areas, were saved by juveniles developing genetic resistance to the virus, an example of evolution in action.

OPPOSITE Estuaries along the Sound serve as critical habitat for migrating shorebirds, like these western sandpipers, that pass through on their way to the Arctic to nest.
ABOVE Hundreds of species of birds, including dunlins, rely on Puget Sound during at least part of their life. Beaches are important habitat for dunlin, which feed on marine worms, small crustaceans, and mollusks.

ABOVE From salmon to salmonberries, the Pacific Northwest landscape offers sustenance.

OPPOSITE Coast Salish tribal members sing to celebrate the 2007 Canoe Journey hosted by the Lummi Tribe at their Stomish Grounds west of Bellingham. This growing annual tradition to celebrate and honor the cultural heritage of the Coast Salish tribes was revived with the Paddle to Seattle in 1989.

Kennedy Creek flows into Oyster Bay between Olympia and Shelton in South Sound. The preserve named for it includes the creek's tidal reaches and adjacent salt marsh, tidal flats, uplands, and riparian flats, which serve as critical feeding areas for more than one hundred forty species of birds and provide food and shelter for coastal cutthroat trout, steelhead, coho salmon, and a robust fall run of chum salmon.

EXTRAORDINARY NATURE

DAVID L. WORKMAN

PEOPLE WHO SPEND THEIR LIVES ALONG OR ON PUGET Sound may fully comprehend the extraordinary nature of this place. For the rest of us, however, the inland sea and its grand surroundings are a mystery that reveals itself as we experience it.

We can exult in the excitement of watching a family of orcas breaching the surface of the Sound, arching backs and dorsal fins slicing the water's surface, on their way to the next meal. We can bask in the cuteness of a harbor seal floating on its back on a calm day, or at the sight of powerful migrating salmon lunging from the water. But to comprehend the nature of Puget Sound, we can also start close to home.

WETLANDS—WILDLIFE NURSERIES OF THE SOUND

A good place to learn about the ecology of Puget Sound is at the edge of a bog or pond, or any wet, marshy place near where you live or work or go to school—even if it's many miles from the saltwater shoreline.

Wetlands are where water covers the soil or is present at or near the surface, either all year or for parts of the year. These areas are some of the most productive habitats on earth— providing food and shelter to mammals, birds, fish, and invertebrates, and often serving as nurseries. They also filter pollution out of water and buffer nearby areas from flooding.

The Washington Department of Ecology has described three basic types of wetlands: Bogs occur in cool, wet areas where the drainage is poor and where there may be floating mats of vegetation and very dark-colored water. Swamps (or forested wetlands) usually occur along rivers with vegetation that is dominated by trees and shrubs. Marshes lack trees and can be either saltwater or freshwater.

All types of wetlands contribute to Puget Sound's health. In addition to creating homes for many wildlife species that are part of the Sound's web of life, wetlands also absorb storm runoff, filtering out toxics and animal waste that are lifted off the ground in rain and storm events. They are nature's sponges.

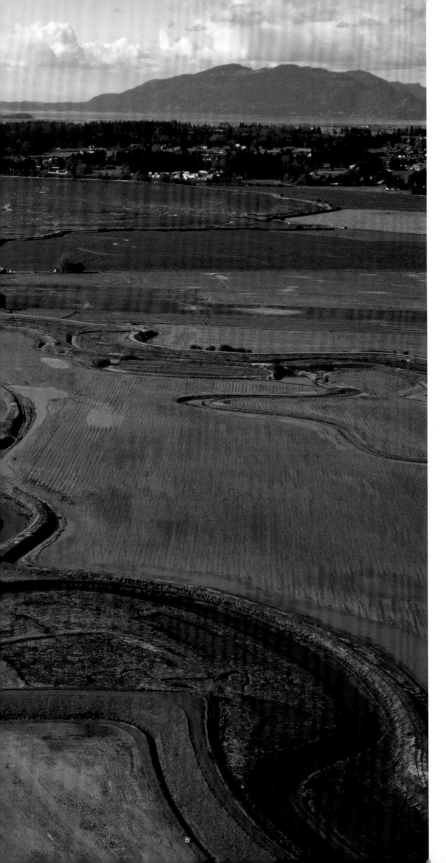

Wetlands are rich with plants, insects, and animals. For example, the Edmonds Marsh, just north of Seattle, is one of the few remaining Puget Sound urban saltwater estuaries—a mixing zone of freshwater and marine species. The twenty-two-acre oasis provides shelter and food for over 225 species of resident and migratory birds, including a nesting colony of great blue herons, a species that is notoriously shy and standoffish around humans.

In King County, Washington's most densely populated region, field inventories of remaining lowland wetlands documented over one hundred species of birds, including thirty species of ducks and geese, nine species of wading birds such as herons and egrets, six species of coots and grebes, plus many species of shorebirds, raptors, and seabirds. They found thirty-five species of mammals, including beavers, muskrats, river otters, cougars, and raccoons, and fourteen species of amphibians, including toads, frogs, salamanders, and newts.

Wetlands are so important that Washington has a goal of achieving an overall "no net loss" in the acreage or functioning capacity of the remaining wetlands around Puget Sound, as well as elsewhere in the state. The state has detailed maps and geographic information system (GIS) data identifying wetlands, rivers, streams, lakes, and other aquatic habitats that must be protected. The US Fish and Wildlife service also has a National Wetland Inventory.

When a highway or housing or commercial development is built, the project plans must address wetlands protection—either avoiding or minimizing damage, or offsetting unavoidable

A slough charged by the Skagit River feeds into Padilla Bay. The Skagit is renowned for its abundant salmon runs, including all five species native to Puget Sound: chinook, chum, coho, pink, and sockeye. Estuarine habitat is critical for rearing juvenile salmon.

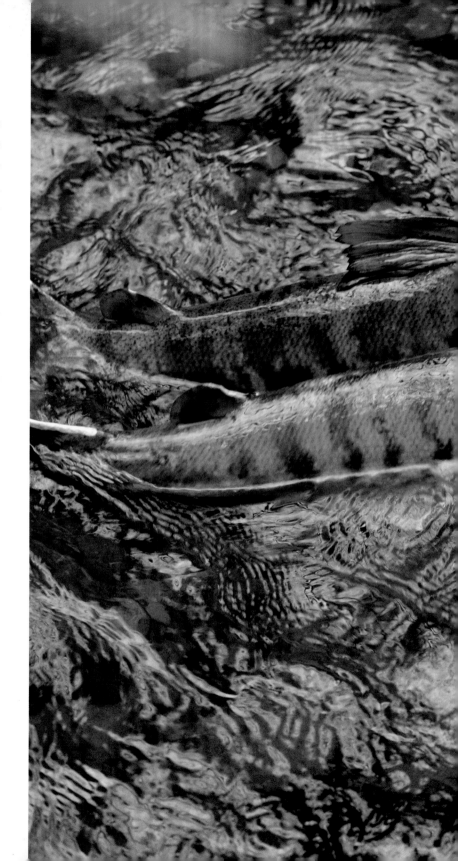

damage through mitigation. In some cases, as a last resort, the state can allow "compensatory mitigation," which means the builder, developer, or landowner must offset unavoidable damage by creating, restoring, enhancing, or preserving other wetlands in a similar area. Every wetland in the Puget Sound watershed contributes to the web of life and the purity of the water in the Sound.

RIVERS AND ESTUARIES, WHERE FRESHWATER AND SEA MEET

Thousands of streams, from the smallest rivulets to the mighty rivers, feed Puget Sound. King County's environmental program explains the importance of rivers and streams in this way: "Many of our Pacific salmon and trout species are anadromous—meaning they are born in our streams, they migrate to the ocean to feed and grow into mature adults, and then they return to their natal stream to spawn. These fish, therefore, are both freshwater and marine species, depending on the time of year. Of this group, the species of Pacific salmon, members of genus *Oncorhynchus*, are by far the most important and iconic." Puget Sound rivers, streams, and nearshore areas support eight species of salmon, seagoing trout, and char. Four of them are listed for protection under the Endangered Species Act: chinook and (summer) chum salmon, bull trout, and steelhead.

The return of these seagoing fish to their natal waters is a sight to behold. In countless places around the Sound, visitors can walk to the water's edge and watch the mighty fish as they work their way up their native streams to a gravelly place where the females will deposit their unfertilized eggs and the males will deposit their sperm.

Between twenty and forty thousand chum salmon spawn annually in Kennedy Creek in the southern reaches of Puget Sound.

Waterfalls and man-made structures, such as dams, reveal the power of a salmon or steelhead to jump and muscle its way up, around, or over obstructions during these seasonal fish runs. The fish will leap until they either clear the obstruction or, for some man-made structures, find a fish ladder (a concrete sluiceway with a series of water baffles allowing fish to pass). The drive to reproduce and continue the species is a truly impressive force.

More than a century and a half of dam building and road construction has blocked fish passage up and down numerous streams. Washington's state Fish and Wildlife agency has estimated there are 18,000 to 20,000 barriers to salmon and steelhead migration in streams across the state. A case brought by the Washington state treaty tribes in 2001 resulted in a 2016 federal court order that Washington must restore salmon habitat by removing or replacing fish-blocking road culverts. In 2018, the US Supreme Court let the order stand.

Meanwhile, 80 percent of tidal marshes and river estuaries in the Sound were diked and drained to take advantage of the rich agricultural soils and flat, easily developed terrain. In recent years, restoring estuaries has gained special focus from fishery and wildlife agencies, tribes, state and federal funding programs, local governments, and conservancy groups. Removal of dikes from former farmland in the Billy Frank Jr. Nisqually National Wildlife Refuge between 2008 and 2011 reestablished hundreds of acres of estuary for fish and other wildlife, including the plants and insects that help make deltas biologically rich. In 2018, another major estuary restoration was celebrated in the Snohomish River delta at Everett. Dike removals at Smith Island opened up 378 acres of

At an underwater viewing window, a child observes sockeye salmon returning to spawn through the Ballard Locks in Seattle.

A well-camouflaged American bittern searches for food at Billy Frank Jr. Nisqually National Wildlife Refuge. Bitterns feed on fish, as well as small vertebrates, crustaceans, and insects, in their wetland habitat.

critical estuary habitat for salmon and other species and provided public access to the estuary through a nearly $30 million project supported by Snohomish County, Everett, and grants from several state and federal agencies. With the completion of the Smith Island project, the county, the city, Port of Everett, Department of Fish and Wildlife, and the Tulalip Tribes have together restored more than 1,200 acres of estuary habitat in the Snohomish delta.

SKAGIT BAY IS AN ESTUARY SOUTHWEST OF MOUNT Vernon, the meeting place of the Skagit River, born in the glaciers and snowfields and lakes of the North Cascades, and the Sound. It is a paradise for birds and for bird-loving people. The bay provides habitat for thousands of migrating waterfowl, including swans and snow geese, plus migrating shorebirds, song birds, and raptors, such as ospreys, bald eagles, peregrine falcons, and northern harriers.

If you walk or paddle along even the smallest of streams as they enter a bay, you may see herons methodically stalking through the shallows in search of an unsuspecting fish or frog for lunch. If you are lucky, a river otter will leave its well-hidden den and dive into the water in search of a meal of fish, mussels, crab, crayfish, amphibians, aquatic beetles, birds, or eggs. A kingfisher may dart from a tree into the water for a meal with fins, all the while making its ratchet-sounding call. You may find any number of species of showy ducks plucking grasses or aquatic plants, or diving for small fish, insects, frogs, or snails.

In a meandering creek or cove, focus your eyes on the tangle of overhanging trees and roots and the jumble of logs and driftwood. Look for the watery passageways where fish and amphibians dart about, out of the reach of airborne predators. Any stream, no matter where or how small, is significant. Streams are so important that several organizations around

Harnessing the Power of People Working Together

CASSANDRA HOUGHTON has never forgotten the day in 2009 when a guest speaker came to her ninth-grade classroom in Maple Valley, Washington, as part of her Pacific Northwest history unit, "Sounding Off on Puget Sound." Peter Donaldson, a sustainability educator, "drew three things on the board that changed my life," she says. It was a diagram of the "triple bottom line" for a healthy Puget Sound—overlapping circles representing ecology, people, social equity, and the economy. From that day on, Cassandra understood that human needs are an essential dimension of sustaining healthy ecosystems, including the breathtaking Sound that has captivated her since her family moved to Washington from Oklahoma.

When she and fellow students were assigned call-to-action projects, she wrote a letter that was published by the Maple Valley Covington *Reporter*, urging her fellow community members to help keep pollution out of Puget Sound. "That's the first time I realized that I could make an impact, that I had power with my voice as a young individual, that I could educate others, and that I could make real change in my community," she says.

Cassandra joined a student leadership program and helped develop an award-winning series of video reports on positive sustainability trends in the Lake Washington and Cedar River watershed, an area encompassing thirteen school districts and twenty-seven schools. She began learning about actions she and other community members can take to keep contaminants out of the Sound, like using biodegradable soap, avoiding car washing on impervious streets and driveways, and creating rain

gardens to increase the amount of rainwater settling into the ground rather than racing off into our waterways with loads of pollution.

Joining a group called Sustainability Ambassadors, Cassandra worked with other students to create rain gardens, lay porous parking surfaces that absorb water, and install a 1,500-gallon rainwater harvesting cistern at a school. A bottom line, Cassandra says, is for students to discover that "you can be problem solvers now."

Cassandra went on to earn a bachelor's degree in science with an emphasis in ecology and sustainable systems from The Evergreen State College in Olympia. She became the first paid intern at Sustainability Ambassadors, working with her early mentor, Peter Donaldson. Later she was hired as the student leadership coordinator for the group. The ambassadors partner with several school districts to equip staff to teach students real-world engineering on a range of sustainable systems including stormwater, water supply, and wastewater solutions.

For Cassandra, the Sound is more than a cause. It's a personal experience. She describes a place on Eld Inlet in the southern reaches of the inland sea, where a zigzag trail leads to a beautiful beach where "bioluminescence comes out in the water this time of year. I've done midnight swims, and I've seen what looks like skylights as my arms move through the water. I've also done midnight kayaking out there, where you dip your paddle and it looks like Harry Potter's wand, with all these glittering bioluminescent algae glowing. It makes me feel connected to the whole of Puget Sound."

the Sound engage thousands of volunteers, adults and children, in an array of activities such as monitoring the health of salmon-bearing creeks and rivers, documenting salmon migration, ridding streams of debris, and working with streamside property owners to help them conserve habitats. Some of these include Stream Teams in the Bellevue area and Thurston County as well as the Adopt-A-Stream Foundation in Snohomish County. Many schools offer outdoor education, including stream study experiences, through a program called FieldSTEM in partnership with the not-for-profit Pacific Education Institute.

In King County, Sustainability Ambassadors is a professional development program for student leaders, teacher leaders, and community leaders committed to educating about sustainability with real-world impact. It provides fellowships to teachers in several school systems who in turn train other schoolteachers about stormwater, water supply, and waste water. The program reaches an estimated four thousand secondary-level students each year. Cassandra Houghton, student leader coordinator for the program, has served as a mentor to high school students in the Kent School District who worked with every seventh grader at Kent's Mill Creek Middle School, just south of Seattle, helping them map their adopted namesake urbanized stream. The students also participated in the design for rain gardens to collect storm runoff and filter out pollutants before they reach the Duwamish River estuary and Puget Sound.

Stealthy hunters, herons eat more than just fish, as this frog dangling from a heron's beak attests.

SHORELINES, FROM ROCKY TO SANDY

The Salish Sea of British Columbia and Washington State has a coastline of more than 4,600 miles, including island shores—almost the distance of a flight from Seattle to New York and back. Puget Sound's share of that is 2,500 miles. That's a lot of beaches, although many of them aren't easily reached because of high natural bluffs or constructed barriers, or because they are private property. And few contain the ocean-tossed fine sands of the Oregon and Washington coasts. Alki Point in West Seattle and Golden Gardens in Seattle are two of the few sandy shores along the Sound, and they are magnets for people.

Going the Extra Mile for the Sound

Fifteen-year-old KYLE PETERSEN lives on a small farm near Sultan, Washington, in the Cascade Range foothills—about forty minutes' drive from the nearest saltwater beach. And yet he is one of the Salish Sea's champions.

As a trained volunteer for the Beach Watchers, Kyle is doing his part to protect Puget Sound from pollution, habitat destruction, and damage to the sea creatures. He may be his family's number one beach volunteer, but his mom and fellow volunteer, Leigh Anne Burford, is right behind him.

"I've always been a big fan of nature," says Kyle, whose family moved to Snohomish County from California when he was ten years old. He got hooked on Puget Sound on his very first visit to the Mukilteo Lighthouse Park, twelve acres of open space with 1,500 feet of sandy beach near the state's Mukilteo ferry landing. "I walked around and played in the water, and I got to see a lot of crabs and stuff," he recalls.

That inspired him to get involved in protecting the Sound. He and his mom signed up for thirteen hours of training plus twelve hours of volunteer time, qualifying them as Beach Naturalists.

Next, they completed an additional ninety hours of training and eighty hours of volunteer service over two years, making them Beach Watchers.

The whole family also does its part back home. They committed themselves to protecting the five acres of old-growth forest surrounding their eighteen-acre property. And they work to keep domestic animal waste cleaned up so it doesn't wash into the Sultan River, a salmon-bearing stream that joins the Snohomish River and flows into the Sound at Everett and Marysville. The family has plenty of animals to clean up after. "We have a horse, three goats, four dogs, two chickens, six cats, two guinea pigs, my little brother's bunny, my lizard, my fish, and my bird," says Kyle.

As Beach Watchers, Kyle and his mom have been trained to speak with people of all ages—offering nature lessons and helping beachgoers do their part to keep the Sound and Salish Sea healthy. Examples of the information they share are the state fisheries rules for harvesting crab, and being careful not to treat precious eelgrass marine habitat as a park lawn at low tide.

Kyle also keeps busy as a student. At fifteen, he enrolled in Sky Valley's Environmental Science School's immersive curriculum in both the sciences and humanities. "I want to become an engineer, but I also want to be a biologist," Kyle says. "I want to get a college major in engineering and a minor in biology." And since he is interested in robotics, you never know what he may someday invent to keep our waters healthy.

Dungeness crabs are native to Puget Sound.

Much of the coastline is composed of the smooth gray cobbles and gravels left by the glaciers. As the tides recede, they expose pools of water and goopy mudflats in sheltered areas such as bays or estuaries. In these special places, watch for both native and introduced species of clams and oysters; hard-shelled barnacles that seem to cement themselves to any surface under the sea; chitons and limpets; moon snails and periwinkle snails; five species of crab; ghost-like shrimp; sand dollars and sea anemones; moon and "fried egg" jellies; kelp and sargassum and eelgrass; and many more.

More than thirty species of sea stars live between the shore and as deep down as a hundred feet below the water's surface. They are voracious predators of animals such as sea urchins, barnacles, clams, mussels, and oysters. Until the massive Pacific coast die-off of these approachable creatures began in 2013, sea stars could be found in the waters of many popular beaches of the Sound. Whether they will fully recover is unknown, and of great concern, to scientists. Laura James, a scuba diver and multimedia documentarian of the undersea world of the Sound, asks a question: If we lose the sea stars, what animals can children touch at the seashore?

Biologists and other marine resource experts include beaches in what they call nearshore habitat, more than 27 percent of which is "armored" with bulkheads, seawalls, dikes, or other engineered structures in Washington State. This habitat is so important—and so disrupted in many areas around the Sound—that the state Department of Fish and Wildlife and the US Army Corps of Engineers have teamed up with many other partners on a long-term Puget Sound Nearshore Ecosystem Restoration Project "to understand how humans have impacted the nearshore zone—our beaches, bluffs, inlets and river deltas—and what opportunities exist to improve the health of the nearshore zone and its ability to support biological features humans value such as shorebirds, shellfish, salmon, orcas, and great blue herons."

The Sound is such a life-intensive environment that Laura James, after thousands of dives in these waters, is struck by this fact: "Wherever you have anything underwater, marine life gloms onto it. If there is a rock, there is an anemone on it. If there's a hard surface, there's an anemone or barnacles on it. If there's a golf ball, it gets barnacles all over it." She brings an important understanding of beaches and shores. "For most people, the place where the water and beach meet is the dividing line. That's where a journey to the beach ends. For me, there is no dividing line."

And that, perhaps, is the key to understanding the Sound and Salish Sea. It is all an ecosystem. So let's go deeper.

CREATURES OF THE SEA

The network of fjords, bays, and inlets in Puget Sound has its share of superlative creatures. Let's start with the giant Pacific octopus, endemic to Puget Sound and the largest of its kind in the world. Its eight arms have a radial span of up to twenty feet, and it commonly weighs between fifty and one hundred pounds. The giant Pacific octopus feeds on shrimp, crabs, clams, snails, fish, and even its own kind. Octopuses are so brainy that some biologists and psychologists, notably Canada's Jennifer Mather, describe them as having personality. These alluring creatures even merited an article published by the American Psychological Association, titled "An Invertebrate with Flair." And the late Roland Anderson, Seattle Aquarium biologist for more than three decades, noted that octopuses are

Consisting of three separate pods—J, K, and L—the Southern Resident orcas, which live in Puget Sound, have been dwindling. Several calves from these pods have died in recent years, most famously a calf that lived less than an hour and then was carried more than two weeks and one thousand miles throughout the Salish Sea by her mother Tahlequah in the summer of 2018.

Leading the Orca Recovery Task Force

As a self-described cowboy from southern Idaho sagebrush country, LES PURCE has never ceased to be amazed by Puget Sound, starting with his first visit while he was an Army Reserve

Officer Training Corps cadet at Fort Lewis, just south of Tacoma.

On a late-summer weekend in 1968, he and some of his ROTC buddies obtained a weekend pass and drove south for the Olympia Brewery tour. "We dropped down into the Nisqually delta, and the view took my breath away," he says. "You looked out into the bay of the southern Puget Sound. The delta was so beautiful." That unforgettable first exposure to the Sound occurred while Les was a senior at Idaho State University, working on his bachelor's degree in psychology. He went on to earn a doctorate in education. In 1989, Les returned to Washington State for the long haul. For several years, he was vice president and interim president at The Evergreen State College, which occupies a forest along three thousand feet of Puget Sound shoreline at the west edge of Olympia. The school has a national reputation for offering programs in sustainability and environmental stewardship. After five years at Washington State University as an executive, he was recruited back to Evergreen in 2000, serving as its president for fifteen years before retiring.

In 2018, Governor Jay Inslee signed an executive order making it a state priority to protect and recover the Southern Resident killer whale population. Even though the orcas have been listed for protection under Canadian and US endangered species laws, the population declined from ninety-five in 1995 to seventy-four in 2018. As part of the executive order, Inslee created the Orca Recovery Task Force, appointing Les Purce and Stephanie Solien as co-chairs to lead representatives of nearly fifty government entities, native tribes, coalitions, and industry groups with an interest in the inland sea.

According to federal and state agencies, the primary threats to the resident orcas are declines in chinook salmon and other fish prey; the presence of toxic contaminants (particularly in stormwater runoff) in the Sound; and disturbance from vessel noise and traffic. The task force was charged with recommending strategies to resolve the survival threats to the orcas.

Les believes education of Puget Sounders, and those who visit the Sound, must play a central role in recovering the orca. "It's essential that we build a coalition of people who are serious about figuring out strategies to increase orca food sources, and about coming to agreement on how we will live with the orcas," he says. "More importantly, we have to reverse the impacts of all the toxics that are in the Sound. The orcas, and how we all experience the Sound, are really at risk. We have to sustain the orcas, and in the process sustain us."

so, well, personable, that they were the only cold-blooded animals on exhibit that earned individual names from aquarium staff members.

There are many more world-record sea creatures in the Sound. The Pacific geoduck is the largest burrowing clam in the world, with a neck siphon that can exceed three feet in length. The giant acorn barnacle, the world's largest barnacle, can reach nearly six inches in diameter and twelve inches in height. Among the world's largest sea stars, the sunflower star can grow to nearly three feet in diameter and can travel up to ten feet per minute, making it one of the fastest-moving sea stars as well. Red urchins can live more than 150 years. The quillback rockfish, one of twenty-eight species of rockfish in our waters, can live ninety years. The copper rockfish can live fifty years. The rougheye rockfish can live more than two hundred years. The lion's mane jellyfish, the largest jelly species in the world, can grow several feet in diameter with a mass of tentacles that can exceed a hundred feet in length.

And nothing spells "WOW" quite like "watching our whales." Puget Sound and the larger Salish Sea host several species of whales. Minke whales, gray whales, and humpbacks appear in the Salish Sea regularly. Humans delight in seeing and hearing blows and spy-hops and feeding behaviors as their tail flukes and fins cut through marine waters. The largest members of the dolphin family, killer whales, or orcas, as they are more commonly called in the region, include distinct populations

OPPOSITE The largest octopus species in the world, the giant Pacific octopus can change the texture and color of its skin to camouflage itself.

RIGHT A crimson sea anemone cradles a candy stripe shrimp, a crustacean whose range extends from Puget Sound north to the Aleutian Islands. This particular shrimp has eggs visible in its abdomen.

The largest jellyfish in the world, the lion's mane jellyfish can reach several feet in diameter.

with vastly different eating habits. Transient orcas, or Bigg's whales, eat marine mammals like seals and sea lions, and their numbers have been increasing recently. Resident orcas subsist almost entirely on salmon—predominantly chinook salmon, the largest, fattiest species in the region. Resident orcas are split into two main groups: the southern group and a northern population centered in Canadian waters, rarely sighted in Washington waters. The endangered Southern Resident orca population consists of three separate pods defined by matrilineal lines: J, K, and L pods. Transients and residents do not interbreed and aren't known to socialize, even though their ranges overlap.

Another marine mammal that, at a glance, resembles an orca is the Dall's porpoise, which has similar black-and-white markings, although its body is much smaller and thicker. These porpoises, and the more common harbor porpoise, typically eat small fish, octopus, and squid.

The most familiar marine mammal in the Sound is the harbor seal. Gray with dark spots, harbor seals are likely to haul out on floating docks and stationary log booms on the water. When they're in large groups, their barks can sometimes be heard across the water's surface. The harbor seal's diet of fish, especially salmon, has been a curse, as it gave seals a reputation as an enemy of salmon fishermen. Until 1960, Washington State paid bounties for killing seals. Even today, some people who fish believe marine mammals are depleting salmon stocks. It's an impressive event to see a herd of seals corralling a school of salmon in a cove, gripping the struggling fish with their sharp teeth and devouring them while the seagulls screech, circle, and dive from above for leftovers.

You may also see California sea lions in our waters dashing after fish, squid, or octopus. Groups of them often rest on the surface of the water in a behavior known as rafting. A related species, the Steller sea lion, is found in our northern waters, and is listed for protection under the Endangered Species Act.

A species that has suffered from hunting is the sea otter. In Washington, their populations have been slowly increasing since their reintroduction in 1969 and 1970 following their extirpation through hunting in the 1900s. While they are more abundant on the open Pacific coast, sea otters have been observed as far east as the Strait of Juan de Fuca.

As of 2015, scientists had identified 253 species of fish in the Sound and the Salish Sea. According to the Environmental Protection Agency (EPA), 37 of those fish species were formally listed as at risk or vulnerable to extinction.

Salmon, steelhead, and other game fish are generally regarded as the "charismatic" species of the fish kingdom. But to exist, they need plentiful schools of smaller forage fish such as herring, smelt, and sand lance to feed on. Since the 1970s, however, forage fish have been declining in much of the Sound for reasons that aren't fully understood by scientists (although habitat destruction and pollution are contributors). For instance, jellyfish, which compete with herring, smelt, and other forage fish for food, became nine times more abundant in some parts of the Sound during the same forty-year period when the forage fish populations were shrinking. Efforts are under way to connect the dots and develop recovery strategies.

A critical thread in the open-water food web is plankton, a food source for young fish, sea birds, and marine mammals. Tiny crustaceans, such as copepods and krill and the early life stages of shrimp, crab, and barnacles, are called zooplankton. Little plant-like organisms called phytoplankton convert energy from the sun to chemical energy that serves as their own food.

They bloom in the spring, clouding the water until they are consumed by zooplankton in the summer.

In the twenty-first century, the plankton bloom in much of the Sound has exceeded the ability of other organisms to consume them. Nutrients such as nitrogen and phosphorous from our wastewater and other human sources are feeding the tiny creatures, causing overabundant blooms. When plankton die, they sink to the bottom, where they decay. This process consumes oxygen and creates zones that can harm fish and other marine life. Because plankton absorb carbon dioxide during their life cycle, the decomposition from die-offs releases carbon dioxide into the water, contributing to acidification.

FORESTS AND MEADOWS UNDER THE SEA

Eelgrass beds and kelp forests provide homes and cover for numerous species in our marine waters. According to the *Encyclopedia of Puget Sound*, the wavy blades of eelgrass may grow in flats, in "expansive, shallow beds typically located in

bays," or in fringe habitats consisting of comparatively narrow, linear beds that follow the shoreline. Eelgrass meadows in Puget Sound can exist from four feet to thirty feet beyond the low-tide line. "The deepest beds are found in the Strait of Juan de Fuca and the San Juan Islands," the encyclopedia reports. Eelgrass provides shelter and food for many marine species such as herring, crab, shrimp, shellfish, waterfowl, and anadromous fish, such as salmon.

Kelp are large seaweeds that form dense canopies in intertidal and subtidal areas, and can extend to about a hundred feet deep. Bull kelp occurs throughout Puget Sound and the Strait of Juan de Fuca, while giant kelp is restricted to the strait. Kelp have been described as a carbon factory for estuaries like the Sound. They take up nutrients and minerals coming down the rivers and, with the help of sunlight, grow into massive structures that feed a multitude of species, from bacteria to sea urchins. "Tiny crustaceans, including buglike amphipods and isopods, grow on the kelp and become prey for many other species, including juvenile salmon and rockfish," says the *Encyclopedia of Puget Sound*. In fact, "this predator-prey dynamic, played out thousands of times, makes a kelp forest one of the most productive habitats on the planet."

Altogether, the many habitats of the Sound serve as a remarkable home for animal and plant life. The Center for Biological Diversity in 2005 recognized about 7,000 species of organisms in the Puget Sound basin, including over 4,200 animals, 1,500 plants, 850 fungi, and 30 algae, and it found that more than 950 species were imperiled. The SeaDoc Society reported the following animals in the Salish Sea marine environment alone: 38 mammal species, more than 170 bird species, and more than 260 fish species; they estimate there are more than 3,000 invertebrate species visible without a microscope.

OPPOSITE Eelgrass serves as critical habitat for many species in Puget Sound, including herring and juvenile salmon, as well as capturing runoff and helping prevent coastal erosion.
RIGHT A school of black rockfish swims through a bull kelp forest.

Making a Difference by Restoring Shellfish Habitat

BETSY PEABODY believes in people power—our ability to save our species and other species as well. And she believes in the power of Puget Sound to sustain us, as a renewing source of life and livelihoods. "This place is still full of resources that literally feed people," she says. "When you are pulling food out of Puget Sound and preparing it and eating it, there is nothing more personal than that."

Although she grew up in and near the Rocky Mountains, Betsy was powerfully influenced by the coral reefs of coastal Australia and the mangroves of Florida. These "living marine habitats imprinted themselves on my brain," she recalls.

When she came to Puget Sound as an adult, she realized it is a living system that—on the whole—still supports humans. But Betsy knows better than most of us that the Sound needs our help. It needs many people working together to restore and protect the inland sea, its beaches, and the creatures and plants that sustain it.

She is an expert at getting people to work together to do just that. After volunteering at the Seattle Aquarium in the 1980s, she became a communicator and educator about the challenges and needs of the Sound and its natural system. Betsy also awarded and managed grants for a state agency that was a forerunner of the Puget Sound Partnership.

In the 1990s, Betsy realized that, as she explains, "I wanted to dig a little deeper, to help recover a place that was becoming increasingly important to me. I didn't just want to talk about Puget Sound."

And she has been doing that ever since. In 1997, she formed a not-for-profit organization called the Puget Sound Restoration Fund, becoming its executive director, and, in 2007, she started serving as president of the Pacific Shellfish Institute. She also served on the Washington State Blue Ribbon Panel on Ocean Acidification in 2012, developing strategies for reducing the human-caused changes in ocean chemistry that devastated the reproduction of shellfish along the West Coast of North America.

Since its creation, the Restoration Fund has worked with many partners to restore the marine species and habitats that are important for a healthy ecosystem. Another major focus is restoring water quality in shellfish-growing areas. Betsy says the work is highly collaborative and implemented "through tangible, on-the-ground projects." With support and engagement from many partners, Betsy's team devotes sustained effort to rebuilding populations of native oysters and abalone. The team is also developing techniques for rebuilding underwater kelp beds that provide vital shelter to aquatic animals.

Restoration Fund projects are designed to spotlight resources that once flourished in coastal waters from Alaska to California, and to reconnect people to these resources. The list of accomplishments is impressive. For example, the group and its partners restored 575 acres of shellfish habitat in the shallow coastal waters of Drayton Harbor near the Peace Arch at the US-Canada border so shellfish can be harvested there again under approved conditions. At the southern end of Puget Sound, the Restoration Fund restored 340 acres of shellfish beds in Henderson Inlet, resulting in resumed harvests. They also enhanced over 60 acres of native oyster habitat with more than one hundred partners as part of Washington State's Olympia oyster rebuilding plan.

Looking ahead, the Restoration Fund is raising and outplanting pinto abalone produced from a conservation hatchery to rebuild breeding populations and restore the health of rocky reef habitat. The organization also established a shellfish restoration and research hatchery with the National Oceanic and Atmospheric Administration (NOAA), launched a five-year project to investigate kelp cultivation as a potential strategy for mitigating ocean acidification, and installed over 150 "shellfish gardens" where Puget Sound residents can grow food on their local tidelands.

A key part of Betsy's work, and a driving force in the creation of the Puget Sound Restoration Fund, has been locating, sustaining, and rebuilding the populations of the tiny, intricate native creatures called the Olympia oyster. It all started in 1998, when Washington Department of Fish and Wildlife biologist Hal Beattie came to her with a challenge. State biologists had developed and secured approval for a native oyster restoration plan, but the plan had no state funding to carry it out. Betsy decided to make the plan a mission for her new nonprofit enterprise. She is glad she accepted the challenge: "I discovered Puget Sound by following the story of Olympia oysters," she says. "Because of the oysters, I've been to very remote little backwater places where I never would have gone. Or if I had gone, I would never have recognized the treasures that still exist there. I have been incredibly lucky to follow this story."

Betsy Peabody (left) and marine biologist Eric Sparkman examine an Olympia oyster restoration site.

The first step on her journey was to learn from "those who know the most about oysters"—the growers and the tribes and scientists around the Sound. "I was taught by a lot of generous people," she says. One of them was state Fish and Wildlife biologist Cedric Lindsey, who spent hours on Puget Sound's cobbled beaches and intertidal waters, teaching Betsy to spot oysters in various environments. He would say, "I see an Olympia oyster within so many yards, and you have to find it." It was her job to see the small, well-camouflaged creature nestled among the rocks and shells of watery tidelands. Other mentors in the ways of the Olympia oyster included shellfish growers Bill and Justin Taylor, who taught Betsy about the habitat conditions that native oysters need in order to thrive.

One result was the Puget Sound Restoration Fund's *Olympia Oyster Field Guide*, developed with help from Brady Blake at

the Department of Fish and Wildlife. The laminated, full-color how-to booklet—which credits numerous funders and contributors—shows in graphic detail what Olympia oysters look like in their natural habitats. It also shows where they are found around the Salish Sea, from Drayton Harbor in the north to the narrow finger inlets of the South Sound and Hood Canal.

Betsy has learned that Olympia oysters—like tropical coral reefs and mangrove forests, and like the Pacific Northwest's undersea kelp forests—provide protective, living habitat for other aquatic animals. Many small animals live under oyster shells and in between the shells. Anemones, barnacles, mussels, and numerous other creatures inhabit oyster reefs—aggregations of oyster shells. "These things not only support other organisms. They support me. They support humans along this coastline," Betsy says. She learned that native oysters "are not a species that's going extinct." They "exist in a lot of places, but they are sparse—an oyster here and an oyster there." She says Washington's largest natural aggregation of native oysters is in North Bay, a shallow tideland near the tiny waterfront town of Allyn in Mason County. Over roughly sixty acres, densities of fifty to seventy-five oysters can be found within an area the size of a Hula-Hoop. A smaller oyster bed in Dyes Inlet between Bremerton and Silverdale supports densities of 150 oysters.

This was the frame of reference for what a reasonably healthy twenty-first century population of Olympia oysters was until Betsy organized an expedition to the storm-tossed western coast of Canada's Vancouver Island. The trip was inspired by Canadian scientist Brian Kingzett, who had mapped out shorelines on the remote coast of North America's largest island fourteen years earlier, and spotted something that made him think there might be healthy populations of native oysters.

In 2008, with funding secured by Betsy and The Nature Conservancy, Kingzett led an expedition that would be chronicled in an engaging book, *The Living Shore: Rediscovering a Lost World*, by Rowan Jacobsen. Provisioning themselves for the difficult journey by boat, the exploratory party set forth from Gold River and motored their way into a rugged and remote fjord named Port Eliza Inlet. What they found there was stunning—beds of native oysters in densities of 650 per Hula-Hoop-size area. They saw oysters and shells "provide structure and spaces and homes for other sea creatures," Betsy recalls.

Equally important, perhaps, was this fact: "Port Eliza is this beautiful, deeply gorged fjord. But it is not pristine," Betsy explains. "There has been a lot of human activity on this coast for a long time. There is still logging activity as well as log rafts, people fishing on these waters, and salmon farming. Still, there are these pocket beaches where Olympia oysters are the dominant habitat form." It gives her hope to know that "you can find these oysters in the strangest of places—places with lots of human activity."

Oysters prove to her that a healthy Puget Sound "isn't about pointing fingers, about identifying bad guys and good guys," she says. "It's about bringing back resources that are important to ecosystem health, and to people. What are the technical things that we can do? What are the financial resources that we might need? What are the project management activities that might be required to move things forward?" Betsy has made it her job to find those resources and those partnerships, because "we can't effectively rebuild resources without rebuilding human connections to resources. That's how you get lasting support."

She is encouraged by the knowledge that "humans are inherently collaborative beasts. We're an adaptive species. We're an innovative species. All of these work in our favor. We have been confronted by big challenges that have challenged the survival of our species, big climate change events that have dwindled our numbers, and we have been able to adapt. We have a lot of genetic history to draw on." And so, Betsy is forging the human connections to protect the Puget Sound experience for all of us, one oyster at a time.

Related to sharks, rays, and skates, the spotted ratfish is the most abundant species in Puget Sound in terms of biomass. It is estimated that more than 200 million of these low-profile bottom feeders live in the depths of the Sound.

OPPOSITE Strawberry sea anemones surround a giant acorn barnacle. Most anemones eat plankton, crabs, and small fish, but some larger species prey on jellyfish and sea stars.

ABOVE Nudibranchs inhabit tide pools, kelp forest, and rocky reefs. These colorful sea slugs feed on algae, anemones, barnacles, corals, and even other nudibranchs.

ABOVE Steller sea lions are the largest of the sea lions, with males weighing on average two thousand pounds.

OPPOSITE A well-camouflaged harbor seal rests on a rocky shore during its first weeks of life.

OPPOSITE Rockfish, such as the copper rockfish, have declined substantially in Puget Sound since the mid-1980s because of overharvesting and habitat loss.
RIGHT Research scientists trawl net specimens to monitor diseases affecting fish, such as these Pacific herring, in Puget Sound.

OPPOSITE, TOP Launched in 1913, the schooner *Adventuress* has become a maritime history icon. It is operated by Sound Experience, a nonprofit organization whose mission is to educate people about Puget Sound and inspire them to care for it.

OPPOSITE, BOTTOM Recreational sailing opportunities abound in Puget Sound, from the multitude of scenic islands and inlets to splendid public beaches.

RIGHT Bulk carrier ships dock at several ports around Puget Sound, including Seattle, Tacoma, Everett, Bellingham, and Port Angeles. They are just one of the many marine vessels that move through Puget Sound every day, including US Navy ships, container ships, cruise ships, ferries, tugboats, and commercial fishing boats.

From its headwaters in the mountains of the Olympic Peninsula, the Hamma Hamma River flows into Hood Canal, an arm of Puget Sound.

Related to rabbits, pikas live in talus slopes in mountain ranges across the United States, including the Olympics and the Cascades. Their limited habitat and intolerance of heat make them an indicator species of the effects of climate change.

Samish tribal canoes are hauled out on the beach at Fidalgo Bay in Anacortes on the annual Canoe Journey, during which tribes navigate the Salish Sea. Held most summers, the journey can last up to several weeks, depending upon which tribe is hosting it.

THE HUMAN CONNECTION

DAVID L. WORKMAN

FOR THOUSANDS OF YEARS, THE BOUNTIFUL LAND AND waters we now call the Puget Sound and the Salish Sea regions have been a remarkably hospitable home for humans. And, especially for the past two centuries, humans have changed this place more than any other species has. Here we will explore many of those changes, and what people are doing about them.

Indigenous people established hundreds of permanent villages along rivers and the sheltered bays and coves of the inland sea. The sea and its surrounding landscape provided everything the people need to live and thrive. They built seasonal camps or villages to hunt, fish, and gather shellfish and gather and process roots, berries, and greens. Today, these indigenous peoples are collectively called Coast Salish people, from their base language, Salish.

After the arrival of Europeans and US settlers, the native groups were designated as "tribes" most often in the United States or "bands" primarily in Canada, though some subgroups in the United States have also been called "bands." Family and tribal groups intermarried with other nearby groups, so that many of the native people in the region today have family roots in multiple tribes or nations. It is estimated there are now 56,000 Coast Salish people in the United States and Canada.

Archaeologists have found remains of ancient villages and camps around Puget Sound and the Salish Sea, revealing important glimpses into ancient lifestyles. One of these sites is at one of the southernmost tips of Puget Sound, in a place called Mud Bay, where Ralph and Karen Munro purchased a farm in 1975. In the late 1990s, the Munros partnered with nearby South Puget Sound Community College (SPSCC) and the Squaxin Island Tribe, who also know themselves as the People of the Water, to research the area's history.

Under the leadership of Dale Croes, the college's archaeology professor, the history sleuths found what John Dodge, in a 2009 report for *Olympian* newspaper, describes as "amazing artifacts, often well preserved in the shoreline mud where they have escaped decay." He describes a toy war club, portions of a cedar bark gill net used to catch salmon, ornamental baskets, arrows, spears, shell jewelry, and, notably, a broken harpoon blade for whale hunting plucked off the eroding beach.

Sally Brownfield, a Squaxin elder and public school educator, spent a summer volunteering at the dig. The archaeological site and artifacts "give us a glimpse into our ancestors' lives," she says. The revelations "added to the honor that I have had to learn from those who came before me."

The staple foods for the native peoples of the Sound were, and are, salmon and other fish, as well as shellfish, such as clams, oysters, and mussels. Much of it could be dried for later use and for trade with distant peoples in the region. Shellfish have been so important to Puget Sound diets that there is an old saying along this coast: When the tide is out, the table is set. In addition to seafood, there has long been an abundance of deer, elk, and other big game; waterfowl and other birds; and edible plant foods like ferns, various greens, roots, bulbs, berries and, where available, acorns.

Over the millennia, skilled artisans perfected the art of weaving not only with cedar bark but also with nettles, milkweed, rushes, reeds, willow bark mountain goat wool, and even dog's hair. Dyes were made from indigenous materials such as stinging nettle.

Beyond food, the forests provided giant cedar trees that could be split into planks and shingles for houses or carved and bent into domestic items like storage chests, bowls, and spoons, as well as large, durable seagoing canoes. The stringy inner bark of the cedar has been prized for thousands of years by the native people: When meticulously peeled off the giant trees, the fibers could be fashioned into fishing nets, baskets, clothing, and blankets.

The rivers and the sea served as a self-stocking supermarket and as a great highway. For thousands of years, beasts of burden were not needed here. In their masterfully carved cedar canoes, the peoples of this region traversed thousands of miles of protected coastline as weather and conditions permitted.

The native peoples of the Northwest coast now openly engage in cultural practices that were long outlawed by the US federal government, exemplified by the Canoe Journey. Many summers, hundreds of paddlers (or "pullers") from dozens of tribes in the United States and Canada come together in a flotilla of large seagoing canoes. The canoes travel great distances, sometimes hundreds of miles for weeks at a time. Each time, a different tribe or nation hosts the canoe pullers as well as the support crews and visitors.

Sally Brownfield says the Canoe Journey helps younger generations learn about the family connections among the many tribes. "I think it has been very powerful in supporting the tribal people," she says. "Way, way back, people had to travel so far for different things. There are records of people from Alaska going down to Northern California. In those days, you would stay for months. It might be for marriage, or it might be a tribute. And there was always trade. The people took care of one another."

Until the arrival of roadbuilding Europeans and Euro-Americans in the early 1800s, the most heavily used native trails in Puget Sound country were the ones connecting canoe routes and those that served as trade routes between the coastal villages and those east of the Cascade Range.

The inland sea and surrounding watersheds offered a great bounty of resources. Working diligently, the native peoples provided for their daily needs, while also preserving foods and materials for the future and for ceremonial needs. As explained

Salmon play an integral role in tribal religion, culture, and physical sustenance. For centuries, Puget Sound tribes have cooked salmon on a wood frame over an open fire. Typically, the salmon is fitted into a split end of a straight, strong cedar or ironwood branch, and then smaller sticks are woven through at right angles to hold the fish flat.

The People of the Water

SALLY BROWNFIELD is a soft-spoken, strong Puget Sound woman. For all but two of her sixty-plus years, her home has been a little peninsula between two narrow inlets at the southern end of the Sound.

Sally is one of the People of the Water, the Squaxin Island Tribe that has lived on and with the water and its plants and animals for thousands of years. Daughter, wife, mother, educator, food gatherer, weaver, salmon fisher, oyster shucker, archaeo-

logical digger—her story is rich with experiences. After college and graduate school in Tacoma, she taught at Washington State University for two years in Pullman, where she felt much like a salmon out of its element. After months of working in the dry Palouse country, "I would just come back and sit by the water and smell it . . . take it in," she recalls vividly. "There is a calming and spiritual presence to being on the water."

As a little girl, she spent many of her days combing the beaches of Little Skookum Inlet, Eld Inlet, and Oyster Bay, where creeks spill into Puget Sound under the bridges of US 101, the Pacific Coast Highway. "The bay was part of our growing up, our childhood," she recalls. "We learned from it and respected it." She and her family would be on the shore when the smelt came in so all could be part of the life-sustaining harvest.

On the Sound, Sally observed the life cycle of the indigenous Olympia oyster. In seventh grade, she learned how to open, or shuck, this Northwest delicacy. "They are just so beautiful, every single one of them," she says. Sally treasures a book published in 1938 by a local game warden. "He tells about observing our native people as they gathered these oysters," she says, "and how careful they were about it because Olympia oysters are very small and very delicate. So our ancestors were very careful. They would lay on their bellies when harvesting oysters to avoid crushing them. When outsiders came, they walked on the beds and crushed them, and overharvested. The oysters almost became extinct . . . But like the native people, those oysters have survived." When asked what Puget Sound means to her, she will tell you "it is our life."

The seven southernmost bands of the Salish peoples came to be called the Squaxin Island Tribe in 1854, at the signing of the Medicine Creek Treaty with the US government. Many of those families were consigned to live on Squaxin Island, a two-square-mile strip of land tucked along the southwest reach of larger Harstine Island.

Before they signed the treaty—importantly reserving their right to hunt and fish in their usual and accustomed places—the Squaxin bands lived in dispersed permanent villages on the shoreline, and they moved to other hunting, gathering, and fishing sites on a seasonal basis.

Sally's immediate family lived at Kamilche Point, the tip of the mainland peninsula where Little Skookum splinters off from Totten Inlet. "It was my great-grandmother's place," Sally explains. "The place is still in our family. My grandfather was born and died on that place—and all his children. My mother was born there."

She reflects: "Sometimes I think it's hard for people who haven't been on the water to have an understanding of, when we talk about treaty rights and fishing rights, what that really means. It's not just about economics. It's about our way of life. It's about our diet. It's about exercise, education, entertainment, and how we see and understand the world around us. It's about a way of living with the land and the water.

"We are always taught that if we are going to harvest something, we only harvest so much of it. We don't take it all. When gathering fiber for weaving, I only take so many plants—and only so much from one area. You leave enough so they can regenerate."

Perhaps nothing speaks more eloquently about the importance of Puget Sound and its resources to the Squaxin and other native peoples than the celebration that occurs each August at Arcadia Point, when the salmon return to spawn in these reaches of the Sound. The people gather for the First Salmon Ceremony to recognize the first run of the season. "We give thanks to the salmon for coming back to us," Sally explains. "We take only the flesh and return the rest of the fish to the water."

Life began to change in a big way for Sally Brownfield and other Squaxin people in 1974. The local Kamilche school had been consolidated into the Shelton School District. With that move, the land and school building were suddenly available for sale. The Squaxin, who had no reservation on the mainland at the time, got a loan from the Bureau of Indian Affairs and bought the property. "That became our center," Sally recalls. In time, the tribe bought an oyster farm on the shore of Harstine, the "big island" of Mason County. Later, the tribe began farming salmon in net pens on the east side of Squaxin Island.

That same year, US District Court Judge George Boldt changed the face of natural resources management in Washington State. In a lawsuit brought by the tribes and the United States against Washington State, he ruled that the 1850s federal treaties reserved the rights to half of the fish harvests for the tribes who signed those treaties. They were entitled to their own separate fishing seasons and regulations regardless of reservation boundaries. The tribes were now co-managers of the state's fish harvests with the government.

In time, a federal Housing and Urban Development grant allowed the tribe to build low-income housing at Kamilche, just off US 101. This allowed the scattered Squaxin people to start to return from the surrounding area and distant places. Then came a gas station serving the community as well as thousands of travelers on the highway. And, after a 1988 federal law allowed tribes to operate casinos under legal compacts with states, a major new source of income opened up to the Squaxin people. They built their Little Creek Casino and hotel right off US 101.

Meanwhile, the Squaxin and four other South Sound and coastal tribes had decided to pool their staffing, expertise, and dollars for social and health services and planning. They formed the South Puget Intertribal Planning Agency to coordinate services for their peoples. Today, Squaxin and other tribes are full partners in managing all manner of resources, including the natural resources that have sustained them for millennia.

As Sally describes the changes that she has witnessed in a generation or two, she observes: "In recent years we have regained a lot of hope, because more people have recognized that what we humans do has a huge impact on the environment, on our life. Not just our livelihood, but our quality of life and being able to breathe clean air and have clean water. We [Squaxin] are continuously having a dialogue between industry and people who watch over the environment. We must have balance in everything. I think there is more of an understanding today than in probably the last several decades."

When asked if there is an aspect of Puget Sound that she finds especially remarkable, she says, after pondering for a moment, "That it has sustained us as much as it has! It has amazing capability for rebuilding itself, but we are pushing it to the brink. If we are responsible with our natural resources, they will sustain us."

by Sally Brownfield, "The peoples developed a great variety of art forms to enhance the beauty of everyday objects, to give reverence to the natural world for providing the resources, and to pass down oral and historical teachings."

Potlatching is one of the ancient ceremonies still practiced by many Northwest coastal tribes. "To native peoples, practicing this ceremonial custom is an expression of giving thanks, gratitude, sharing, and stewardship," she says. "Potlatches always include a great feast, sharing of stories, songs, dance, and the giving of gifts to all. A potlatch may last a day or several days. A protocol, understood by all, is practiced."

The custom is very much a part of the canoe journeys practiced throughout the Northwest today. The host tribe puts on a weeklong potlatch for all those attending—thousands of people from long distances.

Joseph Pavel, a Skokomish Tribe member on Hood Canal at the mouth of the Skokomish River, says: "One of the things the tribes do is share. We share our resources. We share our culture. We share our history. People take great pride in taking care of their guests well. That is our wealth—being recognized as generous."

EXPLORERS AND SETTLERS

Life began to change in momentous ways for the indigenous peoples in the late 1700s with the arrival of large ships with wing-like sails. In 1774, Europeans arrived at the Northwest coast in the form of a Spanish frigate commanded by Juan Pérez Hernández. The Spanish traded with natives at Nootka Sound on what soon become Canada's Vancouver Island. Four years later, British Captain James Cook recorded his arrival at Cape Flattery on Washington's northwest coast, but continued

searching for the elusive Northwest Passage so many explorers journeyed to find. In 1787, British Captain Charles Barkley found the strait that he named after Juan de Fuca, a Greek mariner who claimed to have discovered such a strait two centuries earlier while sailing for Spain.

Change began in earnest in 1792, when British Captain George Vancouver led two ships of the Royal Navy into the strait and began an extensive and well-documented survey in which he mapped the waterways of the region. He named many shoreline and mountain features after friends and allies. Besides bestowing the name of his lieutenant, Peter Puget, on the southern sound of the inland sea, he also gave the name of crew member Joseph Whidbey to the largest island in what would become Washington State.

In 1824, the first visitor from the United States, William Cannon, arrived at Eld Inlet via an overland route from the Chehalis River valley, as part of a Hudson's Bay Company expedition from Astoria on the Columbia River bound for the Fraser River in Canada. Three years later, the company—a British Canadian enterprise that would dominate trade between whites and native peoples in the Pacific Northwest—established Fort Langley on the Fraser River at a site that would become part of Canada's metropolitan Vancouver. Although Hudson's Bay built its posts to trade with natives for fur, it soon found itself trading for salmon to ship to the Hawaiian Islands along with cedar lumber and shakes. The Kwantlen group of the Stó:lō Nation relocated near Fort Langley for this purpose.

In 1832–1833, the company established a trading post named Fort Nisqually in the land of the Nisqually Tribe, near the mouth of a creek north of the Nisqually River delta. It was the first European settlement on Puget Sound. For a quarter

Protecting Hood Canal, Skokomish Tribal Homeland

JOSEPH PAVEL'S birth certificate says "Texas," but his roots run thousands of years deep in Puget Sound country, along the shoreline, tidelands, and waters of Hood Canal. As a son of an Air Force family, Joseph lived as a young boy in many places of the world, as far away as Germany and Panama. At age twelve, he returned with his father, Donald, and mother, Anne, to Skokomish, Washington, where the rushing river of the same name enters the sloughs of its estuary on the southwest shore of Hood Canal. Skokomish is a powerful river, but also a tribe and a Native American reservation created by the Treaty of Point No Point in 1855. That perpetual agreement was signed between the US government and the Twana, S'Klallam, and Chimacum peoples.

After his family returned to the tribe and reservation in the late 1960s following his father's military service, Joseph grew up digging clams and oysters and fishing for salmon in the Skokomish River. "Back then," he recalls, "you could just go out on the beach and dig steamer clams. You can't do that anymore. There are so many shoulder-to-shoulder cabins and fences and signs."

After the epic 1974 Boldt Decision in which a federal judge reaffirmed the tribes' treaty rights to fish in their usual and accustomed places, life changed in a big way for the Skokomish and other Puget Sound tribes. In many ways, it brought the people home. Tribal members were now assured the opportunity to half of the harvest of salmon and steelhead. They would once again have independent sources of income in their own home territory. Families that had moved away in search of jobs and homes began to return to Skokomish and other tribal homelands. As a young man, Joseph and his brother fished from their own skiff, supplementing the income he earned from working in the timber industry. Eventually, life and family obligations and the quest for education led the brothers to give up commercial fishing, but Joseph holds fond memories of those times.

Joseph earned a fisheries science degree at the University of Washington and went on to become director of natural resources for the Skokomish Indian Tribe after a professional career with the Northwest Indian Fisheries Commission.

"Hood Canal is a unique body of water," says Joseph, after a lifetime of experience and scientific learning. "It's considered a fjord—a deep, narrow, glacially formed inlet." The canal is constantly being reinvented by rushing waters from mountains, hills, and the open Pacific Ocean as it rounds the Olympic Peninsula. "Hood Canal is the homeland of the Skokomish people, descendants of the Twana people, who had thirteen major permanent village sites throughout the watershed and many temporary sites," continues Joseph. "The resources of this watershed are a foundation of our life, our history, our culture, our subsistence, our economy."

"The Canal has a great beauty and charm," he reflects. "It's real close to our hearts, for the Skokomish people and for those who have chosen to make Hood Canal their home. On the flat calm of a balmy summer night, the water is just like glass. Or on a stormy November day, the wind and waves seem like they will blow the floating bridge [State Route 104, linking the Kitsap Peninsula and the Olympic Peninsula] down. Hood Canal has its moods from one extreme to the other. We treasure all those moments when we can be out there on the water, floating on a raft, or paddling a canoe, or hook-and-line fishing, or commercial fishing, or tending a crab pot. Whatever chance you have to be out on the water, I feel really blessed to be out there."

Despite declining fish runs, salmon fishing is still significant to the Skokomish people. "Chum is our largest fishery, our bread-and-butter fishery," Joseph says. Most are from the namesake river that flows from the southeastern Olympic Mountains. The summer run of chum is listed by the federal government as a threatened species, as are Hood Canal and other Puget Sound steelhead. The tribe is working with government agencies and partners to restore the species. The fall run of chum represents about 90 percent of chum salmon returning to the Sound, according to the Washington Department of Fish and Wildlife.

The beaches and flats of the intertidal zone are also a rich part of the Hood Canal experience. Oysters and clams live and reproduce there, attracting individuals and families who harvest them for the sheer joy of it, as well as private commercial shellfish growers and tribal members who count on shellfish as an important traditional part of their diet and a source of jobs. "A very significant portion of our Skokomish community and our families rely on the shellfish industry for a major component of their income," Joseph says. Tribal members harvest oysters, Manila clams, littleneck clams, and deepwater geoduck clams.

Shellfish also have their place in the tribes' creation stories. When asked, Joseph recalls the Twana culture's story of the Clam People, retelling it in his own words: "The clams didn't always live under the surface of the ground. They used to live on top of the ground, and they were quite rude. They would talk loudly. They would make fun of bare skinny legs. Humans got tired of it and complained. Creator cursed the Clam People to live in the ground."

Because shellfish and all fish rely on clean water, Joseph says, "We are diligent with all of our partners, the state, and other landowners to try to keep our waters clean." Hood Canal "is not an undisturbed watershed," he says, but the impacts of humans are less dramatic and less visible than in other parts of Puget Sound. The largest town is Belfair, a community of four thousand at the innermost tip of the fjord, at the base of the Kitsap Peninsula. The major man-made facilities on the canal are the US Navy submarine base at Bangor on the eastern shore of the inlet; the Lake Cushman hydro dam and power plant operated by Tacoma Power; and the state's Hood Canal floating bridge, which joins the Olympic Peninsula with much of the population of Puget Sound.

Hood Canal benefits from the fact that much of its watershed is owned by relatively few entities. Prominent among them are the National Park Service, the US Forest Service, the state of Washington, and Green Diamond Resource Company. This has led to a remarkable amount of cooperative action to reduce erosion and the flow of pollutants into the marine environment. In 1985, the governing bodies of Jefferson County, Kitsap County, Mason County, the Port Gamble S'Klallam Tribe, and the Skokomish Tribe formed the first major collaborative effort, the Hood Canal Coordinating Council (HCCC), in response to community concerns about water quality and related natural resources issues. At that time, Joseph's mother, Anne, was Skokomish Tribal Chair and a founding member of the HCCC. In 2006, another coalition of more than twenty organizations formed the Skokomish Watershed Action Team (SWAT) to restore the Skokomish River and its entire drainage area to a healthy condition, thus contributing to a healthier Hood Canal.

With these efforts well under way, perhaps the biggest environmental challenge in Hood Canal is low oxygen levels in the water column, especially during the warmer and calmer summer months. A 2004 University of Washington Sea Grant report explains that oxygen in aquatic environments is released in photosynthesis by algae and other aquatic plants. Oxygen is also absorbed into the water from the air at the canal's surface.

A natural underwater sill near the Hood Canal Bridge restricts the circulation and flow of water throughout the canal. When the winter winds have died down for summer, the confined waters on the surface and on the bottom tend to mix inadequately, causing oxygen to be depleted by fish, shellfish, decaying plant life, and other sea life, the Sea Grant report explains. Rich nutrients flowing into the canal from the ocean and from streams on both sides of the fjord also lead to oxygen deprivation. These nutrients feed aquatic plants, which eventually die, decompose, and sink to the bottom of the canal, where they consume the dissolved oxygen from the water.

Oxygen depletion sometimes causes sudden die-offs of fish, shellfish, octopus, and other aquatic animals. While depleted oxygen—hypoxia—is a natural phenomenon that has occurred for centuries, Joseph says, "We need to be diligent about not adding more oxygen-depleting nutrients to the water."

Particular areas of concern are fecal coliform contamination from failing septic systems at homes and businesses along the shoreline, as well as another surprising source: a large population of seals at the Dosewallips River estuary on the west shore of the canal. Fecal pollution also results in closures of shellfish harvesting.

Joseph says there are other concerns in Hood Canal's near-shore waters, particularly the temptation for residents to change the shoreline. "Everybody wants their own bulkhead. They want their own dock," he says. So the Skokomish Tribe and its partners work with shoreline property owners to minimize their individual impacts and mitigate existing impacts by finding ways to undo earlier near-shore modifications during renovations. "We've been fairly successful in persuading people," Joseph says.

He explains the importance of protecting the watershed this way: "Look at the water as an extension of your body. If you don't take care of Hood Canal and Puget Sound, your quality of life and your survivability will be at risk. Respecting and protecting your air and water is respecting your own body."

The home of the Skokomish Tribe, Hood Canal is a natural fjord separating the Olympic and Kitsap Peninsulas. Stretching almost seventy miles, the canal is famous for its oysters and other shellfish.

century, Fort Nisqually was a busy international trading center between the owners and many tribes, including the nearby Puyallup, Nisqually, and Squaxin Island, and the more distant Suqamish and S'Klallam.

The northwest coast of North America as depicted on a plate from the 1798 atlas that accompanied Captain George Vancouver's *A Voyage of Discovery to the North Pacific Ocean and Around the World*

RESTLESS AMERICANS ARRIVED ON PUGET SOUND IN 1841, in the form of the United States Exploring Expedition (Wilkes Expedition) under the command of Navy Lieutenant Charles Wilkes. They were near the end of a four-year voyage surveying the west coast of South America, the Pacific Islands, and the Pacific Northwest. Wilkes and company named and mapped many features of the Puget Sound region. They also collected scientific specimens for the new Smithsonian Institution.

The first US settlers who came to stay appeared in 1846. The four families, who had crossed the continent on the Oregon Trail, arrived at the very southern tip of Puget Sound, where the Deschutes River spills the waters from the surrounding peaks and forests over a series of pounding waterfalls into Budd Inlet. The new arrivals called their settlement New Market. It later gained the lasting name of Tumwater, derived from the thundering sound of the falls. Future historians would report that this area was a favorite shellfish gathering site for many Salish tribes, including the Nisqually, Squaxin Island, and Duwamish. One of the native names ascribed to the area was Cheetwoot, or "black bear place."

Just as the trickle of American immigrants gave way to a flood in the region south of the Fraser River valley, Great Britain ceded its claim to lands south of the 49th parallel and the United States ceded its claim to lands northward. Puget Sound was now part of the Oregon Territory.

In 1851, settlers arrived by boat in the place that the Wilkes Expedition had named Elliott Bay. They disembarked at a beach they named Alki, near where the Duwamish River enters the sea. This was the land of the Duwamish people. Soon the newcomers packed up and crossed Elliott Bay, settling in the area that became Pioneer Square in Seattle.

In 1853, a businessman named Henry Yesler fired up his steam-powered sawmill in Seattle. As recounted in John Caldbick's essay, at HistoryLink.org, the mill employed native and white workers. The mill helped build Seattle, and its lumber was "exported to California, Hawaii, and other markets." This mill, and another at Port Gamble on the Kitsap Peninsula to the west, launched an industry that helped shape the landscape, economy, and history of this region.

ANOTHER MOMENTOUS EVENT IN THE REGION OCCURRED in 1853. The American region north of the Columbia River and the interior Blue Mountains of Oregon was separated into a new Washington Territory, and Isaac Stevens was dispatched as its territorial governor for the United States. He selected a location near the settlement of New Market, or Tumwater, and declared it to be the territorial capital. Inspired by the view to the north, dominated by the Olympic Mountains on a clear day, he named the capital Olympia. That rugged range derived its name from English sea captain John Meares, who, in 1788, named the nearly eight-thousand-foot Mount Olympus for the mountain home of the mythical Greek gods.

In 1854 and 1855, following clashes between tribes and US immigrant settlers, Governor Stevens convened treaty councils with the tribes, resulting in several treaties: Medicine Creek, Point Elliott, Point No Point, Neah Bay, and many others throughout what is now Washington. In exchange for ceding lands to the US government, the tribes retained their right to fish, hunt, and gather traditional foods. Tribal people were relocated to reservations and promised compensation, medical care, and schools—in many cases provided many years later or never at all. Importantly, the tribes retained their rights to hunt and fish in their usual and accustomed places. The first of the treaties was Medicine Creek, executed in a grove of Douglas-firs on the shore of a small stream that spills its clear spring water into the delta of the Nisqually River. A century later, Interstate 5 would be built right next to the weather-bleached skeleton of one of the original "treaty trees."

For the next century and a quarter, the Washington territorial and state governments interpreted the treaties to mean native people could fish and hunt under the same rules that applied to non-natives. In effect, they were regarded as having no special rights. In 1945, young Nisqually Tribe member Billy Frank Jr. was arrested for fishing with a net—the first of many arrests he, and many others, would face. In the 1960s and 1970s, Puget Sound tribal members and supporters, including celebrities, held a series of fish-ins to protest the state's refusal to recognize the tribes' treaty rights. Actor Marlon Brando was famously arrested for fishing with natives in 1964, drawing national and international attention to the issue.

In 1970, the federal government and the tribes filed a lawsuit against the state for disregarding the treaties, and US District Judge George Boldt in Tacoma studied the intent and meaning of the treaties negotiated by Isaac Stevens. Boldt concluded that, in agreeing to the treaties, the tribes retained their right to

Henry Yesler, 1870

Articles of Agreement and Convention, made and concluded on the She-nah-nam or Medicine Creek, in the Territory of Washington this twenty sixth day of December in the year one thousand eight hundred and fifty four: by Isaac I. Stevens, Governor and Superintendent of Indian Affairs of the said Territory on the part of the United States, and the undersigned Chiefs, headmen and delegates of the Nisqually, Puyallup, Steilacoom, Squawksin, S'Homamish, Stah-chass, T'Peek-sin, Squi-aitl and Sa-heh-wamish tribes and bands of Indians, occupying the lands lying round the head of Puget Sound and the adjacent inlets, who for the purpose of this treaty are to be regarded as one nation, on behalf of said tribes and bands, and duly authorized by them.

Art. I ...

Art. II ...

ABOVE The Treaty of Medicine Creek was the first of several treaties between tribes and the US government in which the tribes relinquished ownership of lands they had lived on since time immemorial but were assured the right to hunt and fish in their usual and accustomed places.

RIGHT Billy Frank Jr. fishing the Nisqually River in 1973

fish as and where they always had. He ruled that the state cannot restrict them, and that they are entitled to half the available harvest. The 1974 Boldt Decision, later upheld by the US Supreme Court, was a landmark ruling for tribal civil rights that transformed fishing and related natural resource management across the state.

As a result of this ruling, the tribes and Washington State entered into a co-manager relationship for fish and other resources. Later rulings recognized the importance of the habitat needed to support healthy fish populations, for tribes and everyone. For example, courts directed the state to begin removing fish-blocking culverts on state-owned roadways. The state appealed the decision to the US Supreme Court, which in 2018 let stand a lower court order. The result of the culvert case is that the state must remove barriers that block access to hundreds of miles of salmon habitat.

A STATE IS BORN

On November 11, 1889, Washington became the forty-second state and received a grant of 3.2 million acres of land from the United States to help establish and support institutions such as public schools, universities, prisons, and capitol buildings. The lands were to be managed in trust for the intended beneficiaries.

The trust lands could be sold, as they had been in other states, or they could be leased, or they could be managed to provide a perpetual source of revenue for the school children, university students, and other citizens of the state. Fortunately for future generations of Washingtonians and for Puget Sound, many of these trust lands were retained by the new state and became an actively managed asset of state forests and agricultural lease lands.

Washington was also granted ownership of all aquatic lands—tidal and submerged lands under the state's navigable waterways, including streams and lakes and marine waters. This gift totaled 2.4 million acres. The new state adopted a constitution that created a voter-elected commissioner of public lands, who in the future would administer and lead the state's Department of Natural Resources.

In 1895, however, the state legislature passed laws allowing the lands commissioner to sell public tidelands and shorelands to private citizens, which encouraged shellfish growing and harvesting, as well as the growth of ports for the new state. Sales of tidelands and shorelands continued until 1971, when the legislature banned future sales to nonpublic entities.

By then, only about 30 percent of the state's tidelands and 75 percent of the state's shorelands remained in public ownership, according to a DNR report from 2000: *Changing Our Water Ways: Trends in Washington's Water Systems.* By contrast, nearly all the bedlands (aquatic lands that are always submerged) in Washington's navigable saltwater and freshwater are owned by the public and managed by DNR.

As early as the 1890s, only a few years after statehood, the magnificent salmon runs of the Pacific Northwest were fast disappearing due to overfishing, habitat destruction, and lack of effective regulation. As the Northwest Power and Conservation Council described in a 2012 historical summary of fish hatcheries in the region: "In 1890, it was legal in Washington to fish with dynamite." Alarmed by the drop in the salmon population, early Washington fish commissioner A. C. Little of Tacoma called for aggressive artificial production—fish hatcheries. But fish declines continued as a result of overfishing and accelerated habitat destruction.

As the state and its economy grew, dams were built on numerous rivers and tributaries in the Olympic Mountains and Cascade Range for hydropower production and municipal water supply. The dams effectively prevented salmon and steelhead from traveling between their ancient upstream spawning grounds and the sea, even though early Washington law required fish passageways wherever salmon migrated upstream.

In a 2000 paper on the status of salmon in the Northeast Pacific region, researchers Ted Gresh, Jim Lichatowich, and

Peter Schoonmaker estimated (based on historical salmon cannery records) that the biomass of salmon-derived nutrients returning to Northwest streams was a mere 6 to 7 percent of historical levels.

In the early years of statehood, oyster harvesting in Puget Sound increased as settlers discovered the food and commercial value of the tasty bivalves whose tiny, intricate shells covered many shores. Before the arrival of settlers with their industrial harvesting techniques, the tiny native oyster of the West Coast of North America flourished in coastal bays and inlets from California to Alaska. It was especially prolific in the maze of shallow tidelands at the southern reaches of Puget Sound. To oystermen and the oyster-buying public, they became known as Olympia oysters, or Olys.

According to the Pacific Shellfish Institute, the Olympia oyster industry reached its peak in the 1890s and then "abruptly" crashed because of "overharvest and declining water quality conditions." By 1915, says the institute, the Oly oyster was "almost extinct in Puget Sound." This near extinction led commercial shellfish producers to introduce Asian varieties of oysters and clams to their shellfish beds, saving the industry.

Half a century later, shellfish farming again gained traction in the region when Kenneth Chew helped launch and grow a world-renowned aquaculture program at the University of Washington School of Fisheries. And then federal and state clean water laws, and shellfish-gathering regulations, also

TOP A net full of salmon in Bellingham, circa 1900
BOTTOM Salmon about to be canned in Bellingham, circa 1904: the advent of salmon canning combined with habitat degradation had devastating effects on salmon populations. Cannery packing peaked in Puget Sound in 1913 at nearly 2.6 million cases.

S'Klallam Leaders

JEROMY SULLIVAN and RON CHARLES represent two generations of the Port Gamble S'Klallam Tribe. The S'Klallam people have lived and subsisted for more than a thousand years on and near the picturesque Port Gamble Bay in north Kitsap County, not far from where Hood Canal meets Admiralty Inlet. Ron was the tribal chair for the better part of three decades, and he counts himself fortunate to be a salmon fisherman. Jeromy succeeded Ron as tribal chair, and says his favorite job is geoduck diver.

They have lived, as the saying goes, in interesting times—for their people, for the tribe's bay, and for the Sound. Jeromy and Ron lived through the last days of the mill era of Port Gamble, and, after the mill closed in 1995, they and other tribal officials have played an important role in the cleanup era. They also live at a time when they and fellow tribal members can exercise their ancient treaty rights to fish, hunt, and gather shellfish in the places where their ancestors did. These rights were specifically reserved and retained in 1855, when tribal representatives signed the Point No Point Treaty with Territorial Governor Isaac Stevens and the US government. For more than a century, the government of Washington State refused to recognize the treaty rights until US District Judge George Boldt upheld the Puget Sound tribes' rights in a landmark ruling in 1974. This, in turn, resulted in the tribes becoming co-managers of fisheries with Washington's state fisheries officials.

Ron says, "I was born in the perfect time because I was a young man and we had this return of our ancestral rights to us. I was able to go out and be one of the ones who harvested. I still do to this day. I count myself as one of the luckiest people because I was able to experience this." Jeromy has been a geoduck diver for more than twenty years. "I love being out on the water and certainly under the water," he says. It is hard, dangerous work. "Seals will push you over when you're underwater. I've learned how much I respect Mother Nature, how much I respect currents, how much I respect wind." He adds, "It's amazing how quickly Mother Nature can show you who is really the boss around here."

Another change Jeromy and Ron have witnessed is the decline in fish, shellfish, and other creatures in Puget Sound waters. Ron, who grew up in the 1940s and 1950s, says: "We used to have huge herring runs to Port Gamble Bay. My dad's and my grandpa's generations would harvest tubs full of them. Port Gamble Bay was known for having one of the largest runs of herring in the state. Now it has dwindled to the point where we are afraid of losing them completely. We used to have a codfish bed just right out there, and people would go out in February and harvest cod. It's gone. They used to go down and harvest critters from the rocks along the bay. We called them sea eggs. They were spiny things, and you would break the shell and eat the roe inside. They are long disappeared. There are several species of different things that were in our diets years ago that are not there anymore."

Jeromy Sullivan

Jeromy says: "The S'Klallam people have been part of Hood Canal and Puget Sound for thousands of years. This body of water is how we survive, even today. It is part of our identity as native people." In addition to hunting and fishing, he says, "We have survived on clams. We have

Ron Charles

been cooking them the same way for at least eight hundred years—cooking on rocks, and steaming them open."

The Port Gamble S'Klallam Tribe is one of the interrelated Klallam and Clallam people who traditionally lived across a wide range of the Salish Sea—along parts of Hood Canal, Puget Sound, and the northern coast of the Olympic Peninsula, and across the water in the San Juan Islands and into Canada. The sea and the sheltered shimmering bay, along with the biologically rich forests, provided everything that the S'Klallam people needed until the 1850s. And then, with the arrival of the US settlers and their government and military might, the S'Klallam people almost lost their ancestral home and livelihoods. At Port Gamble, the tribe's survival during white settlement and Washington's early statehood was tied closely to the sawmill built by newly arriving whites. It operated for nearly a century and a half at Port Gamble.

After the signing of the 1855 treaty, the tribesmen at Port Gamble were told to pack up their belongings and paddle south to live on a reservation called Skokomish, where the river of that name flows from the Olympic Mountains into the sharp bend of Hood Canal. Many tribal members did not want to give up their lives as people of open waters or to live with other tribes at Skokomish. And so it happened that the white men's sawmill provided an escape hatch, enabling them to stay. Frederic Talbot, and his partner Andrew Pope, needed a reliable local workforce for their new logging and milling operation, which started cranking out lumber at the bay in 1853. The natives were available, reliable, good workers, and had no intention of going elsewhere. The company moved the tribal families from their protected shoreline out onto the spit of land known as Point Julia, and provided timber for homes, a school, a church, and a water-delivery trough.

Thus began a mutually beneficial relationship that lasted from the 1850s until the mill's closure in 1995. Ron Charles says the tribe would have disappeared, as many others did, "except our ancestors stayed here to work at the mill." It was central to their lives. "The mill was always with us," he explains. "We knew intimately about it. There used to be a siren that went off when they had an accident at the mill. Because there were so many of us working at the mill, we would worry: Did my dad get hurt? We knew the five o'clock whistle. Parents would tell the kids: Come home when the whistle blows. It was noisy, but you didn't complain about it."

Jeromy says, "My grandpa worked there, and retired from the mill. My dad worked there for thirty-three years. My brother worked at the mill for a year and a half. It was the longest lasting working mill in Washington." Ron's grandfather, Harry Fulton, also retired from the mill. "Until the mill closed, there were Fulton men employed there continuously," he recalls. Over time, mill jobs enabled tribal members to purchase land for homes. Then in 1938, the 1,300-acre Port Gamble S'Klallam Reservation was created by the Indian Reorganization Act. The land is held collectively by the tribe in perpetuity.

For all the benefits that the tribe, the mill owners, and the region gained from the mill's century and a half of continuous operation, the mill closure eventually ushered in a new era of environmental cleanup. The Port Gamble S'Klallam leaders took on another role: co-managers of cleanup, protection, and restoration of the bay and its biological resources. The most visible undertaking has been cleaning up tons of wood waste and 8,500 creosote-treated pilings from Port Gamble Bay, which served for so long as a floating log yard and lumber processing and shipping facility.

Thick layers of wood waste on the bottom of the bay crowded out shellfish and other creatures, and created lifeless zones. Creosote was an effective wood preservative, but led to disease, stunted growth, interfered with reproduction, and shortened lifespans for many marine animals.

Under oversight of the state Department of Ecology and the tribe, Pope Resources—owner of Port Gamble and its former industrial site—spent more than $20 million in company funds removing the environmental contamination from the bay and replacing much of the bay's sediments with clean fill. Thousands of truckloads of contaminated material were trucked to a county-permitted landfill that Pope built nearby for safe disposal of toxic waste, including capping it with clean soil. Both the landfill and the cleanup site will be monitored on a set schedule for continued protection of human health and the environment. The state also provided $9 million for environmental restoration projects, enhanced oyster habitat, and purchase of land to create a 2,000-acre park along the bayshore.

Ron and Jeromy are pleased by the cleanup of the bay at the tribe's front door, but they are keenly aware of how much more must be done to restore the Sound and regain the abundance of food and other sea life that has been lost. They see many reasons for the declines: overharvesting by tribal and non-tribal fishers and gatherers, growth in human population, shoreline bulkheads, hundreds of toxic chemicals and other contaminants entering the Sound from human uses, and changes in sea chemistry caused by the acidification of the planet's vast oceans.

Speaking as a tribal chair and as a harvester of seafood, Jeromy says: "Both the tribes and the state did a really bad job managing for very many years. For us to get back to where we were, with multiple clam digs in a month, we have to change what we were doing. It's hard because our families are hungry. They are wanting to get out onto the beach. Oyster picks are few and far between. Access to beaches is few and far between." Yet he believes sacrifices must be made to ensure sea life, and harvests, in perpetuity.

The tribe is also making changes in its own operations. It built a new sewage system on the reservation, near the tribe's hotel and casino, as far from the water as possible. Sewage is discharged into an engineered drain field, where the sludge is pumped and removed, and safe water percolates into the ground. Jeromy says, "It's scary to learn how much damage humans have done—not just non-natives, but all of us. We didn't have real knowledge of the damage that was being done. It took us a long time to cause the damage. It's going to take us all a lot longer to fix it."

Great blue herons rely on places like Port Gamble Bay for food and habitat.

created healthier conditions for the shellfish industry. The not-for-profit Puget Sound Restoration Fund was formed, taking the lead in implementing the state Fish and Wildlife Commission's native shellfish restoration plan.

As noted in the Washington Shellfish Initiative, many generations of tribal and non-tribal people have harvested and cultivated shellfish from Washington's tidelands. Both commercial and recreational harvests are highly valuable and provide a unique opportunity to eat from the sea. To protect public health, shellfish beds are tested frequently for bacteria that could indicate signs of sewage contamination. Recently, the intensity of aquaculture practices has led some to question its potential impacts on nearshore environments around the Sound and the Salish Sea, and to weigh in on where such operations should be sited.

Raymond Moses tunes his drum before the Tulalip Tribe's ceremony welcoming the first fish of the season. Salmon represent life to the Coast Salish tribes.

Sustainable Shellfish Businesswoman

AHI MARTIN-MCSWEENEY'S immersion in life as a Puget Sounder began, literally as well as figuratively, a few months after she arrived in Seattle as a new college graduate. "It was a beautiful day," she recalls, "and my friends said, 'Let's go to the beach.' I said, 'Great!' I was thinking: I love the beach. I'm from Santa Cruz."

The group of friends went to Alki, that popular crescent in West Seattle on Elliott Bay. Compared to California beaches,

there wasn't much sand at Alki, Ahi recalls. "And there wasn't much surf, but it smelled just right. There was that salty quality to the air. It still had that comforting effect that you get from being near the ocean."

She laughs now at the surprise that awaited her in the waters of the Sound. "We went into the water. It was freezing cold," she recalls with a big, rich grin. "But it didn't matter. We waded in and dunked ourselves." As it turned out, that first frigid exposure to northern Pacific waters wasn't a turnoff for this descendant of Hawaiians and Northern Europeans.

As time went on, Ahi found herself drawn back to the Sound. "For the first ten years of my adult life, the beaches of Puget Sound have been where I would always run off to, to be alone and think. I ended up spending a lot of time at Golden Gardens [a Seattle public park] in the Ballard area, clearing my head." In time, Puget Sound became part of her life in ways she had never expected. Ahi now devotes much of her time and her creative energy to giving others an unforgettable taste of the Sound.

It was two Seattle institutions that brought Ahi to the Pacific Northwest, namely, Starbucks Coffee and the Art Institute of Seattle. She soon realized that art wasn't her calling and decided to devote her energies to her work at Starbucks, which had granted her a transfer to one of its downtown Seattle stores. Eventually, she became a manager of two of the company's stores.

"All of my business acumen I attribute to my time at Starbucks," she says. "I learned a lot about people and about managing, and about being successful in business." She was also strongly influenced by the Starbucks ethic of environmentally sustainable business practices, like attention to recycling and using products made from renewable resources.

As a member of the millennial generation, Ahi was and is plugged in to what's going on in the world around her. After several years at Starbucks, she spotted an online posting for a job that sounded intriguing—setting up a catering business for a company based in Mason County, at a far southwest bend of Puget Sound. The company, Taylor Shellfish Farms, traces its origins back five generations, to 1890. When the first family members began harvesting tiny, tasty Olympia oysters from the inlets of Puget Sound, Washington was a brand-new state.

When Ahi saw that job announcement, Taylor already had a long history as an important producer, seller, and exporter of oysters, clams, and mussels; an influential voice for environmental sustainability; and a strong advocate for the recovery of Puget Sound and clean and healthy water. Ahi applied for the catering job and got it. As it turned out, the shellfish business became not just a job but also a way of life, and a family. Her wife, Michaela, also became a shellfish connoisseur—and expert shellfish shucker—while working at the Taylor Shellfish store in Seattle's Queen Anne neighborhood.

Ahi's job was to build a catering business that helped Taylor take shellfish on the road—and in the air—to events around the region and even across the continent. "We do everything— weddings, birthday parties, funerals. And we do lots of donated events because we're very involved in cleaning up the waterways," she says from the house she and her family are renovating on a gravity-defying street in Seattle's Magnolia neighborhood.

Ahi's catering job even took her to New York City for the Billion Oyster Party, held annually as part of an ambitious project to restore oysters, and oyster-created reefs, in New York Harbor and its waterways. "It's a unique feeling to take something that is so purely of a place and give it to people to eat," she says. For some customers, she has been the person who introduced them to eating oysters. "Many times, when people taste an oyster for the first time, they will say: 'It tastes like Puget Sound,'" she says with a smile. "It's very cool to be able to hand people that experience."

Ahi's job has given her a keen appreciation for the distinctive shapes, textures, tastes, and smells of all sorts of shellfish: oblong-shelled mussels, smooth-shelled clams, gnarly-shelled oysters of various types, and gigantic geoducks. Over time, she was able to distinguish the different types of oysters from their sizes and shells: Shigoku, Kumamoto (commonly called Pacific oysters), and the tiny Olympia oyster—the only oyster native to the West Coast. "There's something really unique about oysters," she marvels. "They take on the flavor of the place where they're grown. Since water is constantly moving, the flavor will vary from time to time."

Working in the seafood business has influenced many of the ways Ahi and her family live in this place. "We like to camp," she says. "We've learned that you can harvest shellfish during appropriate times of the year, so we have started to tailor our camping experiences to be near harvestable beaches so we don't have to pack a bunch of extra protein. We gather oysters, and we grill them with butter and white wine or hot sauce. It's very, very simple."

The business also has shaped her understanding of what it means to have a healthy and sustainable Puget Sound. "It means we humans can swim in the water, and things can grow in it," she says. "If things can grow in it, we can continue to farm and harvest and eat from it."

Why does a healthy Puget Sound matter? Ahi says, "We need water to survive, right? We should all be focused on being not just good stewards of the land, but also of the water around us. We're accustomed to doing certain things on land—trash disposal, recycling, and so on. We don't have those habits formed yet about water. Water makes up how much of our planet? [71 percent, per the US Geological Survey] We need to keep it clean."

With the awareness that they have gained from their work, Ahi and Michaela find themselves thinking and acting differently about water. After all, any water that's used on land upshore from Puget Sound ends up down there, in the Sound. "For me," Ahi says, "the biggest tangible difference is thinking twice about what goes down my drain." That includes sink, tub, and street drains. "I'm much more careful about foreign substances: cooking oil, food scraps, what kinds of products we use for cleaning."

She says unabashedly that there's something else people can do to contribute to a cleaner and healthier Puget Sound: "When we eat local shellfish, we support the local companies doing all this work to restore our bays. The more we consumers interact with them, the more they can do."

When Ahi looks to the future, she is at once apprehensive and optimistic. "What makes me nervous for the future is that we're going into a period of time when the powers that be may not prioritize clean water," she says. "It's kind of unnerving, especially when my life and livelihood are tied to clean water."

But she is encouraged by increased interest in shellfish and other fresh food from our coastal waters. "Consumers have power," she notes. Ahi believes they can force change in how we protect life-giving waters. Through consumer choices, business investments, and advocacy by shellfish growers, she says, "We have been able to reclaim some of our waterways and bays."

Ahi is hopeful that today's children can learn the importance of water and healthy aquatic ecosystems like the Sound. "Kids want to save the world," she observes. "You take kids to a zoo and the first thing they talk about is saving animals so they don't go extinct. We should be supporting kids and helping them to thrive."

Humans aren't the only creatures that enjoy oysters. Sea stars, such as this giant sunflower star, use suction from their powerful tube feet to pry open oyster shells and get to the soft tissue inside. Sea stars also prey on sea urchins like the many surrounding this sunflower star.

Ahi is also encouraged by her own generation. "For millennials, it's part of our group mentality to want to know where 'this' [meaning any particular product or idea] comes from. Information is available to us, so we want answers." She hopes this will lead them to make better choices.

What is clear to her, and she believes will become clearer to others in her generation, is that "one thing we can do to be healthy is to make sure the water is good so it benefits everybody." And for Ahi, there is no doubt that clean water must include a life-giving, life-sustaining Puget Sound.

A BRIEF HISTORY OF THE SOUND

17,000 years ago	Glaciers cover the area that will become Puget Sound and the Salish Sea.
15,000 years ago	The last glacier retreats to what is now Canada.
10,000 years ago	Indigenous people are living in the region, developing a rich culture consisting of numerous tribes in hundreds of seasonal and permanent camps and villages.
1774	Europeans arrive on a Spanish frigate commanded by Juan Pérez Hernández.
1792	Two ships led by British captain George Vancouver enter the area, explore and chart the waterways, and name several geographical features. Vancouver names Puget Sound for his lieutenant Peter Puget.
1827	Hudson's Bay Company establishes a fort and trading post at Langley near future Vancouver, BC. In 1832, the company establishes the Fort Nisqually trading post near the mouth of the Nisqually River.
1841	US Navy Lieutenant Charles Wilkes arrives with his crew in Puget Sound, charting the waters and giving names to many of the places that millions of people will recognize in the future.
1846	Four American families from the Oregon Trail arrive at the southern tip of Puget Sound and found the town of New Market, which will become Tumwater. Britain and the US agree to a boundary on the 49th parallel, which will become the US-Canada border.
1851	US settlers arrive by boat at the future Seattle, named for Chief Sealth, of the Duwamish and Suquamish Tribes.
1853	The US government creates the Washington Territory, with Isaac Stevens as the territorial governor. He founds the capital, naming it Olympia. Sawmills are built at Seattle and at Port Gamble on the Kitsap Peninsula.
1854	Governor Stevens convenes a treaty council with tribes at Medicine Creek at the mouth of the Nisqually River. This treaty, and others that follow, will set the new laws governing tribes and other American citizens. In exchange for relinquishing lands, the tribes retain the right to fish, hunt, and gather traditional foods.
1883	Northern Pacific Railway terminal is built at Tacoma on central Puget Sound, forever changing transportation and trade in the region.
1889	Washington becomes a state, receiving more than five million acres of land and underwater territory from the federal government.
1890	A smelter begins operating at the edge of Tacoma to process mined ore into copper, lead, and arsenic. During nearly a century of operation, its chimney will eventually reach 562 feet and spread toxics over a thousand square miles.
1890s	During this decade, the region's magnificent salmon runs decline alarmingly from overfishing, habitat destruction, and lack of effective regulations.
1895	The state legislature passes laws allowing for the sale of public tidelands and shorelands to private parties.
1897	Gold is discovered in Alaska, and Seattle becomes a major supply and departure point for people, goods, and equipment heading to the gold fields. Seattle's population doubles in ten years.
1898	Hydroelectric diversion dam is built at Snoqualmie Falls, ushering in an era of major damming in the Puget Sound watershed. By 2019, more than five hundred dams of various types exist around the Sound.
1899	Congress creates Mount Rainier National Park, the first of many national and state parks, wilderness and conservation areas, and natural preserves in the Puget Sound region.
1901	The US Navy station at Bremerton becomes Navy Yard Puget Sound, ushering in an era when the region will become home to several major military complexes.

1902	The Pacific oyster is introduced from Japan, following the dramatic decline in native oysters. It becomes the mainstay of the region's oyster industry. Several more non-native oyster and clam species will be introduced to our waters, and our tables, in the decades to come.
1927	The "dread year" for native Puget Sound Olympia oysters, during which the last of the natural population nearly disappears. In decades to come, new water pollution laws plus advances in aquaculture will help commercial growers make the region a major supplier of shellfish again.
1945	A state Pollution Control Commission is established, leading the way for future environmental protection.
1957	The legislature creates the Washington State Department of Natural Resources under the elected commissioner of public lands. With professional stewardship, state forests, lease lands, and aquatic lands become important public resources.
1958	Serious pollution in Lake Washington, resulting from the discharge of sewage of surrounding communities, leads King County voters to create Metro as a regional wastewater treatment authority. New sewage treatment plants and collection systems are built.
1960s	Puget Sound orcas begin to be captured for amusement, parks, and exhibitions. It dramatically reduces the region's historic population.
1970	The state legislature and Governor Dan Evans create the Department of Ecology, the first comprehensive environmental protection agency in the fifty states.
1971	The legislature passes the state's Oil Pollution Act, outlawing the discharge of oil into state waters.
1972	Congress passes the Marine Mammal Protection Act, but doesn't prohibit capturing orcas for commercial purposes. Congress passes the Clean Water Act and puts the new US Environmental Protection Agency in charge of enforcing it nationwide. State voters approve the Shoreline Management Act.
1973	Congress passes the Endangered Species Act in an attempt to halt and reverse the extinction of species occurring nationwide.
1974	The federal court's Boldt Decision affirms tribes' treaty rights to fish in their usual and accustomed locations. The US government creates the Nisqually National Wildlife Refuge in the South Sound. The state legislature passes the Forest Practices Act to protect natural resources during timber and forestry activities on state-owned lands and private timber lands.
1976	The last Puget Sound orca to be captured is taken from the waters of Budd Inlet. Commercial capture of orcas in Washington ends when the state sues SeaWorld in US court.
1980	Scientists document abnormalities in fish in Puget Sound resulting from the effect of toxic chemicals in sediments.
1988	State voters adopt the Model Toxics Control Act to clean up sites contaminated by any of thousands of toxic materials. Puget Sound is designated an Estuary of National Significance for environmental cleanups.
1989	The Washington Wildlife and Recreation Coalition forms and begins raising money for state purchase of land for conservation and recreation.
1993	To great fanfare, the Tacoma smelter stack is demolished and buried in a trench. The last building in the smelter complex is brought down in 2004.
2007	The legislature and Governor Chris Gregoire establish the Puget Sound Partnership, creating a citizen Leadership Council and setting the goal of restoring the Sound to a healthy condition by 2020.
2009	The state receives a $95 million settlement from Asarco to pay for cleanup of the Tacoma smelter stack's plume of toxic waste.
2010	Geographic naming boards in the US and Canada designate the connected inland waters of the Pacific Northwest as the Salish Sea.
2011	The removal of two obsolete dams begins on the Elwha River on the northern Olympic Peninsula, reopening seventy miles of salmon habitat.
2020	This was the target year for returning Puget Sound to a healthy condition under the statute creating the Puget Sound Partnership. Citizens, businesses, and the legislature have recommitted to this vision beyond this timeline.

TOP As mussel shells break down, they release nutrients such as calcium that are essential to the health of terrestrial plants.

BOTTOM Grilled oysters harvested from Puget Sound are a delicacy. Shellfish rely on healthy water. As the ocean and connected waterways absorb carbon dioxide from the atmosphere, the water becomes more acidic, causing some organisms' shells to weaken or even dissolve. Known as ocean acidification, this change can be lethal to young oysters by preventing them from forming shells.

Transformative Educator and Biologist

Since arriving in the Puget Sound region in 1955, DR. KENNETH CHEW has seen just about everything in the inland sea of the Pacific Northwest. What worries him is what he no longer sees.

Ken is a national and international authority on the biology of shellfish and aquaculture (the planting, cultivating, and harvesting of shellfish for commerce). His professional credits are many: University of Washington professor emeritus, retired director of the Western Regional Aquaculture Center, retired associate dean of the UW College of Ocean and Fishery Science, and former member of the Washington State Fish and Wildlife Commission. Oh yes, and NOAA honored him by naming the Kenneth K. Chew Center for Shellfish Research and Restoration (established in partnership with the Puget Sound Restoration Fund) after him.

Early in the summer of '55, Ken arrived in Seattle from his home state of California to study for a master's degree in salmon biology at the UW School of Fisheries. His research project wasn't due to start until September, so the dean arranged for a summer job for him at the Point Whitney Shellfish Laboratory at Dabob Bay on the Olympic Peninsula. "I could not believe the amount of seafood right on the beach," he marvels. "Back in the 1950s, crabs were abundant in Hood Canal. Shrimp was abundant. Oysters and clams were all over the place. That's where I got introduced to eating mussels. You could fish off the dock and get rockfish, piling perch, and sometimes cutthroat trout."

That summer was the start of a life of research and teaching. Biologists at the lab urged Ken to study shellfish, such as oysters, clams, geoducks, mussels, and abalone. At that time, he says, very few people were trained in shellfish biology. Because of the arrangement that had brought him to the university, Ken

devoted his first year of graduate studies to researching the behavior of salmon. But at the end of that year, he "decided to make that leap" to study shellfish and other invertebrates in the Sound. His research and training led to job offers from Oregon, California, and even Venezuela. But the dean of the UW School of Fisheries had other ideas, and put him to work creating a shellfish program at the university with one of his mentors, Dr. Albert K. Sparks.

Ken was particularly interested in the applied aspects of shellfish biology, including basic biology and environmental needs, the best culture or farming techniques, and the commercial and recreational uses of shellfish. The term aquaculture was generally unknown at the time. He recalls, "People would say: Aquaculture? Is that agriculture?" Skeptics didn't understand why he was interested in seafood farming, a common refrain being: "There is always going to be plenty of seafood out in the ocean, so why do we need to farm it?"

It's now apparent how wrong those skeptics were. Many natural stocks of edible sea life are so diminished that farming of shellfish and other seafood has become "absolutely major," Ken notes. "A significant amount of the seafood you see in the stores is farmed, and many types are imported from around the world."

From the beginning, Ken's approach was to go to shellfish growers and ask, "What is your problem? What do you need investigated?" He would then seek funding for graduate students to research those problems. What those students discovered and reported has influenced the understanding of shellfish around the world.

Ken and his students also helped bring about a breakthrough in culinary tastes on the West Coast. Into the 1970s, he says, mussels weren't widely regarded as a delicacy. That began to

A creek runs into Dabob Bay on the Olympic Peninsula at low tide.

Cove on Whidbey Island, which has since become renowned for its shellfish industry.

Another breakthrough from his students' research made it possible for commercial shellfish growers to harvest and sell oysters year-round, including in the warmer summer months when spawning makes oysters mushy and unpalatable. Some of Ken's students learned and documented how to biologically engineer triploid or sexless oysters, which allowed for year-round harvest.

Today, the commercial shellfish industry is a major force in the state's economy. Washington is a top oyster-producing state and the nation's largest producer of hatchery-reared and farmed Pacific oysters. Shellfish also are an important environmental alarm system, and they help protect water quality in Puget Sound. In Ken's words: "If you can legally harvest shellfish, it's an indicator of good water."

So, what has been happening to the sea creatures since young Ken Chew first saw the eye-popping natural abundance of fish and shellfish on Dabob Bay? "Puget Sound is one of the most beautiful estuaries and water bodies in the US," Ken says, but he is concerned about diminished water quality and other changes for the worse. Looking out the window of his home on a bluff overlooking Seattle's Shilshole Bay, Ken points to the marine waters and, at lower tides, a beckoning gravel beach. He

change when he and a student started reaching out to communities and public officials around the Sound to obtain support for mussel research floats in saltwater bays. That research, and more that followed, helped lead to a viable mussel growing and harvesting industry. Some of their early research was at Penn

laments, "I used to go out there in the late eighties and nineties at extreme low tides in July, and I could see several geoduck neck–siphon shows, and numerous siphon holes of horse, cockle, native littleneck, and butter clams. And I usually saw orange succulent sea pens, large sea stars, red rock and shore crabs, to name a few. I usually saw eelgrass and several varieties of macroalgae."

Then he began to see fewer signs of clams, especially horse clams and geoducks, on his beach walks. Various agencies documented that seawater here and elsewhere was becoming more acidic, posing a serious threat to oysters, clams, mussels, and other invertebrates by inhibiting calcium carbonate deposits during larvae shell development. But Ken is careful to point out that the situation on the beach near Shilshole "does not necessarily reflect the same for other Sound beaches, as they are all different."

Ken is encouraged by certain areas of progress in protecting the Sound and its organisms. Treating sewage and reducing industrial pollution have been priorities for federal, state, local, and tribal governments. In addition, fecal coliform and many shellfish toxins are measured and monitored.

Equipment in the Kenneth Chew Center for Shellfish Research and Restoration

But he says many chemicals, hormones, and prescription drugs pass through humans, are flushed down toilets, and end up in our water. "It's the unmeasured component that worries me," Ken says. "It's too expensive perhaps to test for them and study them." He suspects that these contaminants may help explain some of the reduction of popular marine fish species over recent decades. "The recreational fishing for salmon and marine bottom fish such as rockfish and true cod may never be the same as in the fifties," says Ken.

Despite an increase in the acidity of seawater, trends in commercial oyster and clam farming make Ken hopeful. Pinto abalone and sea cucumbers are now being grown in the NOAA hatchery that bears Ken Chew's name, and the young creatures are being replanted in the wild as part of the restoration program. And hatcheries have helped to bring back the native Olympia oyster.

He is also encouraged that oysters and clams are available for recreational harvesting at numerous public beaches. Ken celebrates the successes in saving Puget Sound species, but he also shines a light on the problems. As he sees it, we still have to fight to keep from losing parts of Puget Sound.

OUR GROWING IMPACT ON NATURAL RESOURCES

In 1883, the Northern Pacific Railway completed its roll across the continent, connecting the Atlantic coast with Puget Sound at Tacoma (named for the great mountain that the native peoples called Tahoma, which Captain Vancouver renamed for his admiral friend Rainier). The first rail terminal on Puget Sound was built on Commencement Bay.

A region where people had moved for thousands of years at the speed of canoes had arrived in the industrial age. Puget Sound was now part of a national and global transportation web, at the center of a vast land and sea trade. These developments foreshadowed a time more than a century later, when the communities around the Salish Sea, on both sides of the border, would constitute some of the greatest economic output in North America. In 2017, the combined gross domestic product (value of all goods and services produced) of the twelve Washington counties of the Puget Sound watershed exceeded the GDP of states such as Colorado, Arizona, Tennessee, Minnesota, Indiana, or Wisconsin. In 2016, British Columbia's share of Canada's economic output ranked behind only Ontario, Quebec, and Alberta.

IN 1897, A STEAMSHIP ARRIVED IN SEATTLE FROM ALASKA, carrying news that transformed Seattle and the Puget Sound region. The prospectors that came ashore carried a lot of shiny metal from the Klondike gold fields. The Klondike Gold Rush National Historical Park in Seattle picks up the story from there: "What had been just a few hundred prospectors sailing from Seattle each week soon turned into a stampede of thousands as newspapers spread word, telegraphed from Seattle, that a great quantity of gold had been found along a remote river in what is today the Yukon Territory of Canada."

By 1900, the ten-year census showed 80,000 people living in Seattle—double the 1890 census. It would take a lot of resources to feed and supply all the new arrivals and departing gold rushers. Puget Sound and its watershed was a primary source of food and other resources.

Meanwhile, in 1890, heavy industry arrived on Puget Sound in a big way, bringing with it a toxic legacy of air, water, soil, and sediment pollution. None was more dramatic and far-reaching than the smelters near Tacoma and at Everett. These plants extracted copper and lead, along with arsenic, from ore, making the product easy to ship by water and rail. Although

Asarco's smelter at Everett operated just eighteen years until 1912, it left behind a toxic mess that would have to be cleaned up a century later. The Asarco plant near Tacoma would go on to operate for nearly a century, sending a steady toxic plume up through its massive 562-foot stack and into the air.

Among the many industries that would create long-lasting toxic pollution, leaving behind complex cleanup challenges, are creosote wood-treating facilities, shipyards, pulp and paper mills, lumber mills, coal gasification, landfills, heavy manufacturing, gasoline facilities, and chemical-intensive nurseries. These plants and many other manufacturing facilities provided good-paying jobs while creating products that the world wanted. Over time, the long-term costs to people and the environment became apparent.

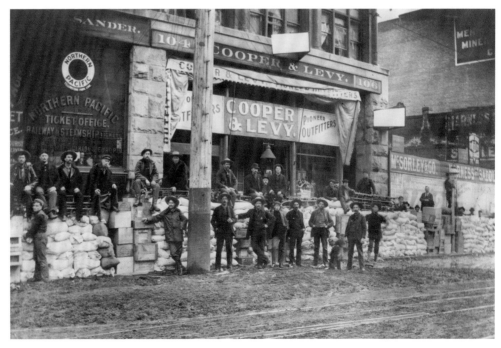

OPPOSITE Paper mills and other industry flourished along the Sound's shores and often contaminated its waters.

RIGHT After news of a major gold strike in the Yukon in 1897, eager prospectors flocked to the port city of Seattle. Here, Pioneer Square bustles with excitement.

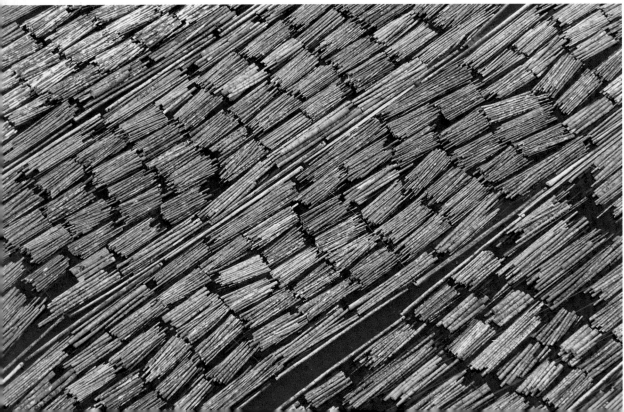

TOP Logging can have serious environmental effects, such as reducing habitat for birds and other wildlife that rely on trees for cover, nesting habitat, and food. Trees also help anchor soil along stream banks; their removal increases the risk of erosion and flooding.

BOTTOM Log rafts float in Commencement Bay in Tacoma. Such rafts can be enormous and can be hazardous to marine life.

OPPOSITE, LEFT Transporting coal in uncovered train cars poses environmental risks from coal dust, fine powder that can contain harmful metals, such as lead, mercury, and arsenic, which can pollute streams and nearby land.

OPPOSITE, RIGHT Oil trains pose environmental risks due to rail safety concerns. If an oil train derails, toxic crude oil may be released, contaminating the rivers feeding into the Sound and the marine waters themselves.

Using Puget Sound as a Classroom

It's the end of March, and a steady rain is falling as school buses arrive at a peninsula that juts out from State Highway 3 into a narrow and shallow inlet of southern Puget Sound known as Oakland Bay. As seventh graders, teachers, and parent volunteers climb out of the buses, they are wearing all manner of foul-weather gear. Mere rain is not going to cancel this day of learning in the Shelton School District. The kids and the adults have arrived at Bayshore, three miles north of their usual classrooms at Olympic Middle School. They are here to experience geology and hydrology, plants and critters, land and sea interacting in a miracle of life.

Welcome to twenty-first century education, delivered in the classroom of the outdoor world. It's a method called FieldSTEM, which takes students outside to integrate a wide range of skills and develop an understanding of complex systems so students can design solutions collaboratively. It was developed by the Pacific Education Institute, a statewide nonprofit organization that provides equitable high-quality learning opportunities for educators.

On this day, the classroom is Bayshore Preserve, with four thousand feet of Puget Sound shoreline and seventy-four acres of land—forty-five of which are being restored and returned to nature following 150 years as a homestead, sawmill, and rural golf course. After acquiring the site with the help of the Squaxin Island Tribe and many other public and private partners, Capitol Land Trust began the diligent process of returning it to a natural condition.

Here, the students can experience natural wonders. With their own eyes, they study Johns Creek, flowing out of the western hills of south Puget Sound into Oakland Bay, an extension of Hammersley Inlet. They see naturally occurring Oregon white oaks, rare in this forested region, but more common farther east and south. They pass huge, widely spaced Douglas-firs, some of them hundreds of years old, with bark fissures as deep as a person's fingers can reach.

In small groups, students wind their way through the preserve, stopping at stations that provide welcoming canopies sheltering them from the rain. At one of the stops, the kids discover some of the insects that serve as food for fish and amphibians. At another, they see tubs of clams, oysters, and shrimp that they can study and touch. Here, they learn about the secrets of the crustaceans and mollusks from Daron Williams, restoration and public access manager of Capitol Land Trust; Tom Terry, former board member and volunteer of the Land Trust; Mary Birchem, outreach and education coordinator with the Land Trust; and Audrey Lamb, biological project manager at Taylor Shellfish Farms and board member of the Land Trust.

Audrey explains that the waters in this region are a major producer of Manila clams, a seafood delicacy to many. Mary holds up a small jar of shrimp and explains that they were eaten by a coho salmon—which Tom caught on his fishing line.

This marker at Shilshole Bay Marina in Seattle reminds people not to dump chemicals into storm drains. Polluted stormwater runoff poses a substantial threat to water quality in Puget Sound.

Tom tells the kids he caught the salmon yesterday while fly fishing at Nisqually, a river and estuary that is many miles and twists and turns away, between Olympia and Tacoma. When Tom opened the coho's stomach, he found it full of shrimp. "Isn't it a good thing that we have shrimp in Puget Sound?" Tom asks the kids, by way of explaining the food web of the region.

All around this landscape, renewal is occurring, as native plants are reestablished where golf greens and fairways dominated for so long. After a 1,400-foot tide-defying dike was removed, broad new channels were dug into the outer shoreline to reintroduce saltwater into the landscape. Telltale signs helped the Land Trust identify where similar channels had historically been located, and new side channels were created to allow Johns Creek to meander to the bay.

Crews for the Land Trust also laid large tree trunks in the channels. Some are anchored with thick braided cables so they will stay in place, providing shelter and protection for salmon and other creatures. Native vegetation was planted along the sides of the channels to stabilize the soil and offer shade, cover, and food.

Daron points out soil indentations that reveal where native prairie vegetation has been seeded. Over time, this golf course will be much as it was before European and American settlers came here and changed the native ecosystem. He describes the planting of more than twenty thousand tree seedlings, including shore pine, Sitka spruce, redcedar, Douglas-fir, and madrona. They're especially noticeable along both sides of Johns Creek.

Pausing a moment, Daron spots something that doesn't belong. He wades into the creek, and on the far side reaches down into the exposed mud bank. He picks up a very old golf ball, buried here ages ago and now exposed by the creek, and takes it to the nearby teaching station. Golf balls, too, can be part of a modern-day education.

Days like this at Bayshore Preserve are only part of the outdoor learning experience for students in Shelton, a town of about ten thousand souls that has survived since 1890 on natural resources—logging, milling, fishing, shellfish aquaculture, farming, livestock, gravel mining, and barging. Because FieldSTEM has been integrated into Shelton schools, elementary and middle school students now gain real-world experience and knowledge about stream flow, Puget Sound beach slopes, wildlife habitat, and the life cycles of salmon and other creatures of the sea. Ninth graders make the trip to the Seattle Aquarium for a

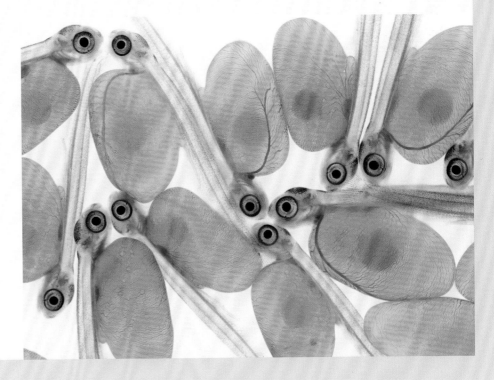

After they hatch, salmon go through a life stage in which they are called alevin. For about a month, these tiny fish absorb nutrients from the large yolk sacs attached to their bellies.

broader understanding of Puget Sound and oceans. Fourth graders receive salmon eggs from the Department of Fish and Wildlife, rear them in classroom aquariums, and ultimately release the young fish (called fry) into the wild.

The students' outdoor FieldSTEM work helps them learn and understand how all things, great and small, fit together as parts of the whole.

Science teacher and curriculum leader at Olympic Middle School WENDY BOLES has the pleasure of watching students learn, grow, and apply what they gain from their studies. She grew up in Tacoma, on the eastern shore of Puget Sound, and has never forgotten the time during her childhood when the news spread that orcas had arrived in the central region of the Sound. She jumped into the car with her family, and they drove to the shore to watch the dramatic breaching of the Sound's most spectacular marine mammals. Her family wasn't alone, Wendy recalls. "There were cars everywhere."

Now, with a lifetime of science study to her credit, Wendy has the opportunity to help hundreds of kids learn about the intricacies, and the majesty, of the Sound, its species, and its landscape. On a spring day, Wendy and fellow science teacher BENJAMIN FLOYD host a conversation between two authors and two Olympic Middle School seventh graders about their own appreciation for the Sound.

In the conversation, students KYLIE WALKER and JACE COLVIN realize they have something very specific in common—a true appreciation for shellfish, which are abundant in the saltwater inlets near Shelton. Oysters, clams, geoducks—they love them all. Both kids have family members who have worked in the shellfish industry, and they both savor the times when shellfish are prepared in special ways at family gatherings.

Reflecting on her studies of Puget Sound and its ecosystem, Kylie says, "It's important for students to know about the wildlife around them from personal experience, and not just in books and pictures." Her own learning was greatly enhanced by her family's move to a home at a point of land where several inlets,

Olympic Middle School students Jace Colvin and Kylie Walker (second and third from left) with science teachers Wendy Boles and Benjamin Floyd

islands, and peninsulas all come together in close proximity. From the beach and from her balcony, Kylie watches a parade of activity on the water—whether passing orcas or tugboats nudging gravel barges headed to distant places.

Both of these seventh graders describe some of the ways they try to help keep the Sound clean and healthy. They pick up trash and garbage littering the ground or beaches before the debris washes or blows into the water. They try to be careful about what they put into drains, which eventually empty into the Sound. They feel an obligation to take care of the water that means so much to them and to their town.

Jace says it this way: "We all need to manage what we take out of Puget Sound and what we put into it. This is like our home in a way. We need to treat it like we would treat anything we care about deeply. You don't want to ruin it by what you take out of it. You want to give back what was lost. You don't want to see this place overrun with garbage." Kylie adds, "If we don't take care of it, a lot of jobs would be lost, too."

The Washington State Department of Ecology reported that toxic metals from the Tacoma smelter had "settled on the surface soil over more than 1,000 square miles of the Puget Sound basin," and that "arsenic, lead, and other heavy metals are still in the soil as a result of this pollution." The State of Washington filed a lawsuit and won a settlement from the overseas owners of Asarco, including nearly $95 million to pay for cleanup related to the Tacoma Smelter Plume. After the smelter and its symbolic stack were torn down, the site and immediate area was remediated and a large complex of waterfront condos, apartments, shops, and restaurants was developed. Today, this waterfront brims with people enjoying the setting.

The Department of Ecology launched a broad, multiyear smelter plume cleanup, including soil testing and replacement for playgrounds, childcare centers, and residential yards within the plume footprint. The agency also provides information on its website about the Tacoma Smelter Plume Project for buyers and sellers of residential properties within the plume area.

IN 1901, THE US NAVY STATION AT BREMERTON WAS designated Navy Yard Puget Sound. In the two world wars that would follow, it played an important part in arming America for victories at sea. It was the birth of a lasting military, and supporting industrial, presence on Puget Sound and in the region.

In 1914, World War I broke out in Europe. The United States sent troops starting in 1917, spurring the growth of Puget Sound industries, including timber, fisheries, and the shipyards. In 1916, William Boeing launched a company to build wings for newfangled contraptions called airplanes. His little company, starting out in a red barn on the Duwamish River, would become the world's largest aircraft manufacturer.

Meanwhile, patriotic and economic-development-minded people in Pierce County raised money through a bond issue to purchase 70,000 acres near the shores of Puget Sound. The county then donated the land to the federal government with the stipulation that the site be used as a permanent military base, later known as Fort Lewis. Nisqually tribal history points out that in 1917, the Army moved onto Nisqually lands and ordered them from their homes. Pierce County later condemned 3,353 acres of Nisqually land and transferred it to the Army to expand the military base.

In 1927, Pierce County raised more money in another bond issue, and purchased land adjacent to the fort, which became McChord Field. Puget Sound's future as one of the world's major military complexes was secured. Over time, the region would become home to a US Navy air station on Whidbey Island, the expanded Navy station and shipyard at Bremerton, Naval Hospital Bremerton, a Navy station at Everett, the submarine base at Bangor on Hood Canal, a Navy station at Keyport near Bremerton, and a Navy munitions handling facility at Indian Island near Port Townsend. Fort Lewis and McChord, and Madigan Military Hospital, are co-located at Joint Base Lewis-McChord. However, one byproduct of military activity was a legacy of toxic pollution found many years later. Today the Department of Defense has multiple cleanups in progress.

IN 1980, THE TOXIC EFFECTS OF HUMAN ACTIVITIES IN AND near the Sound took on new urgency after Donald Malins, at the National Oceanic and Atmospheric Administration (NOAA) Northwest Fisheries Science Center's Montlake Lab in Seattle, published an article in the agency's magazine under

TOP An easy, attractive way to combat stormwater runoff, rain gardens divert water into planted areas that absorb and filter it before it drains into local streams, and ultimately, the Sound. This particular garden, designed by Stone Soup Gardens, also features raised beds with an abundance of fresh vegetables.
BOTTOM In Seattle, Max and Simon Hanson help transform their front yard into a rain garden.

Feeding Refugees, Protecting the Sound

In 1970, at the dawn of America's environmental movement, Joni Mitchell wrote a song about the paving of paradise. Four and a half decades later, an inspirational immigrant, whose family fled war-torn Bangladesh, reversed the process in Kent, Washington. And by doing so, helped to protect Puget Sound.

Soon after arriving in King County in 2016, TAHMINA MARTELLY signed on as manager of Resiliency Programs for World Relief Seattle. Through that program, she envisioned and led an innovative effort at a church to tear up an unused hillside parking lot and replace it with food gardens and a rain-collection system—diverting many thousands of gallons of polluted storm runoff before it could reach the Duwamish River and Elliott Bay on Puget Sound.

With seed money from King Conservation District, Tahmina commissioned a conceptual design by a local firm, Stone Soup Gardens. That effort attracted more partners, including Construction for Change, an international nonprofit that helps leverage infrastructure to improve quality of life; The Nature Conservancy; and Sustainability Ambassadors, which led Rain Garden Design Seminars at nearby Mill Creek Middle School, teaching the seventh graders about the garden project and incorporating them into the rain garden design process.

Tahmina recalls her initial impressions of sitting in the Hillside Church parking lot with Pastor Ev Tustin and brainstorming ideas. "One of the first things I thought was this would make an amazing garden," she says. "It's right in the middle of everything. It's near a transit line. It's officially a food desert, meaning people here have low access to fresh produce or food within a one-mile radius. It's an acre right on a major street. You can get off the bus right there. A lot of refugees and immigrants live nearby."

Depaving began in June 2017. By May 2018, more than forty-five work parties and more than a thousand volunteers had removed twenty-two thousand square feet of asphalt and gravel, built garden plots with cinderblocks, and handlaid irrigation lines. Eighty percent of the water used to irrigate the gardens during dry periods is collected from the expansive roof of the church and piped into aboveground cisterns that hold sixteen thousand gallons, made possible by funding from King County WaterWorks.

For Tahmina, the parking lot plots are more than a garden complex, and more than a pollution prevention project. "Because the people who are served by this garden are asylees, immigrants, and refugees, it's a metaphor," she says. "When you take barriers away, new things can grow." She adds, "Here we are capturing water from this roof that would have rolled off into the stormwater system. And now it is being used for something so amazing. There is something miraculous about it."

a provocative headline: "What's Happening to Our Fish?" While many people who relied on Puget Sound's natural resources were witnessing the decline, it was a wake-up call to many people who thought of Puget Sound as relatively unpolluted compared to other waterways around the nation.

After years of meticulous scientific research, Dr. Malins and his team had established a clear relationship between abnormalities in sole, a major Puget Sound regional resource, and the existence of toxic chemicals in sediments. According to the *Encyclopedia of Puget Sound,* that work "altered the course of marine science and marine resource management in Puget Sound," leading to the Puyallup River estuary in Tacoma and the Duwamish estuary in Seattle being designated as federal "Superfund sites, so contaminated that the federal government intervened to plan, fund, and enforce cleanup efforts."

Every urban bay around Puget Sound, from Bellingham to Budd Inlet, has some level of toxic pollution. The Duwamish River, which empties into Elliott Bay, served as the home of numerous industries that contributed to the region's economic growth. Fish from the Duwamish have among the highest concentrations of PCBs and other pollutants in Puget Sound. In 2001, the federal Environmental Protection Agency established the river's last five miles as a Superfund cleanup site. The Duwamish cleanup currently under way addresses not just historical pollution but also ongoing pollution from stormwater and wastewater.

THE COMBINED IMPACTS OF HUMAN ACTIVITIES RESULTING from the industrial revolution and later developments eventually led federal agencies to list several Puget Sound species for protection under the federal Endangered Species Act, including Southern Resident orcas, Puget Sound and coastal chinook salmon, Hood Canal summer chum, Puget Sound steelhead, and Puget Sound and coastal bull trout.

The number of "species of concern" in the Salish Sea nearly doubled between 2002 and 2013, to 119. Among the species of concern were seabirds and raptors, salmon and trout, rockfish, herons, porpoises, whales, fur seals, Olympia oysters, sea turtles, lampreys, pinto abalone, and purple martins. And that was before the mysterious die-off of the previously plentiful sea stars. Researchers Jacqlynn Zier and Joe Gaydos say "the growing number of species of concern in the Salish Sea suggests ecosystem decay is outpacing recovery." However, even to marine scientists the decline of sea stars was both sudden and bewildering. And it reached far beyond the waters of our inland sea.

In 2013, biologists and divers noticed sea stars "melting into goo," as described by *Seattle Times* reporter Lynda Mapes in a 2016 report on the massive die-off of sea stars in marine waters from Alaska to Mexico. The scourge was called sea star wasting disease, and it was believed to result from a waterborne virus. Mapes reported on a scientific study that also established a link between the sea star die-off and warming ocean temperatures.

Scuba diver and sea-life educator Laura James said the disappearance of sea stars, in particular sunflower stars, resulted, in overpopulation of the animals that the stars eat, such as sea urchins, barnacles, and mollusks. An overabundance of sea urchins, for example, threatens our vital kelp forest habitats, which they devour. "There is no one thing in Puget Sound that isn't connected to something else," she says. "Nothing. It's all connected."

Sea kayaks on the beach at Henry Island in the San Juans

EVOLVING VALUES: PUBLIC LANDS FOR CONSERVATION AND RECREATION

Washington was still a new state when leaders at the state and federal level began to set aside certain remarkable landscapes for public conservation and recreation, a profound shift from the earlier focus on resource extraction.

In 1899, Congress and President William McKinley created Mount Rainier National Park, the fifth in America's national parks system. The new park would protect the headwaters of two of Puget Sound's major water sources: the Puyallup River and the Nisqually River. By 2017, more than two million people were visiting the park each year.

Olympic National Park, the crowning jewel of the Olympic Peninsula, wasn't exactly born. You could say it evolved. In 1897, President Grover Cleveland designated the Olympic Peninsula's ancient forests as the Olympic Forest Reserve. In 1909, President Theodore Roosevelt, an ardent conservationist, used his executive authority to designate part of it as the Mount Olympus National Monument. In 1938, over intense opposition from local interests, Teddy's distant cousin President Franklin Roosevelt signed the act establishing Olympic National Park. In 1981, the park was named a World Heritage Site in recognition of its exceptional beauty and outstanding diversity of plants and animals.

In 1968, with strong leadership from Senator Henry M. Jackson of Washington, Congress and President Lyndon Johnson created the North Cascades National Park, which protects more than a half million acres of remote wilderness, high peaks, glaciers, snowfields, alpine meadows, and streams—including important headwaters for the Puget Sound watershed. Adjacent to this national park is the 117,000-acre Ross Lake National Recreation Area, which provides wilderness fishing, hunting, paddling, climbing, hiking, and camping as well as resource conservation in the northern Puget Sound watershed.

Numerous wilderness areas also protect Puget Sound headwaters along the westward slopes of the Cascades—Mount Baker, Glacier Peak, Wild Sky, Boulder River, Henry M. Jackson, Alpine Lakes, Norse Peak, and Mount Rainier's Clearwater, Glacier View, and Tatoosh wildernesses—as do many national forests, the San Juan Islands National Monument, three national wildlife refuges, and Padilla Bay National Estuarine Reserve. The federal government manages hundreds of thousands of acres of multiuse national forests.

In 1913, Washington's legislature created a State Board of Park Commissioners. Two years later, land was donated to create the first two state parks, one of which is Larrabee State Park on the Salish Sea. Since then, numerous parks have been established on and near the Puget Sound watershed. They give Washingtonians varied and unforgettable places to experience Puget Sound and its history, beauty, diversity, and wildness.

The legislature created the Department of Natural Resources under the commissioner of public lands in 1957. Its immediate job was to replant, and begin managing, millions of acres of previously neglected state-owned forest lands; to train and equip itself to become the wildland fire prevention and suppression force for millions of acres of state and privately owned forest lands; and to actively manage a couple million acres of aquatic lands—notably the tidelands and submerged lands of Puget Sound. The DNR also became responsible for managing and protecting valuable Natural Resources Conservation Areas and Natural Area Preserves, many of them in the Puget Sound watershed.

In 2000, Commissioner of Public Lands Jennifer Belcher designated six areas of state-owned underwater lands of Puget Sound as the state's first state aquatic reserves to protect sensitive habitats and species. Her successor, Doug Sutherland, rescinded those designations, but created a process that resulted in the establishment of four aquatic reserves in the Sound. By 2016, eight DNR-managed reserves had been established in the Sound and its watershed: at Cherry Point, Cypress Island, Fidalgo Bay, Maury Island, Nisqually Reach, Protection Island, and Smith and Minor Islands, as well as Lake Kapowsin in Pierce County. The DNR says these special areas conserve and enhance native aquatic habitats, protect and restore natural functions and processes of shorelines and intertidal zones, and promote stewardship of aquatic habitats and species through collaborative partnerships.

The Nisqually National Wildlife Refuge was created in 1974 at the delta of the Nisqually River, which flows from glaciers on Mount Rainier into Puget Sound. It provides habitat for more than three hundred species of fish and wildlife in the traditional homeland of the Nisqually Tribe. It is a prime location for people to experience the rich diversity of a Puget Sound ecosystem between the urban areas of Olympia and Tacoma.

By 2009, farm dikes had kept the Puget Sound tides from sweeping in and out across the natural tidal area for more than a century. That year, the Nisqually Delta Restoration Project would remove miles of the dikes, and, in subsequent years, the refuge staff, the tribe, and Ducks Unlimited restored twenty-one miles of historical tidal sloughs in the delta. In the process, they increased marsh habitat in the southern reach of Puget Sound by 50 percent, according to Nisqually Delta Restoration Project documentarians. By restoring the tidal influence within the boundaries of the refuge and adjoining land owned by the Nisqually Tribe, the project recreated nine hundred acres of natural estuary for salmon and many other species.

Billy Frank Jr. speaks at the Nisqually National Wildlife Refuge, which was renamed in his honor after his death.

ABOVE Climbers plot their next adventure. The vastness of public lands in Washington allows outdoor enthusiasts to tailor their adventures to match their skill level and desired degree of challenge.

OPPOSITE Legendary among hikers and mountaineers, the Olympic Mountains, seen from a dramatic viewpoint known as Hurricane Ridge, are dappled with sunlight at dawn.

The national wildlife refuge was renamed in 2015 for the late Billy Frank Jr., renowned Nisqually Tribe leader, chairman of the Northwest Indian Fisheries Commission, and champion for protecting Puget Sound. Through the efforts of many people over many decades, the Nisqually River has been preserved as the least-developed large estuary in the heavily populated reaches of Puget Sound.

One of the most important years in conservation and recreation for the Puget Sound region, and all of Washington, was 1989. A group of conservationists and fishing, hunting, and outdoor recreation advocates formed the Washington Wildlife and Recreation Coalition, enlisting as their co-chairs Republican US senator (and former governor) Dan Evans and Democratic congressman (and future governor) Mike Lowry. With support from major corporations and nonprofits, they went to work securing funding for parks, fish and wildlife habitat, and working lands across Washington State.

Over the next three decades, the coalition helped secure more than $1 billion in state, local, and private money. This funding has resulted in more than 1,200 parks, trails, habitat improvements, and other conservation and recreation projects, many of which are in the Puget Sound watershed. In a project completed in 2018, the state Recreation and Conservation Office awarded nearly $18 million from several state grant sources as part of the nearly $30 million Smith Island estuary restoration and dike removal in the Snohomish River delta. That project reopened habitat for tens of thousands of young salmon to feed and find shelter while growing strong for their life at sea.

PROTECTING WATER, NATURAL SPECIES, AND PEOPLE

After World War II, an evolution took place: a growing awareness of the need to protect the environment, including resources such as clean water, salmon and shellfish. Over the next several decades, Washington State and the federal government incrementally passed laws and devoted public resources to protect clean water, soils, sediments, at-risk animal and plant species, clean air, and ultimately human health. And, over time, an environmental movement was inspired and motivated by a series of events.

By 1945, water pollution had become enough of a concern that the state established a Pollution Control Commission, replacing an earlier body. Nowhere would water quality become a more visible and tangible issue than at Lake Washington on the east side of Seattle, where postwar suburban growth turned the state's second-largest natural lake into a place that people stayed *out* of. The problem was sewage, plus phosphate detergents entering the lake, causing massive algae blooms and die-offs. In 1963, the Seattle *Post-Intelligencer* newspaper declared it "Lake Stinko."

A key problem was that ten different sewage treatment plants from separate cities and sewer districts discharged wastewater into the lake. During storms, the systems overflowed and dumped untreated sewage into Lake Washington and other lakes.

Jim Ellis, a local attorney and civic activist, led the way in creating public support for an innovative way to clean up the lake and keep it clean. In 1958, King County voters created and developed a regional wastewater treatment system based

Diver, Stormwater Crusader, and Virtual Guide

Few people on the planet have seen all that LAURA JAMES has seen in the underwater world of the Salish Sea—a problem she is working creatively to solve. A scuba diver, filmmaker, two-time Emmy Award winner, and multimedia visual content creator for the Salish Sea underworld, Laura is a modern-day Jacques Cousteau who devotes her life to introducing people to the marine environment.

Laura has dived all over the world, but she has a special passion for the Sound and the biological richness of these cold waters. She is an ambassador for the Salish Sea and its creatures large and small, including people.  By creating three-dimensional videos, she aims to help the rest of us connect personally with the sea in its greatness and its intimacy. There is no time to waste, Laura says: "We're looking at a body of water that is at a tipping point, if not past it." For the better part of three decades, in more than five thousand dives, she and her video cameras have documented changes in the balance of life throughout the inland sea of Washington and British Columbia. She witnessed close-up the sickening die-off of several species of sea stars after a wasting disease broke out in 2013 in the Pacific coastal waters from Alaska to Mexico, leaving a lasting impact.

Over the decades, Laura's camera has documented big changes. "I definitely see less biomass [the overall mass of living creatures] in the Sound. I see less big fish, less of most species." Except, that is, for barnacles and sea urchins. "We've always had a lot of barnacles, but now we have tons of barnacles without the sea stars eating them," Laura says. These crusty crustaceans attach themselves to almost any hard surface underwater, including rocks, pilings, and boat hulls. After the sea stars vanished, "we had an explosion of green urchins, in places where I had never seen them before," she says. They feed on algae on rocks and other surfaces, along with decomposing matter such as dead fish, mussels, and barnacles.

With other divers and Sound lovers, Laura has witnessed a demoralizing change in the Sound's water clarity, and an explosion of plankton blooms in warm weather. "There are too many nutrients feeding the plankton," Laura says. "They mess up the visibility in the water all summer long. The plankton blooms just go and go. You no longer get those epic days of visibility in late summer."

One way pollution flows into our waterways is through storm runoff. Millions of people and machines deposit tons of trash, chemicals, metals, plastics, and feces from domesticated animals onto the streets, sidewalks, yards, and fields of our landscape. Much of it ends up in the Sound, either blown by wind or sluiced by rainwater into storm drains or into ditches leading to the nearest bay. Laura has filmed what happens when the messes we humans leave on the ground end up in the Sound and has posted these videos online for the world to see. Particularly powerful are her shots of torrents of polluted stormwater blasting from storm pipes jutting into Puget Sound from populated shores.

Laura describes three dramatic impacts of the nasty contents of stormwater entering the Sound. First, there is a water plume contaminated with oils and other chemicals, as well as bacteria, viruses, fertilizers, and pest control products. Then there is the debris flow with heavy plastics that leaves a "black dead zone" on the bottom of the Sound. And there also are the gyres of plastics floating and sometimes swirling about.

When rain falls, it washes pollutants such as leaked oil and pieces of tire tread off roadways and into waterways, where they harm fish, people, and orcas. As our region's population grows, so does the amount of pollutants accumulating in groundwater and the Sound.

Pointing to the water off Seattle's popular Alki Beach, Laura says, "Right out here, we have two gyres of garbage. One is floating, so you can see it, especially where the wind and currents create rip lines. And we also have an underwater garbage patch that is constantly growing. It's full of plastics—little liquor bottles, Christmas ornaments, toys, condoms and wrappers, ketchup packs, disposable coffee lids, and stir straws." She continues, "Divers are your last stand to clean it up. They bring up hundreds of pounds of plastics." Laura makes it a personal priority to bring back at least three pieces of plastic from the garbage patch under Puget Sound on every dive.

She describes what we all can do to keep our waters cleaner. First, don't toss it. If we don't dump it on the ground or flush it down a drain, there's a good chance it won't get into the Sound. Laura refers to the seven simple solutions to urban stormwater pollution described at www.tox-ick.org: (1) Scoop pet poop; (2) use little or no fertilizers, herbicides, or pesticides; (3) wash cars at commercial car washes; (4) when possible, walk, bike, or take public transit to reduce drips and metals from cars; (5) plant and protect native evergreens and shrubs; (6) keep cars well maintained and drip-free; and (7) keep rainwater on-site with rain gardens, cisterns, and green roofs. Some other ideas: If you see it on the ground, pick it up, and dispose of it safely; it's less likely to end up in our waters. Control the flow.

On a community scale, Laura sees impressive results from infrastructure that captures and naturally filters rainwater: "Green infrastructure is rain gardens, bioswales, roots, everything green. All you need is a soil column to make runoff not immediately toxic in the environment. Rain gardens filter the water, and they also slow the fire-hose effect of the stormwater."

In addition to trash, garbage, and toxic chemicals entering the Sound, Laura is concerned with how seawalls and bulkheads, built along shorelines to prevent property erosion, are destroying habitat. Natural shoreline and nearshore areas provide essential food and cover for forage fish such as herring, smelt, and sand lance. But these habitats are often scoured out by waves crashing against seawalls and bulkheads. Laura also sees a strong correlation between natural shorelines and underwater meadows of eelgrass. When she is diving along a shore and there is a gap in the eelgrass, it's a sure sign there's an armored shore, she says.

Scientists and engineers are now teaming up to protect shoreline properties by imitating nature with slopes and terraces that absorb the energy of rushing water. In 2015, more than 3,000 feet of old armoring were removed from the Sound, compared to 2,231 feet of new construction permitted that year.

This gives Laura hope. She witnessed dramatic results after changes were made to the Elliott Bay shoreline in creating Olympic Sculpture Park in downtown Seattle, leading up to the park's opening in 2007. A thousand feet of seawall was removed and replaced with a three-level underwater slope designed to absorb the energy of crashing waves and to create a stable intertidal zone for sea life. "Almost immediately," says Laura, "kelp beds began to flourish, eelgrass beds returned, and forage fish started swimming and spawning there again." And she is confident it was

A plume of pollutants and sediments billows from a stormwater outfall in Seattle's Elliott Bay. Stormwater contains toxic chemicals, metals, oil, and sediment, which contaminate the marine environment.

no coincidence that, in 2017, Laura and other divers discovered "a massive herring spawn" on Alki Beach, a couple of miles across Elliott Bay from the sculpture park. "Everywhere we sampled, we found eggs. There was no [recent] record of that happening before," Laura says. In the undersea world, a couple of miles isn't an obstacle for animals when habitat becomes available, as occurred with the shoreline restoration at the sculpture park.

Something else that gives Laura hope is that ocean advocates can use modern imaging technologies to bring the depths of the Sound to "millions of people who are lining our shores." Her goal is to engage people in knowing and valuing the Salish Sea so they will "get onboard to protect it."

In addition to in-person presentations, Laura has done 360-degree, live-streaming presentations from underwater, and produced under-the-Sound educational experiences using XR (extended reality) that include real and virtual elements generated by computer graphics and wearable visual technology. She says, "I believe that if humanity has good information, they will make good decisions." And she believes the future of the Sound depends on it.

Proper wastewater treatment is crucial to the health of Puget Sound. Viewed abstractly, as in this aerial perspective of an aerated pond in the South Sound region, it's easy to see that this process often happens on a grand scale.

on watersheds rather than political boundaries. Soon after, construction began on two regional treatment plants, West Point in Seattle's Magnolia neighborhood and the South Treatment Plant in Renton, which were operating by 1966. The plants originally used the standard of the time, primary treatment, which removed about half the pollution. In the decades that followed, the success story of Lake Washington gave hope to future leaders and conservationists that polluted waters could be cleaned up.

In the 1980s, the state attorney general updated what constituted acceptable sewage treatment in light of improved information and technology. A legal opinion said the law required wastewater treatment plants to employ all reasonable and available treatment technology, in this case, secondary treatment, a biological step where helpful organisms break down even more pollution. The extent of wastewater treatment in the Salish Sea has been hotly debated for decades.

The twenty-first century has seen public and scientific pressure mount for even more stringent sewage treatment. A big problem is the overabundance of nutrients, such as nitrogen, in water. Nutrients feed tiny organisms called plankton at the base of the food web. These nutrients arrive in the Sound from natural sources, including rivers and streams and especially from upwellings of deep water from the Pacific Ocean into the Salish Sea. Millions of people add excess nutrients through on-site sewage disposal systems, storm runoff, and wastewater from sewage treatment plants, few of which remove nutrients. An exception is the Lacey, Olympia, Tumwater, and Thurston County (LOTT) Clean Water Alliance, a wastewater treatment plant that removes more than 90 percent of the nitrogen from the sewage.

In search of collaborative solutions to the nutrient problem, in 2018 the state's Department of Ecology convened a Puget Sound Nutrient Forum—a large advisory group representing wastewater treatment plant operators, municipalities and counties, tribes, environmental groups, industry groups, watershed and salmon restoration organizations, state and federal agencies, and other members of the public. Its goal is to develop a broadly supported nutrient reduction plan that protects Puget Sound's fish, shellfish, and people.

In the past decade, a growing number of sewage treatment utilities around the Sound built facilities to reclaim, or recycle, wastewater from homes, businesses, and industries. Thurston County's LOTT Clean Water Alliance diverts some treated wastewater to a reclamation plant that cleans it even further, making it high-quality water for irrigating parks and a golf course. In 2006, the county cooperative also built an upland treatment plant that discharges treated water into wetland ponds that drain into gravel basins to replenish underground water supplies.

The cities of Blaine, Sequim, and Yelm, plus the Kitsap Recycled Water consortium, also built systems that produce reclaimed water for legally approved uses such as irrigating, toilet flushing in some types of buildings and commercial and industrial operations, recharging underground water supplies, and replenishing wetlands and some surface waters. King County, the major population center along the Sound, provides recycled water to customers from two of its five treatment facilities—the South Plant at Renton and the Brightwater plant in neighboring Snohomish County. A third King County facility at Carnation produces reclaimed wastewater used in a nearby wetland restoration project.

An American mink peeks out from some barnacle- and limpet-encrusted rocks in the rich intertidal zone of a beach on Orcas Island. These semiaquatic mammals eat crustaceans, fish, frogs, rodents, and birds.

Sound Champion and Steward

RALPH MUNRO'S hometown newspaper, the *Bainbridge Island Review*, said it with eloquent simplicity in a December 27, 2004, headline: "Orcas have a friend in Munro."

Indeed they do. And so do the shellfish, salmon, bald eagles, and other wild critters of the Puget Sound basin. As do the beaches, tidelands, and shorelands. And the children, the ancient people, and lovers of the Sound, present and future.

It would be difficult to find an individual who has done more to protect Puget Sound and its biological and cultural diversity than this Bainbridge Island native. Ralph Munro has been both a public champion and a personal steward of the Sound and its resources for decades. He became a staff member to Washington governor Dan Evans in the 1970s, and in 1976, lit the fuse that ended commercial whale captures in United States waters. He later served as Washington's elected secretary of state from 1981 to 2001. After retiring from public office, Ralph continued to express his lifelong commitment to stewardship of the Sound. In 2006, he and his wife, Karen, executed a perpetual conservation easement on 203 acres of their Triple Creek Farm and its 3.5 miles of sinuous shoreline on one of the Sound's southernmost bays.

Ralph's commitment to improving the health of the Sound is driven by a lifetime of treasured memories and by a disturbing reality. "It's in much worse shape than people realize," Ralph explains. "It's beautiful, but the water quality has dropped dramatically. If the ecosystem collapses, we've got problems for the whole state."

In the late 1800s, there were an estimated two hundred Southern Resident orcas living in Washington waters. Salmon were plentiful. As the second decade of the twenty-first century draws to an end, the orca population living in the state's waters has dropped below seventy-five, leading to warnings that the Southern Resident killer whales could become extinct. They have been listed as endangered under the Endangered Species Act. Meanwhile, some of the seagoing fish that return to spawning streams—another key indicator of the health of the Sound and its intricate watershed—have also been listed for protection under the Endangered Species Act. They include Puget Sound and coastal chinook salmon, Hood Canal summer chum, Puget Sound steelhead, and Puget Sound and coastal bull trout.

As the apex species with their spectacular breaching displays, orcas are icons of the inland sea of Washington and British Columbia. Ralph Munro's love of orcas began in earnest when he was four or five years old in the 1940s, living with his family in a cottage on the southwest shore of Bainbridge Island. He remembers one night when he could hear a group of the marine mammals in the bay outside his window. As he described the experience in a 2004 interview with the *Bainbridge Island Review*: "They were sleeping, but I wasn't. I was just—for hours—lying in my bed listening to them breathe . . . ."

In the 1960s, Puget Sound orcas became targets of capture for amusement parks. Dozens of the mammals were removed from Puget Sound and nearby waters, causing an immediate and lasting decline in the overall population.

The last straw for killer whale capture came on a March day in 1976, when Ralph and Karen Munro were sailing with friends on a small sloop in Budd Inlet just north of Olympia. They suddenly saw orcas speeding by, chased by power boats and aircraft commissioned by SeaWorld. Ralph vividly recalls the human pursuers repeatedly dropping explosives to herd the orcas into a net, separating mother orcas from their babies. "It was gruesome," Ralph recalls. "And they were going to take that whale out of

Puget Sound and put it in a swimming pool somewhere. I had the feeling enough was enough."

At the time, Governor Evans was out of state on a ski vacation, but Ralph was convinced the orcas couldn't wait for his boss's return. He immediately set to work with Attorney General Slade Gorton's legal team in filing a lawsuit in the US District Court. "I was skating on thin ice," Ralph says. "But Dan Evans agreed with me that we had to take action." The state prevailed, and SeaWorld was forced to release the orca. Ralph says, with unmistakable finality: "That was the last whale capture in the United States."

In 1975, Ralph and Karen took a big chance and bought some privately owned shoreline and adjoining pastureland just outside Olympia. Getting along on a 1970s state-employee salary, the purchase stretched them financially, he recalls, but they were able to pay the previous owner in installments—$450 a month for years to come. This purchase began a lifelong process of transforming the property into a family home as well as a diverse network of habitats for saltwater, freshwater, wetland, and upland species. Over time, they purchased a neighboring pasture and tidelands, where they hauled out hundreds of discarded tires.

Over the years, the Munros have hosted numerous events, welcoming guests and visitors, many of them for conservation fundraisers, to this piece of Puget Sound paradise. Ralph sees people as an essential and natural part of the equation of a healthy Sound, and encourages visitors to Triple Creek Farm to walk around the property.

On a walk with Ralph along the creeks and shoreline, you see numerous passageways where fish and other aquatic animals find protection among tangles of roots, logs, branches, overhanging banks, and marshland vegetation. Five species of seagoing fish are regular neighbors here, as are bald eagles, red-tailed hawks, great blue herons, cougars, coyotes, and of course deer. In a shallow tidal creek near the house, there are remnants of ancient cedar posts that were part of weirs—fence traps—used by Squaxin tribal fishermen for centuries.

In time, Ralph came to suspect that the land here had been used by native people as encampments for fishing and for gathering clams and oysters. He invited a noted archaeologist from nearby South Puget Sound Community College to visit the property, and his suspicions were confirmed. In the muddy shoreline between a pair of creeks, they found surefire evidence of human habitation: fist-size rocks that had been split open by the heat in shellfish-baking pits.

For eleven summers ending in 2009, Triple Creek Farm became an important upland and tideland archaeological dig, revealing stories about the lives of the ancestors of today's native people. Among other things, the digs yielded fragments of ancient fishnets made from woven cedar bark. Because of the meticulous research, it is now known that Squaxin ancestors lived and worked here in seasonal encampments as far back as nine centuries ago.

In gratitude, the tribe commissioned Quinault-Squaxin master carver Randy Capoeman to carve a "welcome pole" from redcedar as a gift to Karen and Ralph. It stands on the point of land at the water's edge, looking out on the body of water now known as Eld Inlet in southwest Puget Sound.

Given the natural, cultural, and historical significance of this place, it is fitting that the Munros decided to protect it in a conservation easement, which went into effect in 2006. The easement was created in partnership with the Capitol Land Trust in Thurston County, with the support of the Trust for Public Land, US Fish and Wildlife Service, state Department of Ecology, Squaxin Island Tribe, and South Puget Sound Community College.

Ralph credits the remarkable conserved habitats of Triple Creek Farm for helping him recover from life-threatening open-heart surgery in 2011. "I was in the hospital, almost dead," he recalls while treading one of the paths at Triple Creek. "A friend sent a note, reporting there were more than a hundred eagles at McLane Creek right near here. I thought: I've got to get out of here and see that." His promise to himself worked. In the years that followed, he saw with his own eyes eagles congregate to feed on salmon carcasses around the place that he and Karen purchased so long ago.

Once endangered but now flourishing, bald eagles inhabit the Puget Sound region year-round.

When asked what success in restoring Puget Sound to a healthy condition would look like, Ralph recalls the words of the governor who set the original challenge: "I think Chris Gregoire said it very well," Ralph says. "We need to make sure the Sound is swimmable, diggable, fishable."

We have a long way to go, he says. Orcas, as the top of the Puget Sound food chain, have accumulated vast amounts of toxic residue in their tissues from chemicals, including polychlorinated biphenyls (PCBs) that flowed into the Sound for decades and continue today despite being banned in the US in 1976. Because they persist in the environment, these chemicals present a continuing threat. Nonetheless, Ralph has seen progress in how people treat the Sound. "We used to carry a net on the bow of the boat," he says. "We would pick up the bottles and cans floating out there. Now you can spend a week in the San Juans and not see a can or a bottle on the water."

And he says kids have a conservation ethic that their elders could learn from. "All this environmental education is paying off. They want to do the right thing. It shows up in how they live later in life," he says of his experience working with thousands of kids in Scouting and with elementary students on conservation projects.

But he believes the best teachers have lived in the Puget Sound region for thousands of years. "We can learn lots from the native people, their history, how they lived off the land, and how they would regenerate the land," he says. "I think we have too long neglected how much they can teach us." Thanks to the Munro family, these lessons are on display in perpetuity at Triple Creek on the shore of Eld Inlet in Puget Sound.

Although reclaimed water represents a small percentage of the 6.5 billion gallons of wastewater treated and released from Brightwater into the Sound, the county's wastewater experts say the recycling rate has steadily increased each year since it opened in 2011. Recycling water not only diverts wastewater from the Sound but also reduces the amount of well water that is drawn from the underground aquifers and other drinking water sources. The goal is to treat water as a resource.

AS LATE AS THE 1960s, THE SALISH SEA WAS LITERALLY the municipal garbage dump for Bellingham. In 1963, three Western Washington State College students were appalled at the sight of the city's garbage being bulldozed into Bellingham Bay. "It was awful," one of them recalled half a century later. "It was raw garbage, including oil cans, paint buckets, dead animals, et cetera. Gross." That student, Ralph Munro from Bainbridge Island, went on to serve on the staff of Governor Dan Evans, and later was elected as Washington's secretary of state, a position in which he served for twenty years.

Ralph and his college buddies got the idea of dressing like regulators. Ralph donned a hard hat, declaring himself to be a "scientist." His buddy Chuck carried a clipboard and announced himself as affiliated with the fictional "Ecology Protection Association." Phil, the "official photographer," carried a single-lens reflex camera.

As Ralph described the scene many years later, the official-looking students told the bulldozer operator: "This is illegal. You can't do this! We are shutting you down right now!" The operator said words to the effect of "Fine by me," climbed down from his rig, and posed for a photo with his "regulators."

The next day, the dozing resumed, but within a couple of years, the city discontinued dumping trash into the bay. Although their daring pretense did not cause the closure, it taught Ralph Munro and his pals some lessons about citizen involvement in protecting the Sound. And half a century later, federal, tribal, state, and local governments and liable parties are carrying out a Bellingham Bay cleanup and prevention program for twelve different pollution areas, including garbage, shipyard waste, industrial pollution, and petroleum fuel storage under the state Model Toxics Control Act. Like many waterfronts with such a long economic history, pollution includes arsenic, lead, mercury, copper, polycyclic aromatic hydrocarbons, PCBs, dioxin, benzene, and diesel fuel.

A TURNING POINT IN ENVIRONMENTAL PROTECTION FOR Washington waters, including the Sound, occurred in 1969 at an oil drilling platform off the coast of Santa Barbara, California. A blowout caused the largest oil spill in US history to that date. Meanwhile, oil fields had been discovered in Alaska's North

If not properly maintained, gasoline-powered vehicles can deposit oil on pavement, from where it washes into storm drains and pollutes Puget Sound.

Transporting oil via tankers like this one near Port Angeles poses risks to Puget Sound. In the event of an accident, millions of gallons of toxic crude oil could be released into the marine environment, resulting in devastating impacts to birds, fish, marine mammals, and other organisms. Washington state has made spill prevention and response a high priority. The Department of Ecology requires spill prevention plans; inspects vessels, facilities, and oil transfers; and issues penalties.

The North American river otter lives in both freshwater and marine environments, including rivers that flow into Puget Sound. Through the Woodland Park Zoo's Living Northwest conservation program, citizen scientists in Washington state have submitted hundreds of otter sightings to help the zoo study how populations are faring. The zoo in Seattle also cares for captive otters, like the one shown here.

Protection Agency in charge of enforcement and set ambitious goals, including eliminating pollution discharges into the nation's waters.

Political leaders of Washington State also took aim in the 1970s at oil supertankers—to keep them out of Puget Sound. As explained in a 2016 Sightline Institute article by Samir Junejo and Eric de Place, Republican governor Evans "inserted a rule into Washington's landmark coastal zone management program that banned oil port development anywhere east of Port Angeles."

Democratic senator Warren Magnuson of Washington stood on the floor of the Senate in 1977 with what he called a "little amendment" to a routine funding reauthorization for the Marine Mammal Protection Act. The next day it passed

Slope at Prudhoe Bay. The next year, the Washington legislature and Governor Dan Evans established the Department of Ecology, bringing together a wide range of environmental protection powers and responsibilities. Ecology was the first comprehensive environmental protection agency in the fifty states.

In 1971, the legislature passed the Washington Oil Pollution Act—making it illegal to discharge any oil into the state's waters, providing for unlimited liability for spills, and setting in motion a state oil spill response program. A year later, Congress passed the Clean Water Act, replacing a series of federal laws adopted in the previous two decades. It put the new Environmental

the US House of Representatives, and twelve days later President Jimmy Carter signed it. The Magnuson Amendment thus became the law of the land, prohibiting federal agencies from granting permits that would expand oil terminals in Washington east of Port Angeles. In 1982, in spite of promised jobs and economic development during a major regional economic recession, Republican governor John Spellman—who was personally committed to environmental protection—rejected two major Puget Sound oil-related projects, to the consternation of many legislators in his own party, which controlled the legislature.

Sound Protector and Salmon Fisherman

NORM DICKS has spent most of his adult life on the national stage, notably as a member of the United States Congress for thirty-six years until 2013. He has been a major force in federal funding, natural resources conservation, and national defense. But he still sees himself as a "Bremerton kid" and a citizen of Puget Sound and its western arm, Hood Canal.

In Congress, Norm helped secure hundreds of millions of dollars for protecting and cleaning up the Sound. But he gauges our success or failure in protecting these marine waters by salmon and steelhead.

As a kid in the 1940s and early 1950s, Norm spent a lot of time at Twanoh State Park on the south shore of Hood Canal's east-west channel, between the town of Belfair and the wide spot named Union. Growing up in Bremerton, he also shared many a fishing trip with his dad, an avid angler. "We would go across the Manette Bridge in East Bremerton to a marina that would open up at like four o'clock in the morning, and you could get live bait," he recalls. "And then we would drive from there out to Point No Point [at the northeast tip of the Kitsap Peninsula] and fish. We had a fourteen-foot Bell Boy Boat with a forty-horsepower Johnson motor. We fished there. We fished at Manchester. We fished at Seabeck. And then we would go every year on a big trip to Neah Bay on the Strait of Juan de Fuca." In those years, he says, Washington was a "salmon fishing capital" for the nation, if not the world.

A lifetime later, Norm Dicks still loves salmon fishing, and he is a board director of Long Live the Kings, a salmon recovery group that carries out restoration projects and invests in resource management innovations. He manages to get out on a few local fishing trips each year, but his best fishing these days is in Alaska waters. "Fishing up there is still very, very good, and it's because they don't have the people and the pollution that

people create. In Alaska, the habitat that supports salmon is still healthy," he says.

In Washington's waters, "You've seen a big decrease in salmon. There used to be a lot of salmon out there. The quality of the water has deteriorated. It used to be much more pristine than it is now. Part of it is population growth—the number of people around the Sound. And it's also the deterioration of habitat, the armoring of shorelines with bulkheads, and runoff of pollution into the Sound." He explains, "You add a million people. In my lifetime it has to be a couple of million, with the prospect of even more people coming. Unless we do something that is scientifically correct and from an engineering perspective plausible, and unless we figure out how to finance it, Puget Sound is going to continue to slowly decline, which is tragic."

Norm hopes he and other fishermen can have more days like the one he had on Hood Canal in 2003. He was out in his fishing boat following a big run of chinook salmon up the Skokomish River. "They were literally jumping out of the water," he remembers. "I was catching eighteen- to twenty-five-pound fish, one after another, and then I would release them."

Back on shore later that day, his son David—who would become the first executive director of the state's Puget Sound Partnership—thought his father was spinning a fisherman's tale. So, the next morning, the two of them headed out in the boat before daylight. Norm picks up the story: "He had his Point Defiance dart jig. It's a beautiful green. And on the first pull, bam! A twenty-five-pounder!" Norm smiles at the memory. On that fisherman's morning, "David became a believer."

When it comes to saving one of the great estuaries of America, Norm says: "We can do it, but it has to become a much

A coho salmon leaps up a waterfall.

bigger priority with the State of Washington, the counties, and the federal government." For inspiration, he points to a historic success story in reversing the death throes of another important water body. When Norm was growing up, his family would take the ferry to Seattle to watch the Rainiers baseball team play at Sick's Stadium. "We would go to have lunch on Lake Washington," he recalls, "and there were signs up. You couldn't swim in Lake Washington because of the pollution."

And then a local attorney and activist named Jim Ellis galvanized political and public support for cleaning up Washington's greatest urban lake—and keeping it clean. In 1958, voters created a regional sewage collection and treatment authority that was called Metro, to build and operate a wastewater system based on how water flowed, rather than on political jurisdictions and boundaries. An infinite number of separate wastewater systems were replaced by a regional system of collecting and discharging wastes, and eventually treating the wastes before they were discharged into Puget Sound. "The community gathered together and cleaned up Lake Washington," says Norm. "Yes, they diverted the discharges to Puget Sound, and that's an issue. But just think of the value that was protected and created there, by creating a clean lake." Six decades later, it remains a jewel of Washington's most urbanized area.

Norm also points to the hugely successful effort in bringing the Elwha River, historically a great salmon habitat, back to life in 2014 after a century of near-death. Norm, who as a member of Congress was instrumental in finding the federal funds to pay for removal of two dams on the river, recalls, "It took fifteen separate federal appropriations" to bring down the dams and reopen a river system that once supported six hundred thousand returning salmon a year.

"We're doing a lot of work on restoration of habitat on rivers, which is helpful to salmon," says Norm. But in his view, the number one problem for Puget Sound is the toxic mix of chemicals and other pollutants that enter the Sound when rain, especially storm runoff, washes over hard surfaces and carries the mixture down ditches and gullies and creeks and rivers, out into our marine waters. "There is no single culprit. It's all of us, and the products we use," he points out. Pollution in stormwater is "caused by this very large population that is living so close to the Sound," he says. "A big problem is Interstate 5—storm drains taking oil, copper, all this terrible stuff off the roadway directly into the Sound. We just haven't had the will to come up with the resources to solve the problem."

He continues, "You can create a lot of jobs with a good, credible cleanup program. We've got the wealth to do it. We've just got to figure out the way to raise the money, to use a flush tax on land parcels or something like that to get started, and then to put together a plan with the state, local, and federal governments. We have to get all the counties around the Sound involved."

Norm points out that in 2016, nine California counties surrounding San Francisco Bay passed a tax on land parcels, with a 70 percent yes vote, to protect the wetlands that buffer the bay from human impacts. To keep pollution out of the Sound in the future, "you have to have some revenue stream so you can sell bonds to do the projects we need," he says. "There are creative solutions, such as bioswales, that trap the stormwater before it reaches the Sound, but they all cost money. We need to have pilot projects to test solutions. Well over 90 percent of our pollutants can be kept on land through the swales. We all have to take responsibility and get the job done."

If we do so, we will protect our future, he says. "There are a lot of recreational fishermen on Puget Sound. It's a multibillion-dollar industry. The boating industry is depending on keeping

Untreated runoff drains from the Highway 520 bridge into Lake Washington.

that recreational fishery. If Puget Sound declines, the value of homes and marinas and other businesses declines. Puget Sound is a great attraction. We have a lot of industry on the Sound."

And there's this fact as well: "Doing something now is the future of salmon. This is the future of orcas. You've got all kinds of species depending on this. It would be a tragedy and a failure of our leadership to let Puget Sound continue to deteriorate."

At Cherry Point in Whatcom County, Chicago Bridge & Iron pushed hard for changes in state shoreline protections so it could build a large facility for manufacturing and shipping offshore oil drilling rigs. Cherry Point is also home to a unique Salish Sea marine habitat, including eelgrass beds that are critical for herring spawning and therefore salmon survival. The governor stopped the plant in its tracks. The same year, Spellman vetoed the proposed Northern Tier Pipeline for oil, including a tanker facility at Port Angeles, and an under-the-Sound pipeline that would cross the state and head east. Even now, the battle to prevent the expansion of the Cherry Point oil terminal continues.

IN 1973, CONGRESS ENACTED THE ENDANGERED SPECIES Act in an effort to halt and reverse the trend toward species extinction. The Washington State Legislature adopted the state Forest Practices Act in 1974, to protect public resources while maintaining a viable forest products industry. The law regulates growing and harvesting timber, building and maintaining forest roads, thinning forests, replanting, and using fertilizers and pesticides. The rules are intended to protect soils, water, fish, wildlife, and roads and power lines affected by state and private forestry.

Beginning in 1986, the state Timber Fish Wildlife Agreement offered "a new way to manage state and private forests by allowing all the stakeholders—tribes, loggers, environmentalists, government agencies—to develop logging practices together," as described in a HistoryLink.org essay by David Wilma.

The largest burrowing clams in the world, Pacific geoducks can live longer than a century. These clams were harvested near McNeil Island by the Squaxin Island Tribe.

Protecting marine mammals gained urgency as populations plummeted throughout the world. In 1972, Congress adopted the Marine Mammal Protection Act, making it illegal to feed or harass animals such as seals, sea lions, porpoises, dolphins, orcas, and other whales. This new law marked a major reversal of the state's practice, from 1947 to 1960, of treating seals as an enemy to fishermen, including bounties for killing seals.

Federal protections did not stop the capture of orcas in the Sound and northern straits for commercial purposes. Beginning in the 1960s, the Sound's orcas became targets of capture for commercial exhibitions at amusement parks. Historically, two hundred orcas lived in these southern waters at any one time, but according to the Washington Department of Fish and Wildlife, nearly seventy killer whales were captured and taken from Puget Sound and nearby waters by exhibitors, or were killed in the process, causing a lasting decline in the overall population.

Despite laws to protect the orca population, NOAA Fisheries in 2005 listed Puget Sound orcas as endangered under the federal Endangered Species Act. They were found to be among the most contaminated marine mammals in the world because of the presence of long-lasting toxic chemicals concentrated in their bodies. NOAA began a recovery effort that includes new vessel-approach regulations and oil spill contingencies to protect the whales.

In 2018, Washington governor Jay Inslee, remembering times in his youth when he and his dad experienced orcas up close on the Sound, signed an executive order to devote state resources to protecting the species. He directed state agencies to outline immediate steps and long-term solutions to recover the orcas. In that year, the orca population dropped to seventy-four, the lowest since the capture era.

TACKLING URBAN AND RURAL POLLUTION SOURCES

For many decades, the most intense sources of pollution were industrial activities, often associated with port areas. However, another threat grew as millions of people spread out across the landscape and along our shores. Degradation of natural habitat, hard-armoring of shorelines, soil erosion, and waterborne flow of litter and contaminants from our everyday lives into the Sound have emerged as major environmental concerns.

In 1971, the legislature adopted the state Shoreline Management Act "to prevent the inherent harm in an uncoordinated and piecemeal development of the state's shorelines" as a referendum to the people. Voters aproved it in 1972. In 1990, the legislature adopted the Growth Management Act, requiring state and local governments to adopt Comprehensive Plans and to address specific threats from unplanned growth at the local level. Counties and cities must identify critical areas like wetlands for further protection, and local governments must designate Urban Growth Areas where more intense development should be located.

As habitat degradation and pollution increased, new approaches and alliances formed across many organizations that may not always agree on the best way to counter the degradation of the Puget Sound ecosystem. For example, in 1985, the governing bodies of Jefferson County, Kitsap County, Mason County, the Port Gamble S'Klallam Tribe, and the Skokomish Tribe formed the Hood Canal Coordinating Council in response to community concerns about water quality and related natural resources issues. The council went on to set the environmental goals of improving populations of summer chum salmon, stopping the net loss of forest cover in the

Harnessing the Power of Plants to Restore Urban Areas

When ANDREW SCHIFFER came to Seattle in 2004, he was focused on social justice, cultural issues, and identity politics. But the bustling, beautiful city on Puget Sound expanded his focus to the environment around him. "Doing environmental work transcends the divisions of identity politics," he says.

Andrew enrolled in Seattle's Antioch University, where he earned a master's degree in environment and community while living in the heavily industrialized Georgetown district. There he found affordable housing, friendly neighbors, and a sense of belonging. As a result, Andrew has enthusiastically devoted himself to creating a healthier environment and quality of life for some of Puget Sound's most polluted communities—the Georgetown and South Park neighborhoods on opposite shores of the Duwamish River.

At Antioch, adjunct professor Cari Simson told the graduate students about the Duwamish Tree Canopy Enhancement Project to help area residents plant and care for inner-city trees. Andrew signed on with Cari to help create urban green spaces filled with native trees and shrubs carefully chosen to filter air pollutants and absorb polluted stormwater before it enters the Sound. Efforts such as these have placed Georgetown and South Park at the center of a major effort by federal, state, and local governments to clean up the Duwamish River, contaminated by many decades of exposure to toxic industrial chemicals and heavy metals.

According to the technical advisory group for the Duwamish River Cleanup Coalition (DRCC), local residents "are constantly exposed to pollution sources from industries, automobiles, trucks, and other sources," including "the highest citywide air concentration of diesel particulates and benzene." A health impacts analysis by the DRCC and Just Health Action, in consultation with other groups, showed high lung disease rates and much shorter life spans in the Duwamish Valley than in other parts of Seattle and King County.

Motivated by his Antioch studies, Andrew worked on projects with the Duwamish Valley Youth Corps and Duwamish Infrastructure Restoration Training Corps (DIRT Corps), providing hands-on training with a focus on rain gardens and cisterns, vegetation management, and ecological restoration. In time, Andrew created his own environmental consulting business, Bricktree LLC. He chose the name to suggest the paradox of cities and nature being intimately connected.

Some of his favorite projects have been "green walls" or "green screens" in Georgetown and South Park. They were designed in consultation with community members concerned about cleaning toxics out of the air they breathe. The walls or screens consist of metal trellises that support fast-growing vines. One of them is 126 feet long and 13 feet tall, and helps shield homes from industrial dust.

Andrew explains: "Plants are a very powerful pollution mitigation tool. They remove air pollution through their leaves. They soak up a lot of water and stormwater pollution through their roots, and the more you plant, the more they soak up." According to Andrew, removing any pollution from air and water helps the Sound. And it helps his Duwamish neighbors live healthier lives.

TOP Volunteers plant native plants, such as Oregon grape, sword fern, and salal, along the Duwamish River at Herring's House Park in Seattle as part of the twice-a-year Duwamish Alive! restoration day. Flourishing native plants and restored habitat are crucial to the health of Puget Sound. **BOTTOM** Biologists net juvenile salmon at North Wind's Weir along the Duwamish River in Tukwila to research the effectiveness of a restoration project in the area.

watershed, and achieving healthy, harvestable shellfish beds in Hood Canal. Three decades later, the council's report card showed improvements in all three areas.

Regulations play important roles in galvanizing action. However, seed funding often will jump start groups tackling complex problems. In 1986, the legislature created the Centennial Clean Water Grant Program, funded by a tax on cigarettes, and later state construction bonds. The program has since funded local wastewater treatment facilities, agricultural practices to prevent water pollution, water quality monitoring, lake water quality planning, and education and stewardship.

Other efforts bridge state and federal funding programs. In 1987, Congress created the Clean Water State Revolving Fund to support states' efforts to clean up and protect waterways. Each state, including Washington, received an interest-earning source of funds that can provide loans to local governments for building and repairing wastewater treatment facilities, controlling pollution from stormwater runoff, and protecting estuaries such as Puget Sound. The fund remains an important federal commitment to the goal of clean water.

As new environmental laws took effect and conservation-minded people formed land trusts to purchase and restore critical habitat along shorelines, the shellfish industry once again began to flourish. By 2007, commercial shellfish growing—aided by advances in aquaculture pioneered by University of Washington scientists—had made Washington the second largest oyster producer in the nation and the home of the most economically valuable clam fishery (geoduck), according to the state Puget Sound Action Team. And according to the Pacific Shellfish Institute, the state had become the largest producer of hatchery-reared and farmed shellfish in the US, with more than three hundred farms.

BY THE 1970s AND 1980s, TOXIC POLLUTION HAD RISEN TO prominence amid such terrible incidents as Love Canal that sickened hundreds of people whose homes were built on top of a landfill. Such incidents spurred the passage of the federal Superfund Law, called the Comprehensive Environmental Response, Compensation, and Liability Act of 1980, which led to a process for cleaning up toxic waste sites. However, more was needed in Washington State.

After several attempts to pass a bill in the Washington State legislature, environmental groups including the Washington Environmental Council drafted a ballot initiative that voters passed in 1988. The Model Toxics Control Act (MTCA) is a key statewide tool for cleaning up contaminated sites in water and on land. The law puts the onus for cleanup on the polluter, with a hazardous substance tax that pays for toxic pollution prevention, management, and cleanup. Since MTCA was enacted, more than seven thousand toxic waste sites, including industrial sites, gas stations, and dry cleaners, have been cleaned up across the state.

That same year, the Environmental Protection Agency designated Puget Sound as an Estuary of National Significance, giving it annual National Estuary Program grants for cleanup and protection. Major toxic cleanups with federal oversight have taken place in Tacoma's Commencement Bay and Seattle's Lower Duwamish Waterway, two areas highly contaminated by industrial operations over many decades.

In Tacoma's port area, two waterways at the mouth of the Puyallup River were cleaned up over two decades—including investigating, planning, sediment removal, and pollution source control costing $105 million. The cost was paid by city, state, private, and corporate contributions. The project removed nearly half a million cubic yards of contaminated sediments that were dredged and confined behind a containment berm. The success of the effort led the city to proclaim that "the Thea Foss and Wheeler-Osgood waterways sparkle with new life today."

In Seattle, the lower five miles of the Duwamish River were designated a federal Superfund site in 2001. The EPA oversees the cleanup of toxic sediments, and the state's Department of Ecology is responsible for controlling sources of pollution. By 2018, about half the toxic contamination from industrial coolants known as PCBs had been dealt with in the river's sediments. While the cleanup continues, the EPA entered into a cooperative agreement with Seattle–King County health officials to work with the community to develop a program to encourage healthy choices for consumption of fish from the river, since some may not be safe to eat.

INTENSE INDUSTRIAL IMPACTS AND LESS OBVIOUS but also damaging impacts from land development have accumulated over decades. Reversing those declines requires a combination of regulations and incentives. And complex problems require innovative approaches developed by governments, tribes, businesses, and nonprofits, approaches that are often slow to manifest obvious improvements. Every once in a while, however, conditions improve rapidly.

Between 2011 and 2014, something remarkable happened in the Salish Sea watershed. Two hydropower dams on the Elwha River were brought tumbling down, opening up seventy miles of fish habitat.

All of this garbage was collected in a single day from the beach at the mouth of the Elwha River on the Olympic Peninsula. Plastic pollution has increased tenfold since 1980. Petroleum-based plastics persist in marine environments both underwater and on the water's surface, wash up on shorelines, and are sometimes consumed by marine creatures and birds. Some plastics in the ocean degrade into smaller and smaller pieces, contributing to enormous garbage patches across the planet.

For more than a century, the Elwha Dam prevented salmon from reaching their spawning grounds in the upper reaches of the Elwha River. Following the dam's removal in 2012 and the removal of the Glines Canyon Dam eight miles upstream two years later, the Elwha River flows naturally again from its headwaters in the Olympic Mountains to the Strait of Juan de Fuca.

Olympic National Park notes that "prior to dam construction in the Elwha River, the chinook salmon runs were legendary for their size and numbers," with some individual fish reaching one hundred pounds. In her "Elwha: Roaring Back to Life" report for the *Seattle Times*, Lynda Mapes wrote: "The $325 million Elwha experiment remains the biggest dam removal project ever. With 83 percent of the Elwha watershed permanently protected in Olympic National Park, it offered a unique chance to start over." When the dams came down, fish began returning to the watershed.

Decades of concerted effort by federal, state, local, and tribal governments, with the private sector, have significantly reduced water pollution from single-point sources such as industrial facilities and sewage discharge points. Today, there is emphasis on "green chemistry"—designed to reduce or eliminate toxics before they are piped to treatment facilities.

The bigger challenges now come from millions of people living and working around the Sound—and the resulting pollution from litter, plastics, chemicals, other toxics, and feces from domesticated animals that float off the ground in storm runoff and are sluiced into the Sound.

IN 2007, GOVERNOR CHRIS GREGOIRE AND THE LEGISLATURE replaced the Puget Sound Action Team with the new Puget Sound Partnership, led by a governor-appointed citizen Leadership Council, charged with developing an action plan for restoring the Sound to a healthy condition by 2020. The first members of the council were Bill Ruckelshaus (first administrator of the federal EPA), tribal leader Billy Frank Jr., former state fisheries and revenue director Bill Wilkerson, environmental champion Martha Kongsgaard, Transportation Commission Chairman Dan O'Neal, Puget Sound farmer Steve Sakuma, and former Seattle utilities director Diana Gale.

Guided by its professional staff and a diverse group of community leaders and experts on an advisory Ecosystem Coordination Board, the council adopted three strategic initiatives in the action plan for the Sound: (1) Protect and restore habitat (Habitat Initiative). (2) Prevent pollution from urban stormwater runoff (Stormwater Initiative). (3) Restore and reopen shellfish beds (Shellfish Initiative).

Although 2020 is the year by which the legislature directed the partnership to achieve recovery of Puget Sound, Martha Kongsgaard assesses the issue this way: "Nobody thinks Puget Sound is going to be restored to health by 2020, but the statutory deadline is important. You get results when you're in campaign mode." Because of the goal, many eyes will be focused on how much progress has been made by 2020, and how much remains to be done.

A pod of orcas gathers at sunset. The Southern Resident orcas belong to a large extended family made up of three pods, J, K, and L. Within pods, grandmothers or great-grandmothers occupy a central role in the family structure.

THE FUTURE
OF THE SALISH SEA

LEONARD FORSMAN AND MINDY ROBERTS

WE STAND AT A GENERATIONAL CROSSROADS FOR THE recovery of Puget Sound and, by extension, the greater Salish Sea. These bountiful waters of the Pacific Northwest have sustained people for millennia, providing clams, salmon, and other foods, first for the tribal people and then the pioneer families, who found bounty and a place that is woven into their identity. Since the days of Chief Seattle and Doc Maynard in the villages of Seattle and beyond, the Sound has lured people and businesses into making this area their home. More than eight million people live and work in Washington and British Columbia, drawing inspiration from the international landscapes and waters of the Salish Sea region. The health of these shared waters reflects our individual and collective decisions, as well as the decisions of those who came before us.

Through exploitation and innocent neglect, we have made a mess, and together we have to clean it up. Our societal decisions in the next few years will determine the future of Puget Sound's health, and the experience of future generations.

Our goal is to grow a shared vision of a vibrant Puget Sound. To succeed, we will need people connected to their communities and to the region's rich natural resources—resources that have come to define our common cultural values. Many people here already know and value this place, whether they are recent transplants or those whose ancestors stretch back hundreds of generations. Our vision of the future includes equitable communities and a shared understanding that a healthy economy and individual well-being are intricately interwoven. We want future generations to experience the vibrant salmon runs and thriving orcas that have been and will be fundamental to our regional identity. And we recognize that a few generations of human activities have damaged the natural resource systems that support our iconic local wildlife and the people of Puget Sound. The two of us are personally and professionally committed to this vision, yet we cannot achieve it alone: as a region, we need to change course.

LEFT Prolific filter feeders, mussels clean the water they inhabit. Because they accumulate contaminants in their tissues, they make great tools for researchers to study the health of Puget Sound.
OPPOSITE The health of Puget Sound starts far from its shores at alpine lakes, such as Royal Lake in the Olympic Peninsula's Dungeness watershed, where this young fisherman caught some brook trout.

The future of Puget Sound has yet to be written, but what's at risk is too valuable and sacred to lose. If we fail, future generations will not know the unique experience of eating food from the Sound. If we fail, we will tear apart the fabric of rural economies that depend on sustainable natural resources. If we fail, our cities and towns will lose their Pacific Northwest culture and identity, and we will violate tribal treaties that require protection of fish and clam habitat.

In the noise of daily life, it's easy to lose sight of progress we have made. But by looking back on the damage caused over the past two centuries, we are also reminded of our successes. Often, they are frustratingly slow to manifest in measurable ways in the complex world of the Salish Sea. Clean water and healthy habitat often require years and even decades of steady investments before we see positive results. Merchants of doubt point to this lack of evidence as proof of failure. Only when we look across the years do we recognize the gains made thanks to people before us who made decisions and sometimes personal sacrifices that now benefit all of us.

We share with you these ideas, grounded in science and informed by cultural identity, to prompt discussion and reflection on how you can contribute to the recovery effort. It's up to each of us, the people of the Salish Sea, to take action so that future generations can experience clean water, abundant salmon, resident orcas, and thriving communities.

TAKING ACTION FOR PUGET SOUND

The individual actions of people like you will determine the fate of Puget Sound. Lack of political will and of funding have stymied previous efforts, but the inspiring people introduced in the profiles throughout these pages show that we can and will prevail. However, for our communities, resources, and region to thrive, we need to accelerate the adoption of effective practices. Your contribution is critical—change must start now. Here are ten actions you can take personally to help recover Puget Sound's health.

TEN THINGS YOU CAN DO

Change begins with each of us, and now is the time to act individually and collectively. We challenge you to join us to help protect Puget Sound. We encourage you to focus on one action each month, and share your experience with family and friends to motivate and energize them.

1. **VOTE IN LOCAL, STATE, AND FEDERAL ELECTIONS.** The greatest leverage you have to contribute to the recovery of Puget Sound is voting for candidates who believe in this goal and champion it. Look into organizations you trust that vet and endorse candidates. A few hours of your time spent researching candidates and issues during election season makes a big difference.

2. **HOLD YOUR ELECTED OFFICIALS ACCOUNTABLE.** Engage your elected officials through meetings, social media, phone calls, and emails. Ask them to develop and support legislation and budget priorities that value our region's natural resources and the communities that depend on them. Thank them when they safeguard clean water, support sustainable farms and forests, build strong and durable rural economies, increase urban tree canopy, reduce carbon pollution, protect wildlife, and strengthen vulnerable communities. Remind elected officials that clean water is good for the economy and that restoring Puget Sound creates jobs.

3. **UNDERSTAND AND SUPPORT TRIBAL TREATY RIGHTS.** The treaties signed by the US government and Northwest tribes in the 1850s established critical protections for salmon and for people. These protections include salmon's access to high-quality habitat for spawning. Supporting tribal treaty rights means understanding the cultural relevance of salmon to tribes. Greater access to habitat means more salmon for everyone.

4. **REWARD BUSINESSES THAT PROTECT THE SOUND AND ITS PEOPLE.** Spend your money at businesses that expressly support Puget Sound recovery. Several certification programs identify business practices that positively affect the Sound, including reducing single-use plastics and energy consumption, practicing salmon-safe approaches, and improving supply chain sustainability. Reward businesses that participate in such programs with your consumer spending, and avoid businesses that harm Puget Sound, its people, and its wildlife.

5. **EAT LOCAL.** We are fortunate to live in a region with a rich and varied food network, including cultivated crops and foraged foods. Shop at farmers markets where you can support local farmers and fishers who grow and harvest food in ways that do not negatively affect our shared waters. These local food entrepreneurs strengthen local economies and improve food security.

6. **SUPPORT ORGANIZATIONS THAT WORK FOR POSITIVE CHANGE.** The Northwest enjoys an extensive array of organizations advocating for Puget Sound's recovery. They range in geographic scale from individual neighborhoods to international programs, and from focusing on single issues like protecting a local park to the varied actions needed to address climate change. These organizations employ a variety of tools and tactics from nuanced policy development to grassroots actions to litigation. Reward them with your financial support

or volunteer to help them. For every large organization you support, contribute to at least one small organization that advocates for these interests at the local level.

7. **INCLUDE AND EMPOWER COMMUNITIES OF COLOR.** Puget Sound recovery must include solutions for everyone; we will fail if we leave some communities behind. Learn what equality, equity, and justice mean. As we work on common goals like reducing toxic pollution, we must do so in a way that breaks down the structures that led to disproportionate impacts in the first place. In other words, focus efforts on the most affected people, often communities of color and low-income neighborhoods.

8. **EMPOWER YOUNG PEOPLE.** In a rapidly changing world, young people are the voice for change because they will live in the world that we create based on our collective decisions. Volunteer to help youth groups that engage in work you are passionate about and collaborate with young people to

effect change—whether that's through outdoor recreation, faith-based groups, or a group devoted to a particular social cause.

9. **REDUCE YOUR OWN IMPACTS.** Find one way to reduce your environmental footprint each year. Reduce personal vehicle use. Be mindful about what you pour down the drain. Evaluate the products you use inside and outside of your home. Substitute one locally produced harmless product for another harmful one. Small changes add up over time.

10. **EXPERIENCE YOUR PUGET SOUND, AND SHARE IT WITH SOMEONE YOU KNOW.** We live in a remarkably diverse area that offers ample opportunities for outdoor experiences. Learn by experiencing—picnic with your family or friends at a local park, walk along the waterfront, catch your dinner in the Sound, plant trees, go tide-pooling, or volunteer for programs that get kids outside. Explore and enjoy this place you call home.

For more ways to explore your Puget Sound, and more actions that you can take to help, visit www.wearepugetsound.org.

To develop this list, we interviewed a number of influencers in our region, including journalists, federal and state government leaders, elected officials, tribal leaders, non-governmental organizations, and community leaders. The resulting list represents the collective wisdom of the overall group and does not reflect individual opinions or endorsements by any of these individuals. Many thanks to the following people: Anji Moraes, Bellamy Pailthorp, Betsy Peabody, Brian Walsh, Chris Dunagan, Chris Wilke, Dave Herrera, David Workman, Dennis McLerran, Jamie Stephens, Joe Gaydos, Lylianna Allala, Lynda Mapes, Jay Manning, Mike Sato, Ryley Fee, Sally Jewell, Sheida Sahandy, Stephanie Solien, and Will Hall.

HOW PUGET SOUND HAS TRANSFORMED

How we got to where we are today is the result of both the millennia-long human desire for natural resources and our deep spiritual and cultural connection with the unique lands and waters of our region. The Puget Sound tribes relied on their voices to preserve their traditions, history, and social values. Stories passed from generation to generation told the origins of their ancient lands and waters and the plant and animals that inhabit these places.

Transformation stories, such as the one below, remind us that the first people of this land are interconnected with the landscape and carry a responsibility to care for it and its creatures. Leonard Forsman adapted this version of the story from "The Story of the Blackfish" by Ernest Bertelson as told by Suquamish elders, which appeared in the *Seattle Sunday Times* on January 16, 1949:

The Blackfish Were Once Human

In what is now Gig Harbor there lived two brothers who were once great seal hunters. Their rival, another accomplished seal harvester, lived there too. He resented the brothers' skill and decided to get rid of them by carving a fake seal made from cedar. He fooled the brothers, who harpooned the lifelike decoy, and then the figure, which had been spiritually empowered by the rival, pulled the brothers way up north into unknown and frigid waters.

Lost, stranded, and hungry, the brothers sought food and shelter. Eventually they spotted a small man expertly diving for halibut from a large canoe. They waited until the odd-looking diver was underwater and raced out to his canoe and took a halibut. He caught the brothers stealing, captured them, and towed them farther north, to his village. The people here were small like him and ate only spoiled halibut and clams.

They kept the brothers as servants for their crime until they were instrumental in saving the village from a swarm of mallard ducks that usually wreaked havoc on them. Now that they were heroes, the chief allowed the brothers to return home. As they traveled, they waited to comfort their grieving mother and plot revenge on their enemy. The brothers decided to become blackfish (killer whales) by draining all of their blood on a sandy beach at what we know now as Point No Point. After the bloodletting, they went into the water and became blackfish. They attacked the trickster in his canoe back near their old village near Gig Harbor, tearing him to pieces. A rock near this place represents their grateful mother.

This story explores origins and what some may view as anguishing changes and events. Moreover, it weaves together contemporary issues like taking things that do not belong to you, consequences of personal actions, and redemption. At its root, the Blackfish story reminds us of the deep spiritual connections among people, places, and animals. Change has always happened, and how we came to this point in time is fascinating and compelling.

OPPOSITE Birders share a discovery in Seward Park in Seattle. As we observe and learn about the natural world, our drive to protect it will grow.

HEALTH IS NOT ONE-DIMENSIONAL

The English word *health* refers to the general condition of the body or mind and connotes wholeness and vitality. Similarly, the Lushootseed word *həliʔil* means "become well" or "heal." In Lushootseed, English, and other languages as well, health reflects both a condition and a process of moving toward a more connected and complete state of being.

Why is health important? How do we define and measure health? What behavioral changes would improve our health? What exactly is required to be deemed healthy?

These questions apply equally to a doctor assessing your personal health and to the region's best minds as they assess the health of Puget Sound and the broader Salish Sea. Multiple indicators are needed to describe personal health, and a suite of general behaviors nudge us toward better health. However, defining the most effective actions needed to *həliʔil* requires constant adjustments and tailoring to circumstance and location.

People from government agencies, academia, businesses, tribes, nonprofit organizations, and the public have identified twenty-five different, complementary indicators of Puget Sound health, including the number of Southern Resident orcas and opportunities for outdoor recreation.

These Vital Signs show a mix of improving, worsening, and stagnant conditions. This slow progress frustrates many of us. For example, our region has focused on salmon recovery for decades, yet we have consistently underfunded the necessary work—at times funding only 15 percent of what is needed. We would not expect our personal health to improve if we did not commit time and resources to it. Similarly, solutions for the recovery of Puget Sound require a mix of behavioral changes and institutional programs at all levels of government.

WHO IS RESPONSIBLE FOR PUGET SOUND?

No single agency can enforce every aspect of Puget Sound and Salish Sea recovery. The Washington State legislature created the Puget Sound Partnership to foster coordination across government and with the private sector, including businesses, nonprofit organizations, and the broader public. Critical regulatory authorities necessary to recover Puget Sound span multiple levels of government—federal, state, local, tribal, and even international.

State laws, such as the Model Toxics Control Act and Shoreline Management Act, represent hard-fought battles to combat toxic substances and protect the natural functions of our shorelines. Federal laws, such as the Clean Water Act and Endangered Species Act—currently under attack at the national level—provide strong foundations for preventing pollution and protecting native species. Treaties with tribes guarantee protections for treaty-reserved resources and habitat recovery on both tribal and non-tribal lands. And international agreements govern trade and other transboundary issues with Canada. Local government statutes and land use codes help implement federal and state law and also tailor application of these laws to the values of individual communities. A healthy Puget Sound and Salish Sea require clean water, healthy habitat, thriving human communities, and species recovery, yet responsibility spans all levels of government as well as decisions by individuals, businesses, and organizations.

Part of the struggle is that multiple jurisdictions play a role in the recovery of Puget Sound, but their responsibilities are not clearly defined. Moreover, because of the interconnected nature of water, air, and lands, actions that positively benefit one area economically may negatively affect public health or species recovery in other political jurisdictions. To change our ways, the public will have to speak up and hold elected officials accountable.

Current regulations reflect both proactive and reactive policies. They often represent what was politically feasible at the time rather than what we need today, ecologically and socially. The private sector needs to engage with state, federal, and tribal regulators to find common ground. Industry and business must balance profit with environmental stewardship responsibilities. While some people have developed a distaste for politics, particularly in our contemporary partisan society, political reforms and elected officials are essential to advance solutions for the Puget Sound region. Let's remember that salmon and orcas do not respect political boundaries, and opinion polls show strong support for clean water across all political leanings and geographies.

Tribal, federal, state, and local environmental laws protect our shared water, air, and lands, as well as the health of our neighbors and communities. But new or strengthened regulations can trigger intense battles at any level of government. Until the United States held polluters accountable under the Clean Water Act and Superfund program, businesses had few incentives to change practices. Until tribes sued to prevent habitat degradation in their treaty-protected fishing grounds, in-water development was unchecked and poorly managed. Market forces do not typically value the public's health, and without regulation, businesses maximizing profit have no reason to reduce pollution.

Regulations play an important role; however, regulations alone will not lead to the recovery of Puget Sound. We need innovative approaches to achieve our goal, yet the risk of failure can hinder innovation. For example, for many decades,

Green infrastructure like these rain gardens along apartments in Seattle's South Lake Union neighborhood help filter out pollutants. Instead of rushing unfiltered into a drain, stormwater is absorbed into the soil where contaminants can be filtered out and the water can nourish plants.

stormwater management focused on pipes that quickly routed rain away from farms and homes to avoid flooding, sending water to the nearest waterway as fast as possible. When rain falls on pavement and hard surfaces, the water runs off rapidly, picks up pollution like bits of tire tread and leaked motor oil, and delivers that pollution to rivers, lakes, and Puget Sound. Solutions to stormwater runoff that imitate nature, like rain gardens, use plants and soils to slow down and clean the water. But even as green stormwater infrastructure gains traction, some engineers continue to build in concrete pipes and other "gray infrastructure" as a backup. This outdated approach substantially increases costs, which can make implementing green stormwater infrastructure appear prohibitive rather than innovative.

Incentive-based approaches remove barriers to adopting better, greener practices. Rebates on cleaner technologies like solar power and electric vehicles can prime the pump of new ideas and lead to the development of new business sectors that advance Puget Sound recovery. As the price of clean energy declines and the price of fossil fuels reflects their true costs to society, interim financial incentives can be phased out.

Transitioning to clean energy sources reduces the greenhouse gas emissions that contribute to ocean acidification and the risk of an oil spill that would devastate the Southern Resident orca population. Solar power technology, for example, continues to improve every year, and the time it takes to pay off the initial investment with energy savings continues to decrease, spurred in part by financial incentive programs. As more residential homeowners have installed solar power in our region, our local solar industry has grown. Moreover, many solar energy products are manufactured locally or pass through our ports.

But it's not enough. Our region is not making progress fast enough to address past damage and plan for future growth. We need strong regulations applied fairly, coupled with incentive programs that accelerate transitions to better ecological and business practices for the Sound. Incentives accelerate actions while regulations level the playing field. The protection and recovery of the Sound require both.

Several nonprofit organizations have championed Puget Sound recovery over the years, including People For Puget Sound. Founded in 1991 on the premise of speaking for the Sound, the organization grew from a few committed and passionate people to a robust agenda working together to protect orcas, hold the line on unchecked land development, and prevent oil spills that would devastate the ecosystem. Even after the organization closed its doors in 2012, its legacy remains in policy and public engagement at the Washington Environmental Council and hands-on restoration work at EarthCorps.

Many organizations are committed to recovering Puget Sound using a variety of approaches. Some work to strengthen protections through regulations at city and county councils. Others lead through incentivizing better practices by institutions, businesses, and personal behavior change. Several litigate under federal, state, or local law to effect change and to stop egregious behavior.

Over the years, these organizations have succeeded individually and collectively, effecting change from the scale of local neighborhoods to the region to internationally. Grassroots activism galvanized public support and lobbying grew political support for regulations like the State Environmental Policy Act, Shoreline Management Act, and Model Toxics Control Act, each of which happened because people took action. Coalitions

A great blue heron stands near a drain pouring stormwater runoff into the Duwamish River.

comprising tribes, communities of color, labor, public health, faith-based groups, and conservationists have pushed for protections to leave a legacy for future generations to know and appreciate.

A PROMISING NEW CHAPTER

When Governor Chris Gregoire established 2020 as the Sound's recovery deadline back in 2007, there was no solid definition of recovery, let alone how to measure it. Since then, a vast number of dedicated people and organizations have built a robust roadmap for action, with each phase building on the work of what came before. Collaborative approaches take time to build and resources to sustain, yet they are the only way forward. The recent focus on Puget Sound has turned the tide in a few important areas like increasing harvestable shellfish beds, but elsewhere damage still outpaces recovery.

What's next for Puget Sound recovery? This critical question drives our personal interest in this book and campaign, because what comes next will depend on people who take action—including you.

SALMON AS SENTINELS

After fattening up in the Pacific Ocean for several years, coho salmon return to the streams where they began life as eggs. This final journey begins with adult coho gathering in estuaries at the mouths of streams and rivers, waiting for fall rains to replenish their flows. As the storms begin, the salmon head upstream. Once they find suitable habitat, they dig redds, or nests, in the gravel, spawn the next generation, then die within a few days. But their bodies continue to support the ecosystem in other ways. The decaying bodies of the coho provide nutrients that support an intricate web in nature. Aquatic insects feed on these nutrients, and in turn nourish the young salmon that emerge from the gravels. Wildlife drag the salmon carcasses out of the water to eat, where the remnants (and ensuing scat) fertilize the trees whose shade will keep the water cool for the young coho the following summer.

In the early 2000s, people who spent time in the urban creeks around King County began to notice a disturbing pattern. Adult coho were dying before they could spawn. After swimming for even a short time in creeks carrying urban stormwater, they grew disoriented, dying within hours. (Puzzlingly, chum salmon swam right past and successfully spawned in those same streams.) Pre-spawn mortality now affects coho streams throughout the Puget Sound basin, but that early observation triggered investigations into why it was happening.

The culprit turned out to be polluted stormwater. We do not yet know which pollutants in stormwater are behind these declines, but scientific research has increased our understanding and provided solutions. For instance, if polluted stormwater first passes through layers of plants and soils, the resulting clean stormwater is no longer toxic to coho. This simple system—plants and soil—naturally filters stormwater. Stormwater engineers can design systems that achieve what plants and soils provide naturally.

These green infrastructure solutions, including rain gardens and tree canopy cover, benefit communities in many ways. In schools, rain gardens serve as outdoor classrooms and examples of science in action. In both public and private spaces, research has demonstrated that simply seeing green tree canopy lowers people's blood pressure compared

Tahlequah, the mother orca also known as J35, carries her dead infant calf for the sixteenth straight day. The next day, she released the calf's body. Images of this somber, heart-wrenching vigil sparked an international outpouring of sympathy and grief for the endangered Southern Resident orcas. (Photographed under NMFS permit 21114)

with being surrounded with concrete. People linger longer in shaded, tree-lined shopping areas, with increased economic benefits for nearby commerce.

But simply knowing the answer to this problem has not compelled action fast enough. Costs to manage stormwater were not factored into older subdivisions or road projects. Puget Sound cities and counties are only now adopting these practices for new development, triggered by the Clean Water Act and local regulatory requirements that continue to evolve in light of new knowledge.

What if we applied known stormwater technology, including green infrastructure, to public and private lands? Could we prevent and reverse damage? A study of urban and rural areas in King County, which accounts for more than 40 percent of the region's US population, looked into these questions. The results were astonishing: modernizing our approach to treating stormwater would not only prevent further declines but lead to healthy stream conditions like the ones present in naturally

forested areas. We have the technology to prevent and reverse impacts from urban stormwater runoff. How much are we willing to pay to implement these changes? If we don't, salmon and orcas will pay the price instead.

FACING THE CONSEQUENCES OF DAMAGE

In the summer of 2018, a member of the Southern Resident orca J pod, Tahlequah, gave birth to a calf. The newborn orca lived less than an hour. Over the next seventeen days, Tahlequah carried her dead calf throughout the Salish Sea. She swam more than one thousand miles, growing thinner as she was unable to feed herself. Each day brought devastating photos of a mother's grief, as her calf's body slowly decayed in view of the world, rather than sinking to the ocean's depths to be forgotten. Orcas recognize humans—perhaps Tahlequah was reminding all of us about the damage we have caused.

Tahlequah and her lifeless calf became the face of human damage to Puget Sound. Thousands of people in the region, nationally, and internationally, followed this mother's haunting parade. Yet Tahlequah's calf was not the only fatality that year. Crewser, a member of L pod, died in June. Then Scarlet, also of J pod, died in September, despite efforts to feed her and treat her poor health. The loss of these animals and the deaths of several calves after a brief baby boom several years prior has awakened a new resolve to clean up our messes so these critically endangered orcas can survive and recover.

The Southern Resident orcas are starving. Historically, they fed on chinook salmon in a territory that extends from Alaska and the Fraser River in Canada, throughout Puget Sound, the Columbia River, and down into Northern California. When one salmon run was low, the pod's matriarch would guide her family to another run. The cold reality is that, for myriad reasons, many of the salmon stocks the orcas rely on are depleted. Salmon returns have declined to less than 10 percent of the rich bounty that sustained earlier generations of both humans and orcas throughout the Pacific Northwest. These orcas have nowhere else to go to find the salmon they need to survive.

Reduced salmon populations are the biggest cause of the decline in the endangered orca population. Another threat is toxic pollution, which affects the health of adult and juvenile orcas, as well as the survival of what they eat. PCBs (polychlorinated biphenyls), for example, are so dangerous that even very small amounts in water bioaccumulate through the food web to the point that they affect the survival of juvenile chinook salmon and the reproductive and immune systems of orcas; they also increase the risk of cancer in people who eat contaminated fish. Phytoplankton concentrate PCBs from water, then zooplankton eat phytoplankton; herring and juvenile salmon eat zooplankton, and orcas eat salmon. PCBs increase at each level. Though banned for decades, legacy sources of PCBs, like toxic waste sites, as well as untreated stormwater running off our roadways, continue to release PCBs and other toxic substances into our shared waters and the food web. Juvenile orcas have the highest concentrations of PCBs before they are weaned because they pick up the chemicals from their mother's milk.

The dual effects of food shortages and toxic substances demonstrate how threats can compound to jeopardize the survival of a species. Transient orcas that eat marine mammals have even higher concentrations of PCBs. Because transients have plenty to eat, the PCBs they consume are stored in their fatty tissues, where they cause less harm to the animals. When the Southern Residents go hungry, the PCBs released from their blubber cause harm. In addition to improving salmon runs, the long-term recovery of orcas requires us to reduce toxic pollution now.

Finally, boats in the Sound produce noise and disturb orcas, interfering with their ability to find food and communicate with each other. Orcas use echolocation, communicating using sound frequencies that are also produced by vessel engines and other equipment like echosounders used to measure depth and to find fish. Here, the solution is uncomplicated: simply slowing down and avoiding orcas gives them the space they need to forage without intrusion from people.

Orcas and salmon are the canaries in the coal mine, and they are ailing. Pollution, noise, disturbance, and lack of food collectively threaten the immediate survival of the Southern Resident orcas. We cannot afford to lose them or the chinook salmon that have sustained them for thousands of years. When we act to reverse their declines, we will also recover the health of Puget Sound. The stakes have never been higher.

Hundreds of people gathered in Olympia for Environmental Lobby Day in January 2019. Hosted by the Environmental Priorities Coalition, the event offered people opportunities to speak with legislators about why we need environmental programs that protect the health and well-being of both orcas and human communities.

WE CAN ALL INVEST IN PROTECTION AND RECOVERY

Tahlequah's grief clearly showed people the reality of our many impacts on the Salish Sea. Yet, too many people and organizations continue to see our waters as a dumping ground where wastes "go away" to some mysterious repository. Science tells us otherwise, and much of the pollution that reaches the Sound stays there for years and even decades.

The Sound looks so lovely on the surface that many people have a hard time believing its health is in jeopardy. Few have directly witnessed doomed coho salmon returning from the Pacific Ocean to attempt to spawn in Puget Sound rivers and streams. But images of billowing black stormwater from pipes beneath Puget Sound, filmed by scuba divers, provide visible evidence of those impacts. Videos have surfaced featuring adult coho struggling and hopelessly swimming in circles, unable to complete their final life act to spawn the next generation of salmon. Photos of Tahlequah have galvanized more people than ever before to fight for the health of Puget Sound.

No single sector has caused Puget Sound's health to decline, and we are all responsible for its recovery. Adopting new practices and transitioning from old ways of doing business will never be cheaper, and the costs of community and environmental damage must be internalized into the costs of doing business. Anything less shifts the burdens to communities that do not receive the economic benefits that drive commerce. Private business has a role and a responsibility, and we are heartened by the early actions of a few industry leaders to operationalize best practices into how they do business. For example, private developers are incorporating green infrastructure elements that treat polluted stormwater from adjacent areas into their project designs, garnering praise and positive publicity.

To date, attempts to provide dedicated government funding for Puget Sound recovery have focused on single revenue sources—and none have been enacted. We need solutions that address funding gaps through a suite of approaches, from federal to state, regional to local. Let's learn from other states that have successfully adopted new revenue sources. Pollution-based fees, taxes on parcels and real estate, bond measures, private challenge funding, committing 2 percent of the state budget to a Puget Sound Trust Fund, public-private partnerships, innovation competitions, fees on goods and services, dedicated regional funding, development fees, utility rates—everything needs to be on the table. As we approach the 2020 deadline for recovering Puget Sound, now is the time to boost investments in protection and recovery.

PUGET SOUND BEGINS RECOVERING TODAY

We face a daunting task in reversing declines and building the resiliency of our inland waters. Distributed oversight and a lack of accountability are both responsible for our failure to take action. But we cannot bequeath these known problems to the next generation to solve. We cannot wait for the system to collapse and then expect to build it back up successfully. We must learn from the experiences of other regions like New England, Chesapeake

Bay, and the Great Lakes, each of which suffered ecosystem crashes that galvanized action. Rebuilding a broken system is far from optimal, yet it is too often the default approach.

Puget Sound is currently experiencing the tragedy of the commons: some of the people receiving economic benefits from shared natural resources do not pay for the damage their activities cause to those resources. The public value of the commons—Puget Sound—has not been given financial value, yet economic value drives resource extraction. History tells us that an eventual catastrophe could trigger action, but generally only after decades of declining measurements and dire warnings. We should heed these red flags now and recognize the financial value and intrinsic value of natural resources. Chief Seattle said, "Every part of this country is sacred to my people. Every hillside, every valley, every plain and grove has been hallowed by some fond memory or some sad experience of my tribe."

The plight of the endangered orcas has galvanized public support and provoked demands to improve the health of Puget Sound, because the future of these creatures, the Sound, and its communities are intertwined. We must act quickly to leave a legacy of Southern Resident orcas for future generations. In fact, these whales came desperately close to the brink of extinction in the 1960s and early 1970s. At that time, people captured or killed at least sixty-seven orcas throughout the Salish Sea, bringing the Southern Resident population to a low of seventy-one animals. Ending the capture of orcas required a multiyear push driven by the public's demands for action, activist testimony, responses by state agencies and the legislature, and legal actions.

After orcas were no longer being captured, the Southern Resident orca population rebounded in just twenty years to a high of ninety-eight animals in 1995. The increase in this population

A child enjoys a field of blooming tulips in the Skagit Valley. More than ninety different crops are grown in Skagit County, from tulips to blueberries to red potatoes. Practices on such farms directly affect the health of Puget Sound.

through the mid-1990s gives us hope today. When we address threats, natural systems respond, and orcas are no different.

The two of us serve on Governor Jay Inslee's Orca Recovery Task Force, and we are pushing for bold actions that address the lack of food, toxic substances in the water and in fish, and noise and disturbance. The list of actions is long because the need is so great. Few of these actions require new authority. We do not need to build programs from scratch. In fact, salmon restoration and pollution reduction programs have been successful locally for many years. But, if these programs have been in place for years, why haven't we done more to increase salmon and reduce pollution in Puget Sound?

In short, we have not made Puget Sound and orcas a political priority, nor have we adequately invested in the programs needed to turn the tide for orcas. That has to change. Tahlequah and her calf remind us that we cannot revert to business as usual in the face of such compelling grief. The current groundswell of public support is resulting in renewed calls for bold actions.

A proverb attributed to Chinese philosopher Lao Tzu captures our thinking on these challenges: "A journey of a thousand miles begins with one step." We cannot see the end of our journey here at the beginning, but unless we begin in earnest, nothing will change.

For thousands of years, Coast Salish and First Nations peoples have set off in wooden canoes to make long trade journeys without modern navigation tools along the Pacific Northwest coast. These canoe journeys are not one-way, one-time trips—

they represent collaborative community efforts that connect people to each other and to the remarkable places in this region. The resulting bonds and human connections are in many ways as important as the economic trade those connections enable.

Whether these personal connections and journeys continue to be a part of our region's story depends on how we answer some critical questions. Will we reverse the stunning declines of chinook salmon, on which people and Southern Resident orcas feed? Will we decrease toxic substances that increase the risk of cancer and negatively affect the health of those who eat the Sound's fish? Will we adapt our business practices and personal choices to build resilient communities for an equitable future?

We need to adopt a value system that puts this ancient inland Sound and its shorelines first. The Creator made this place for the people. The tribes were the first peoples here and now we are all here together in this place known as Washington State. Let's leave a fruitful legacy for our children.

Yet to be written, the future of Puget Sound begins the day you read this passage. It begins with your votes, the businesses you support, the communities you build, and your personal actions toward *həliʔil*. We are hopeful, because we have seen positive change in our lifetimes, thanks to forward-looking decisions made by people before us when faced with threats to their core values. With your help, we will pull together and move faster toward recovery. Now more than ever, we need you to take action, collectively and individually. Join us in deciding the future of Puget Sound and the Salish Sea.

Snohomish tribal members paddle their Blue Heron Canoe through Elliott Bay along the Seattle waterfront.

Fishing from the rocks at Deception Pass, with Deception Island in the background

EXPLORING AND ENJOYING PUGET SOUND

BRIAN J. CANTWELL

EVEN BEFORE IT WAS CALLED PUGET SOUND, THIS INLAND sea provided people with food, transportation, and other basic needs. Today, many treasure its expanded role as a splendid venue for boating, fishing, and other water sports, as well as near-shore hiking and camping. This sampling of recreational gems spotlights more than thirty key locations across Western Washington. These sites were chosen to represent geographic, cultural, and recreational diversity—from moorings for an idyllic night on a sailboat to an estuary you can tour from a wheelchair and beaches where dogs can run. Select destinations include detailed maps.

Knowing our neighbors' recreational appetites, in this list we reach a bit beyond what some call Puget Sound, taking in some of the wider Salish Sea. What these sites have in common is their rich potential for education, cultural enrichment, or just good fun—a key to why so many of us value these shared waters as our own.

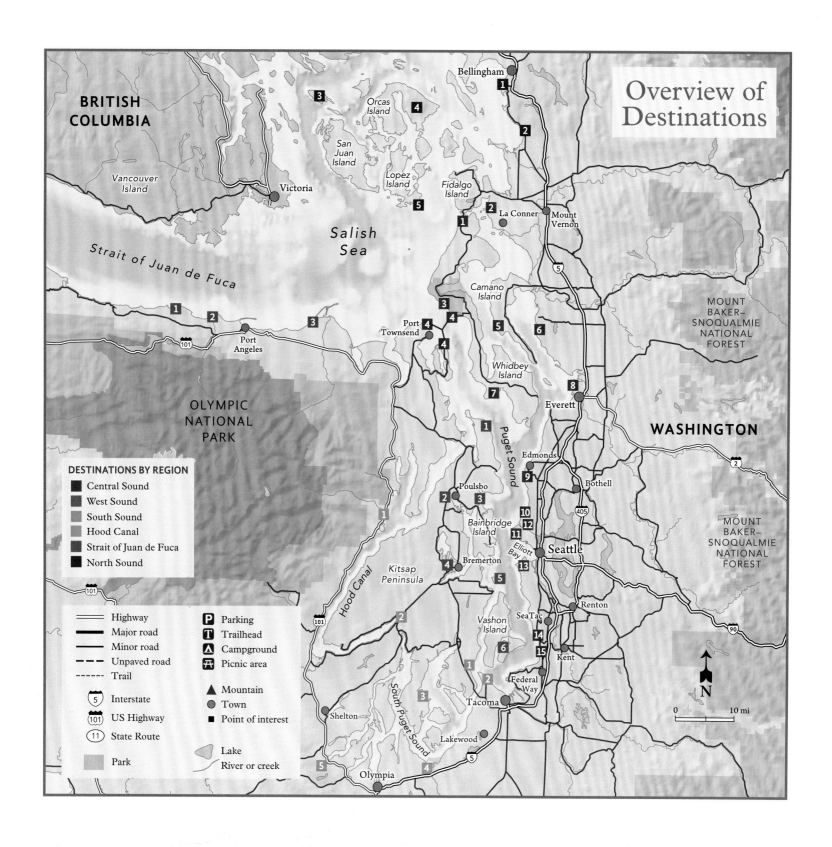

Overview of Destinations

BRITISH COLUMBIA

WASHINGTON

Vancouver Island

Victoria

Strait of Juan de Fuca

Salish Sea

San Juan Island

Orcas Island

Lopez Island

Fidalgo Island

Bellingham

La Conner

Mount Vernon

Port Angeles

Port Townsend

Camano Island

Whidbey Island

Everett

Edmonds

Bothell

OLYMPIC NATIONAL PARK

Puget Sound

Hood Canal

Kitsap Peninsula

Poulsbo

Bainbridge Island

Elliott Bay

Seattle

Bremerton

Vashon Island

Renton

SeaTac

Kent

Federal Way

MOUNT BAKER– SNOQUALMIE NATIONAL FOREST

MOUNT BAKER– SNOQUALMIE NATIONAL FOREST

Shelton

South Puget Sound

Tacoma

Lakewood

Olympia

DESTINATIONS BY REGION
- ■ Central Sound
- ■ West Sound
- ■ South Sound
- ■ Hood Canal
- ■ Strait of Juan de Fuca
- ■ North Sound

═══ Highway
▬▬▬ Major road
──── Minor road
– – – Unpaved road
········ Trail

🛡5 Interstate
🛡101 US Highway
⬭11 State Route

▨ Park

🅿 Parking
🆃 Trailhead
⛺ Campground
🎪 Picnic area

▲ Mountain
● Town
■ Point of interest

▨ Lake
〜 River or creek

0   10 mi

N

CENTRAL SOUND

1 DECEPTION PASS STATE PARK

On the Water: Deception Pass, Strait of
Juan de Fuca, Rosario Strait, Similk Bay
On the Globe: 48.3912°N, 122.6470°W

Deception Pass isn't merely the most-visited state park in Washington. It's also like the diamond in the tiara of the entire park system—at least if a park ranger ever wore a tiara instead of a Smokey Bear hat. Explore rocky ramparts, wade on salty shores, and marvel at rushing tidewaters and ancient trees, all amid vintage Civilian Conservation Corps structures.

The pass got its name during a 1792 expedition, when English explorer Captain George Vancouver was deceived into thinking the narrow saltwater strait separating Whidbey Island from Fidalgo Island was merely a river.

THE BRIDGE

Even if you're just driving State Route 20 from Fidalgo Island to Whidbey Island, the **DECEPTION PASS BRIDGE** (circa 1935) is worth a stop. Tiptoe onto the narrow walkway to peer 180 feet down to see the cliff-hugged waterway roil like a rushing river during tidal changes.

HIKING

Don flip-flops before hitting sandy, cobbled **WEST BEACH** or **NORTH BEACH**, along the 3,854-acre park's more than fourteen miles of saltwater shoreline. Or pull on boots to explore **HOYPUS POINT**, one of Washington's largest remaining old-growth forests.

If you have more time, trek **NORTH BEACH TRAIL** to some premium picnic sites and a front-row view of the bridge, then head upward past stone walls for a troll's-eye view beneath the bridge's base. Or, from Bowman Bay, walk to **LIGHTHOUSE POINT** for spectacular sunsets over the Strait of Juan de Fuca, or to watch tourist-carrying jet boats navigate the pass.

CAMPING

Camp among old-growth firs in **CRANBERRY LAKE CAMPGROUND** or near the protected cove at **BOWMAN BAY CAMPGROUND**. Rent cabins at **QUARRY POND CAMPGROUND** or remote **BEN URE ISLAND**. A caveat for campers: Noise from Whidbey Island Naval Air Station jets sometimes booms through the park late into the night.

Dog walkers stroll along North Beach, beneath the Deception Pass Bridge.

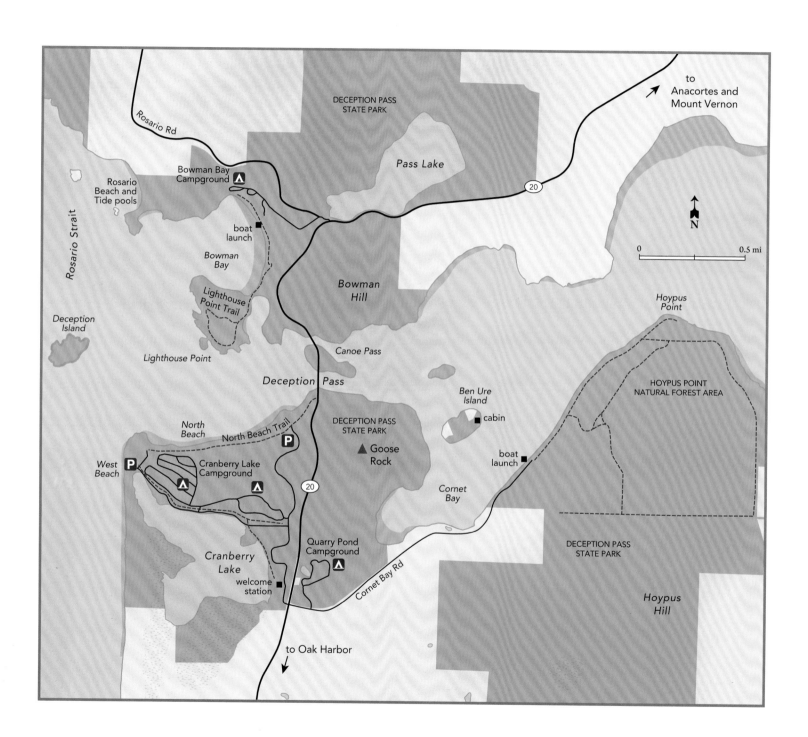

DECEPTION PASS
STATE PARK

Rosario Rd

Pass Lake

to
Anacortes and
Mount Vernon

20

N

0   0.5 mi

Bowman Bay
Campground

Rosario Strait

Rosario
Beach and
Tide pools

boat
launch

Bowman
Bay

Bowman
Hill

Hoypus
Point

Lighthouse
Point Trail

Deception
Island

Canoe Pass

HOYPUS POINT
NATURAL FOREST AREA

Lighthouse Point

Deception   Pass

Ben Ure
Island   cabin

North Beach Trail

North
Beach

P

DECEPTION PASS
STATE PARK

boat
launch

West
Beach

P

Cranberry Lake
Campground

Goose
Rock

20

Cornet
Bay

Cranberry
Lake

Quarry Pond
Campground

Cornet Bay Rd

DECEPTION PASS
STATE PARK

welcome
station

Hoypus
Hill

to Oak Harbor

BOATING, FISHING

Launch boats from one of the park's five saltwater sites, rent kayaks at **BOWMAN BAY**, or take your own craft out for peaceful fishing on **CRANBERRY LAKE** (limited to electric motors) or **PASS LAKE** (human-powered only).

BY BUS

ISLAND TRANSIT'S Route 411 serves the park Monday–Saturday from Oak Harbor or March's Point.

2 KUKUTALI PRESERVE

On the Water: Similk Bay, Kiket Bay
On the Globe: 48.4209°N, 122.5532°W

Opened in 2014, Kukutali Preserve, near La Conner in Skagit County, is Washington's first state park site to be jointly managed with a native tribe (the Swinomish). Its name means "place of cattail mats," which were historically erected as shelters during shellfish gathering.

Cross a tombolo, a narrow sandbar restored to its natural, tide-washed state in 2018, to reach eighty-four-acre forested **KIKET ISLAND**, purchased by Seattle City Light in 1969 as the site for an eventually shelved nuclear power plant (a flyer at the time promoted the effluent's potential for creating warm, swimmable waters here). At the far end, Flagstaff Point's tidelands offer a view of the east side of the **DECEPTION PASS BRIDGE**—and bracingly cold water for visitors to wade or kayak through.

HIKING, BIRDING, BOATING

From a small parking lot off Snee Oosh Road, three miles south of State Route 20, hike along a dirt road to a saltwater lagoon to look for wading great blue herons. Across the tombolo (best at low tide) lies a one-mile trek to the island's west end. Just past a landing site for paddle-craft, huge drift logs piled here like a jumbled game of pick-up sticks make for an inviting spot to sit and enjoy the view of Kiket Bay's islands. Watch for grebes, cormorants, and other seabirds. Beyond this beach, **FLAGSTAFF POINT'S** uplands are closed year-round to protect spring-blooming wildflowers, worth glimpsing from the south tidelands, which are accessible to the public as tides permit.

NEARBY ATTRACTION

About five miles away, enjoy historical **LA CONNER'S** wheelchair-accessible boardwalk overlooking the **SWINOMISH CHANNEL** and the neighboring tribal village, including park pavilions whimsically modeled after traditional woven-cedar hats.

A crabbing boat heads up Swinomish Channel past the Swinomish Tribe's community park with pavilions shaped like woven-cedar hats, as seen from La Conner.

3 EBEY'S LANDING NATIONAL HISTORICAL RESERVE

On the Water: Strait of Juan de Fuca, Admiralty Inlet, Penn Cove
On the Globe: 48.1923°N, 122.7082°W

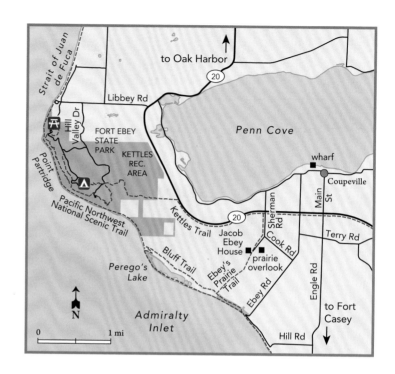

Whidbey Island's fertile farmland, sweeping mountain views, and protected harbor attracted some of the region's earliest Euro-American pioneers. At the threshold of Puget Sound, this reserve encompasses three state parks, more than thirty miles of Island County trails, and the historic seaport of Coupeville.

WALKS, DINING

Trek the windswept **BLUFF TRAIL**, adjoining scenic farms with wide vistas of Admiralty Inlet, the Strait of Juan de Fuca, and Perego's Lake. Beyond are the Olympic Mountains and Port Townsend. A side trip on **EBEY'S PRAIRIE TRAIL** leads to the Jacob Ebey House, circa 1856. Jacob's son was Isaac Ebey, the first permanent white settler on Whidbey Island. He was beheaded here in 1857 by raiding northern natives in revenge for tribal members killed by American soldiers.

Explore **COUPEVILLE'S** wharf and take a self-guided tour of sixty-five historic sites and Victorian-era homes. Catch **PENN COVE MUSSELFEST**, traditionally held each March, or enjoy a restaurant meal of the shellfish farmed here.

SHORE FISHING

The reserve's Admiralty Inlet beach is a popular spot to cast for salmon.

In Ebey's Landing National Historical Reserve, edging Admiralty Inlet, Ebey's Prairie Trail offers a look at the rich farmland—still being worked today—that attracted nineteenth-century settlers.

MOUNTAIN BIKING

Find meandering paths for cyclists and hikers in Island County's **KETTLES RECREATION AREA** and **FORT EBEY STATE PARK**.

BY BUS

ISLAND TRANSIT'S Route 1 serves Coupeville Monday–Saturday from the Clinton Ferry Terminal.

4 TRIANGLE OF FIRE FORTS

On the Water: Admiralty Inlet, Kilisut Harbor, Port Townsend Bay
On the Globe: Fort Worden, 48.1317°N, 122.7633°W; Fort Flagler, 48.0859°N, 122.7017°W; Fort Casey, 48.1638°N, 122.6783°W

The *other* Washington—on the Potomac—didn't worry too much about Puget Sound in the nineteenth century, but establishment of a naval yard here in 1891 finally distinguished these waters as worth defending. The 1898 Spanish-American War sped the construction of forts at three strategic points by the Sound's entrance. Yes, what came to be known as the "Triangle of Fire"—**FORT WORDEN**, at Port Townsend; **FORT FLAGLER**, on nearby Marrowstone Island; and **FORT CASEY**, on the western shore of Whidbey Island—was spurred on by worries that a latter-day version of the Spanish Armada might lay siege to Bremerton.

Largely used for training, the forts were militarily obsolete by the mid-twentieth century and became state parks.

HISTORIC FORTIFICATIONS

See the forts' "disappearing guns," innovative for their day, which after being fired rocked back in cradles hidden below the walls to protect both gun and crew during reloading.

CAMPING AND LODGING

Fort Casey has 35 beachfront campsites. Fort Worden offers 80 campsites and Fort Flagler another 117, in beach and forest settings. Forts Worden and Flagler also offer vacation rentals in military housing, and Worden

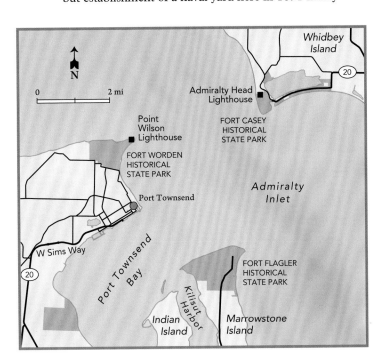

Admiralty Head Lighthouse perches above the waters of Admiralty Inlet at Fort Casey Historical State Park.

has conference facilities. Seattle Pacific University manages Fort Casey's housing as **CAMP CASEY**.

SCENIC LIGHTHOUSES

Fort Worden has the **POINT WILSON LIGHTHOUSE** and Fort Casey has the **ADMIRALTY HEAD LIGHTHOUSE** (with a seasonal interpretive center and gift shop).

EVENTS

At Fort Worden, the **CENTRUM** organization stages art and music events. At Fort Casey, costumed reenactors lead free **LIVING-HISTORY TOURS** on summer weekends.

OTHER ATTRACTIONS

Fort Worden is home to the **PORT TOWNSEND MARINE SCIENCE CENTER**, the **COAST ARTILLERY MUSEUM**, and the restored **COMMANDING OFFICERS QUARTERS**. Nearby Port Townsend hosts a prestigious **WOODEN BOAT FESTIVAL** each September.

OTHER ACTIVITIES

Visitors can find picnicking and hiking at each park. There is also a paragliding zone at Fort Flagler and a remote-control glider area at Fort Casey. Fort Worden is home to kayak and bicycle rentals.

5 CAMA BEACH HISTORICAL STATE PARK
On the Water: Saratoga Passage
On the Globe: 48.1452°N, 122.5088°W

A private fishing resort from the 1930s to '80s with rustic cabins fronting Camano Island's Saratoga Passage shoreline, **CAMA BEACH** has enjoyed a renaissance since Washington State Parks reopened it for family fun in 2008. On the National Register of Historic Places, the 486-acre park retains a cozy yesteryear look. To get there, take exit 212 from Interstate 5 and follow the clearly posted signs.

BEACH TIME

Whether you score a summer rental of one of the cabins feet from the water or just visit for a day, you can enjoy the pebbled beach with views of the Olympics rising beyond Whidbey Island. Gray whales frequent these waters in spring.

BOAT BUILDING, RENTALS

Rent a boat with a crab pot, take a sailing lesson, or join in toy-boat building at an outpost of the Seattle-based **CENTER FOR WOODEN BOATS**. Some fees apply.

PICNICKING, HIKING

Several tables offer waterfront views. Hike fifteen miles of trails, including a path to **CRANBERRY LAKE**, a beaver pond teeming with lily pads and bird life.

NEARBY PARK, PUB

Extend your adventure to nearby **CAMANO ISLAND STATE PARK** (with camping) or a homeward stop at **NAKED CITY BREWERY** at Terry's Corner.

BY BUS

ISLAND TRANSIT Routes 1 and 5 stop by request at Cama Beach, Monday–Saturday.

At Cama Beach Historical State Park, rustic cabins are just feet from the water of Saratoga Passage.

6 KAYAK POINT REGIONAL PARK

On the Water: Port Susan
On the Globe: 48.1386°N, 122.3595°W

This 670-acre site includes 3,300 feet of shoreline on Port Susan, the protected saltwater bay tucked into the mainland side of Camano Island. It was slated to be an oil refinery until Snohomish County bought it for a park in 1972. To get there, take exit 199 from Interstate 5 at Marysville, go west on Marine Drive, and continue thirteen miles.

CAMPING, LODGING

A thirty-site wooded campground is supplemented by a ten-unit **YURT VILLAGE** and the three-bedroom **KAYAK KOTTAGE**. Cascadia Marine Trail campsites are available for paddlers.

PICNICKING

Roast a hot dog over one of the shoreline fire pits or nab one of ten beachfront picnic shelters. A day-use fee applies.

FISHING PIER, BOAT LAUNCH

Catch crab or fish from a three-hundred-foot pier, or launch your boat from the park's ramp.

Waterfront picnic sites and a fishing pier on Port Susan are among the attractions at Kayak Point Regional Park. Camano Island is in the distance.

WINTER BIRDING

In colder months, watch for birds ranging from bald eagles to Barrow's goldeneyes. Audubon Washington lists the park as a stop on its **GREAT WASHINGTON STATE BIRDING TRAIL**.

7 DOUBLE BLUFF PARK

On the Water: Admiralty Inlet, Useless Bay
On the Globe: 47.9819°N, 122.514°W

This sandy beach near Freeland on south Whidbey Island offers neck-swiveling views of water and mountains, with a bonus for dog lovers: it's a designated off-leash area. To get there, turn south from State Route 525 to Double Bluff Road and continue 1.9 miles to the road's end.

BEACH TIME

With your free-ranging tail wagger, you can hike a two-mile beach with a southward view of Mount Rainier, Seattle, the Cascade Range, and Olympic Mountains. (Be sure to heed the leash requirement near the park entrance.)

CLAMMING

Dig clams on adjacent tidelands (state license required).

PICNICKING

Bring a lunch to the park's picnic area or sit on one of the many drift logs with a view.

8 JETTY ISLAND

On the Water: Snohomish River, Possession Sound
On the Globe: 48.0035°N, 122.2277°W

To the fifty thousand or so who visit annually, nothing says summer like Everett's **JETTY ISLAND**. This man-made island is composed of about 1,800 acres of river-dredged sand at the Snohomish River's mouth. Access is primarily by a free passenger ferry operated each summer by the Port of Everett, the island's owner.

BEACH TIME

Bring your towel, sunscreen, and lunch for an off-the-grid day in the sun. (The island's only structure is a seasonal floating restroom.) Warm sand, shallow water, and nature trails make it a family-friendly escape, as well as a popular location for **KITEBOARDING**.

FERRY

The ferry makes the quarter-mile run daily July 5–Labor Day, departing **JETTY LANDING**, adjacent to the boat launch at Tenth Street and West Marine View Drive, just north of downtown Everett. Get boarding passes at the Jetty Island kiosk. Reservations are recommended; check the Port of Everett website for details.

NATURE WALKS, CLASSES

Park naturalists lead free walks and classes on raptors, wildflowers, and other island phenomena.

9 MARINA BEACH PARK

On the Water: Puget Sound
On the Globe: 47.8049°N, 122.3929°W

Tucked south of the Port of Edmonds Marina at **EDWARDS POINT**, not far from downtown Edmonds, this delightful beach park is a favorite among Snohomish County urbanites.

BEACH TIME

A sand-and-pebble beach strewn with silver logs offers sunset views of the Olympics animated by ferries crossing between Edmonds and Kingston. When kids tire of sand castles, there's a playground and volleyball court.

Sometimes nothing beats a good book, not even the view from the beach at Golden Gardens in Seattle.

PICNICKING

There are a number of tables on the grass or beachside with barbecue stands.

OFF-LEASH BEACH

Directly south of the park is an off-leash area for any retriever who just has to chase a tennis ball into the waves.

BY BUS

COMMUNITY TRANSIT routes 116, 130, 196, and 416 serve Edmonds Station, 0.7 mile away.

10 GOLDEN GARDENS

On the Water: Shilshole Bay, Puget Sound
On the Globe: 47.6879°N, 122.4026°W

The eighty-eight-acre park called **GOLDEN GARDENS** is a favorite Seattle sunset-watching spot and beach-party venue.

BEACH TIME

There's volleyball, kite flying, playing suntan rotisserie in the sand, or lapping ice cream from the neighboring **LITTLE CONEY** stand. Kids love the playground structure in the shape of a pirate ship.

DRIVE-UP SUNSETS

Sit in your car in a westward-facing lot or loll on a park bench while feasting your eyes on the sun as it sinks behind **MOUNT OLYMPUS,** with side helpings of spinnaker-flying sailboats (races occur most Wednesday evenings April–September) and swooping herons.

PICNICS, BONFIRES

Reservable shelters are popular for birthday picnics, or rent the historical bathhouse. Enjoy a bonfire in a beach-front firebox (open after 4:00 p.m.; natural firewood and charcoal only).

MORE RECREATION

A multilane boat-launch ramp adjoins a fishing pier. Rent paddle-craft seasonally from a vendor at neighboring **SHILSHOLE BAY MARINA.** Kiteboarders catch winds from **MEADOW POINT,** at the park's north end.

WALK TO WILDLIFE

Stroll to the Meadow Point **DUCK POND,** where tree-gnawing beavers reshape the landscape.

DOG PARK

Find an **OFF-LEASH AREA** in the upper park off Golden Gardens Drive.

BY BUS

KING COUNTY METRO TRANSIT routes 18 and 45 stop near the top of a long public staircase descending to the park from the west end of Northwest Eighty-Fifth Street.

11 DISCOVERY PARK

On the Water: Elliott Bay, Shilshole Bay
On the Globe: 47.6583°N, 122.4037°W

Formerly Fort Lawton, this 534-acre expanse edging Magnolia Bluff has been called the "everything park," and it is Seattle's largest. Here are forests, meadows, a spaghetti-tangle of trails, hundreds of documented bird species, and two miles of wild beach, with a scenic 1881-vintage lighthouse, a tribal cultural center, and historic military structures to boot. There's even a wastewater-treatment plant.

BEACH TIME

This is an isolated beach for contemplative walks among driftwood and cobbles, offering a recharge for the urban soul—along with saltwater vistas. (For auto access, get a permit from the visitor center. Otherwise, hike or bike in.)

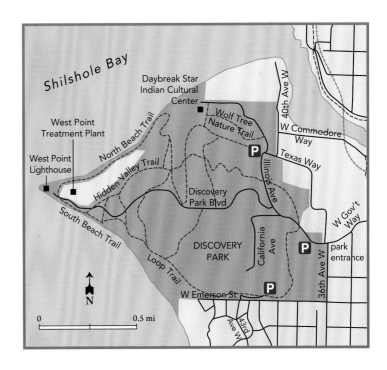

HIKING

Among visitor favorites, the **NORTH BEACH TRAIL** is a two-mile loop, while the **SOUTH BEACH TRAIL** offers direct views of Mount Rainier. Both take you out near the **WEST POINT LIGHTHOUSE**.

CULTURAL CENTER

Among other offerings, **DAYBREAK STAR INDIAN CULTURAL CENTER** hosts the annual **SEAFAIR INDIAN DAYS POW WOW**, traditionally the third weekend in July, featuring dancing, drumming, and a salmon bake.

BY BUS

KING COUNTY METRO TRANSIT Route 33 connects Discovery Park and downtown Seattle.

A boater passes the West Point Lighthouse at Discovery Park in Seattle. The sailboat masts of Shilshole Bay Marina bristle in the background.

12 BALLARD LOCKS AND SEATTLE'S URBAN WATERFRONT

On the Water: Salmon Bay, Elliott Bay
On the Globe: 47.6656°N, 122.3975°W

As the local timber industry and residents' interest in touring their watery world both grew in the early twentieth century, Seattleites yearned for a way to move commercial vessels and pleasure craft between Lake Washington, Lake Union, and Puget Sound. Ambitious engineers dug a canal linking the waters, but that wasn't enough. Since the two lakes are about twenty feet above sea level, locks were needed to maintain lake levels and prevent saltwater intrusion from the Sound. In 1917, the US Army Corps of Engineers opened **HIRAM M. CHITTENDEN LOCKS**, known informally as the Ballard Locks after the adjoining neighborhood. Today, the locks remain a key transportation link as well as a source of geeky fascination for both locals and visitors who come to watch boats of all sizes go up and down.

To extend your urban-shore adventure, Seattle's **ELLIOTT BAY WATERFRONT** along Alaskan Way is a popular place to walk, watch ferries, shop for curios, ride Pier 57's 175-foot **SEATTLE GREAT WHEEL**, visit Pier 59's **SEATTLE AQUARIUM**, or munch on fish-and-chips.

CYCLING CONNECTION

It's easy to pedal between the locks and the downtown waterfront. Protected bike lanes through the Interbay neighborhood link the locks to the **ELLIOTT BAY TRAIL**, which continues south along the shore through **CENTENNIAL** and **MYRTLE EDWARDS PARKS** to Alaskan Way, 4.5 miles away.

WALKING

The waterfront parks offer scenic paths, public art, and benches. Downtown skyscrapers looming overhead add drama to a stroll along Alaskan Way sidewalks.

A vintage motor vessel bound for Puget Sound exits the Ballard Locks as waiting boats jockey for position on their way toward Lake Union.

SALMON VIEWING

In autumn, don't miss the locks' **FISH LADDER** and subterranean viewing room where visitors can see salmon heading for spawning streams that flow into Lake Washington.

GARDEN AND ART

Adjoining the locks is the seven-acre **CARL S. ENGLISH JR. BOTANICAL GARDEN** (with mammoth rhododendron bushes abloom in spring and free weekend band concerts in summer). At the north end of the downtown waterfront, Seattle Art Museum's free **OLYMPIC SCULPTURE PARK** offers outdoor sculpture and glorious views of mountains and water.

DINING

A Pier 54 institution, **IVAR'S ACRES OF CLAMS** has inside dining as well as an informal Fish Bar with views of city firefighting boats. Near the locks, **RED MILL TOTEM HOUSE** and **THE LOCKSPOT** offer atmospheric Northwest dining.

BY BUS

KING COUNTY METRO TRANSIT routes 17 and 44 stop at the locks. Route 12 stops within two blocks of Pier 54.

13 ALKI POINT

On the Water: Elliott Bay, Puget Sound
On the Globe: 47.5819°N, 122.4045°W

Widely considered the birthplace of Seattle, Alki Point is where the city's founders, the Denny Party, disembarked from the schooner *Exact* on a cold, rainy day in November 1851—and stayed anyway. Today, Alki is Seattle's own little beach town, with sandy shores, a miles-long promenade, and a lineup of coffee shops and eateries both humble and fancy.

WALKING, SKATING, BIKING

Make a day of it by starting from **SEACREST PARK** (a passenger ferry will drop you here from downtown). Walk, jog,

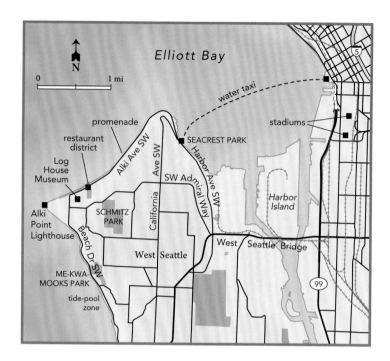

A young visitor peers through a public spotting scope along the promenade on Alki Beach, as a state ferry plies Elliott Bay.

skate, or bike paved paths toward Alki Point as the view changes over 2.5 miles from city skyline to Elliott Bay and Puget Sound. Watch ferries scoot with platoons of commuters to and from Bainbridge Island and Bremerton.

PICNICS, BONFIRES, BEACH GAMES
Spread out along Alki Beach are picnic tables, fireboxes, and volleyball nets.

DINING
Choices range from flip-flop-friendly hangouts such as **SPUD FISH & CHIPS** and **PEPPERDOCK** (for burgers) to popular water-view bars.

MUSEUM AND LIGHTHOUSE
A block off the beach is the **LOG HOUSE MUSEUM** (admission by donation), dedicated to stories of the West Seattle peninsula. Take a free tour of the small **ALKI POINT LIGHTHOUSE** on Sundays, Memorial Day–Labor Day.

PADDLING
Rent paddle-craft from vendors near Seacrest Park or watch for beach concessions in summer.

NEARBY ATTRACTION
A five-minute drive away is **ME-KWA-MOOKS PARK**, where naturalists lead seasonal tours of tide pools.

BY BUS OR WATER TAXI
KING COUNTY METRO TRANSIT routes 773 and 775 serve Alki, connecting with the RapidRide C Line. Or hop the seasonal **WEST SEATTLE WATER TAXI** from the Alaskan Way waterfront.

14 DES MOINES PIER
On the Water: East Passage, Puget Sound
On the Globe: 47.4023°N, 122.3314°W

For a certain part of the Puget Sound populace, jigging isn't dancing—it's fishing. A popular way to put sashimi or calamari on the table, jigging involves bobbing a hooked lure up and down to attract squid. Shoreside piers are the preferred fishing spot.

This fall-and-winter activity is prompted by the annual spawning migration of market squid into Puget Sound. Also known as *Loligo opalescens*, this squid typically measures six to nine inches. They are most easily caught during their nightly feeding, when they are attracted to the lights shone from nearby piers, such as the **DES MOINES PIER**. A state-issued license is required.

FACILITIES
This 670-foot pier, part of the municipal marina in Des Moines, south of SeaTac, is ADA accessible and features night lighting, a fish-cleaning station, and restrooms.

OTHER PIERS TO TRY
Among other Puget Sound fishing piers popular for squid jigging are those at **REDONDO, POINT DEFIANCE PARK, EDMONDS, SHILSHOLE BAY MARINA, SEACREST PARK, DASH POINT PARK**, and **INDIANOLA**, as well as any public pier along Seattle's Elliott Bay.

15 SALTWATER STATE PARK
On the Water: East Passage, Puget Sound, McSorley Creek
On the Globe: 47.3728°N, 122.3233°W

This is South King County's saltwater beach, a pleasant place to picnic or wade, with sunset views over Vashon and Maury Islands. Off Marine View Drive south of Des Moines, halfway between Seattle and Tacoma, it's also the spot where representatives of the two cities called off a bitter rivalry, literally burying a hatchet at the park's dedication. Today's multicultural visitor base inspires park events such as **FLUTE QUEST**, celebrating Native American flute music, and a **CAMBODIAN CULTURAL CELEBRATION**.

BEACH TIME

Enjoy 1,445 feet of saltwater shoreline in sight of Tacoma-bound ships rounding **POINT ROBINSON**. In fall, salmon splash their way up **McSORLEY CREEK**.

DIVING

An underwater **ARTIFICIAL REEF** near day-use mooring buoys is popular with divers.

CAMPING

Forty-seven campsites edge the creek. It lies beneath Seattle-Tacoma International Airport's flight path, so don't count on quiet, but it's a convenient destination for urban campers.

TRAILS

Three trails open to hikers and bikers navigate the park's 137 acres.

WEST SOUND

1 POINT NO POINT LIGHTHOUSE

On the Water: Admiralty Inlet, Puget Sound
On the Globe: 47.9113°N, 122.5301°W

What early explorers thought was a major point, but turned out to be less substantial, **POINT NO POINT** intrigues with more than its quirky name. Here, at the tip of the Kitsap Peninsula, is one of the sandy gems of Puget Sound beaches, with views of Whidbey Island's bluffs and the distant Cascades. Bonus: Little more than a half mile separates you from the Sound's main shipping lane for wave-at-the-crew views of freighters and cruise ships.

LIGHTHOUSE, LODGING

Circa 1880, this squat structure is considered the oldest Puget Sound lighthouse. Built to be seen *below* fog level, it's open for weekend tours April–September. The lightkeeper's quarters house the nonprofit, preservation-oriented **UNITED STATES LIGHTHOUSE SOCIETY**, which also rents vacation lodging here.

BEACH TIME

Choose from a number of activities: fly kites, build sandcastles, or construct driftwood huts.

BIRDING

Fierce tide rips churn up fish and food (best at tidal changes), making this an **IMPORTANT BIRD AREA** on Audubon's **GREAT WASHINGTON STATE BIRDING TRAIL**. Besides seabirds, look for songbirds around a marsh.

2 POULSBO WATERFRONT

On the Water: Liberty Bay
On the Globe: 47.7343°N, 122.6474°W

LIBERTY BAY attracted immigrant homesteader Jorgen Eliason for its resemblance to his native fjords, and he founded the town of Poulsbo there in the 1880s. It's been celebrating its Norwegian heritage ever since. Souvenir shops here may be the best place in the Northwest to buy a Viking-style horned hat.

ACTIVITIES

From **AMERICAN LEGION PARK**, savor the views of the Olympics as you follow a paved path and wheelchair-friendly boardwalk edging Liberty Bay 0.3 mile into town. Along the way, pass by **SONS OF NORWAY HALL** and stroll through manicured **WATERFRONT PARK**, with perhaps the cleanest public restrooms this side of Oslo.

SLIPPERY PIG BREWERY'S downtown pub specializes in **LUTEFISK TACOS**, which are about as good as you'd expect of fusion cuisine made with dried codfish soaked in water and caustic lye until it smells like dirty socks. Stroll the Scandinavian-themed shopping district, including the landmark **SLUYS BAKERY**.

From the park where you started, it's 0.6 mile north to **POULSBO'S FISH PARK**, near where the native Suquamish had summer fishing camps. Watch salmon spawn in **DOGFISH CREEK** in fall.

BOATING
Rent a kayak or pilot your own vessel around the bay, popular with boaters who dock in the public marina or anchor offshore.

MARINE CENTER
Visit the touch tank to get familiar with sea anemones and urchins at Western Washington University's free **SEA DISCOVERY CENTER**.

BY FERRY AND BUS
From Seattle, walk onto a Washington State ferry to Bainbridge Island and catch a **KITSAP TRANSIT** Route 90 bus, which runs Monday–Saturday.

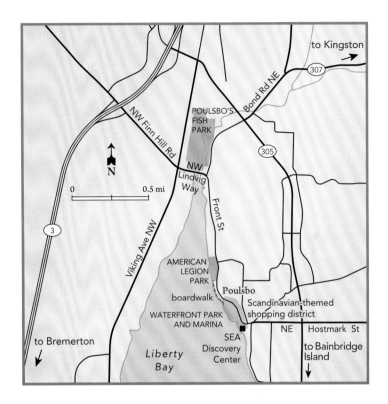

A boardwalk over Liberty Bay leads to Poulsbo's Waterfront Park.

3 OLD MAN HOUSE PARK

On the Water: Agate Passage, Port Madison
On the Globe: 47.7244°N, 122.5583°W

The clamshell-strewn beach at this tiny park at **SUQUAMISH** on Port Madison Indian Reservation offers atmospheric insights into the lives of the region's early inhabitants. This was the site of Old Man House, circa 1800, believed to have been Puget Sound's largest longhouse—as long as the Space Needle is high—and winter home to Chief Seattle, the tribal leader for whom the city was named.

BEACH TIME

Admire the current-scoured waters of narrow **AGATE PASSAGE**, with views of the distant Cascades and the nearby scenic bridge to Bainbridge Island. In the Lushootseed language, the site was D'Suq'Wub, or "place of clear saltwater." Perch on a log as you ponder

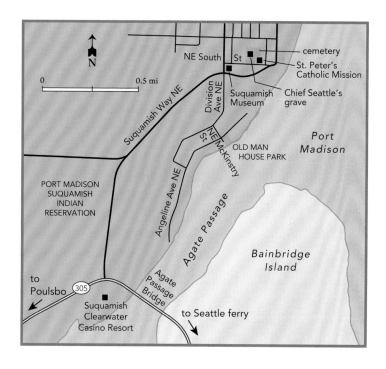

Story poles flank the marble gravestone of Chief Seattle, also known as Sealth, a variation on his Lushootseed name.

the vantage point from which a long-ago native leader took in his world, perhaps inspiring his widely credited belief that his people's spirits would forever inhabit these lands and waters.

MUSEUM AND GRAVE

Learn more at the nearby **SUQUAMISH MUSEUM** (admission fee). Just down South Street in the cemetery adjoining **ST. PETER'S CATHOLIC MISSION** (circa 1904), an old marble marker at the chief's grave has been supplemented in modern times by twelve-foot story poles artfully carved from cedar.

4 BREMERTON WATERFRONT

On the Water: Sinclair Inlet
On the Globe: 47.5633°N, 122.6237°W

It's not surprising that Puget Sound's protected waters and strategic location have drawn a military presence. Bremerton, home since the 1890s to the **PUGET SOUND NAVAL SHIPYARD**, is a quintessential Navy town. Now in the twenty-first century, the city has redeveloped its waterfront to welcome visitors. From the cross-sound ferry (you can leave your car at home), glimpse submarines, aircraft carriers, and other moored naval vessels before exploring the shoreline promenade for a taste of how national defense has shaped this corner of the Sound.

SCENIC WALK, SHIP TOUR

From the ferry terminal, walk the **BREMERTON BOARDWALK**, site of summer festivals and concerts. End up at the **USS TURNER JOY**, a Vietnam War–era destroyer and the only naval ship here regularly open for public tours (partially wheelchair accessible; admission fee). See if you fit the captain's bunk or if you're just one of the swabs.

WADING POOLS, FOUNTAINS, MUSEUM

Kids in tow? Tucked between the ferry terminal and shipyard, **HARBORSIDE FOUNTAIN PARK** has brilliantly designed wading pools and fountains reminiscent of a flotilla of submarines or battleships (but they spout like whales). Adjacent is the free **PUGET SOUND NAVY MUSEUM**.

5 BLAKE ISLAND MARINE STATE PARK

On the Water: Puget Sound, Rich Passage, Colvos Passage
On the Globe: 47.5382°N, 122.4920°W

Whether you arrive from Seattle by tour boat to Native American–themed **TILLICUM VILLAGE** for fire-roasted salmon, or take your private yacht, runabout, or kayak out for some quiet island time, mostly undeveloped Blake

On Bremerton's waterfront boardwalk, a bronze sculpture of a shipyard worker and a boy sharing a model of an aircraft carrier commemorates the 1991 centennial of the city's Puget Sound Naval Shipyard.

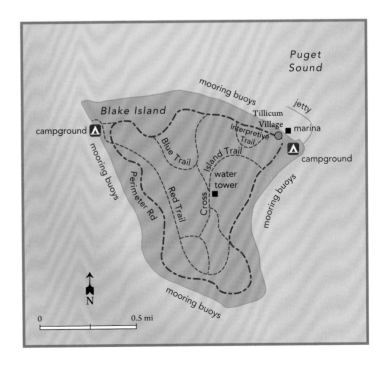

The moon rises over boats moored on state-park buoys at Blake Island.

Island is a favorite for quick getaways from the city. Some historical accounts say Chief Seattle was born here.

SALTWATER EXPERIENCE

From Seattle, take a forty-five-minute tour-boat ride or a leisurely cruise on a private vessel for eye-goggling views of the city skyline and Mount Rainier.

From your own boat, camp at the sandy beach on the island's west point, tie up to 1,500 feet of dock at Tillicum Village, or snag one of the park's many mooring buoys. From the west side, this 475-acre forested island blocks all view of the city, creating a feeling of serene remoteness.

Ask about kayak rentals and tours at the island's marina.

WILDLIFE

At low tide, raccoons dig for clams on the west beach. Visitors may also dig for clams depending on the seasonal water quality (license required). Aquatic birds frequent the area. Watch for pileated woodpeckers in the woods.

HIKING, BIKING, CAMPING

Eight miles of hiking trails (7.5 miles open to bicycles) wind through alder and cedar forest. Campgrounds include beachfront sites.

6 QUARTERMASTER HARBOR

On the Water: Puget Sound
On the Globe: 47.3787°N, 122.4568°W

Shaped like a seahorse when viewed from the air, protected **QUARTERMASTER HARBOR** separates southern Vashon Island from Maury Island (a four-hundred-foot-wide isthmus at a community called Portage connects the two).

ANCHORAGE

A snug overnight nook for boaters, the inner harbor north of **BURTON PENINSULA** protects from all but northerly winds, which can sweep across at Portage.

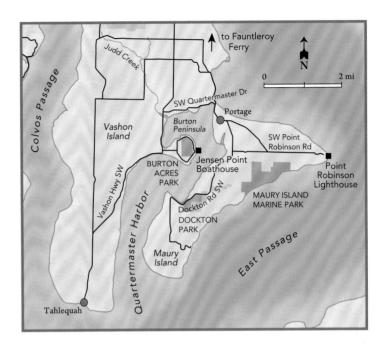

PADDLING

In warmer months, rent paddle-craft and launch from **JENSEN POINT BOATHOUSE**. (There's a launching ramp for trailered boats, too.) A guide service is also available here, including full-moon kayaking. Skirt shorelines of opulent homes while counting sea jellies below you and kingfishers above, explore lazy **JUDD CREEK**, or venture out to East Passage to camp at **MAURY ISLAND MARINE PARK**.

PARKS, LIGHTHOUSE

DOCKTON COUNTY PARK has public moorage, picnicking, swimming, a playground, boat launch, and trails. **BURTON ACRES PARK** is sixty-four wooded acres with trails. At nearby **POINT ROBINSON**, tour the red-roofed lighthouse on Sundays in summer or rent the lightkeeper's quarters.

BY BUS

King County Metro Transit **ROUTE 119** passes Dockton County Park. **ROUTE 118** can drop you a mile from Jensen Point Boathouse.

SOUTH SOUND

1 GIG HARBOR WATERFRONT

On the Water: Gig Harbor, where the
Narrows meets Dalco Passage
On the Globe: 47.3308°N, 122.5813°W

An appendix of saltwater near the Tacoma Narrows is
home to one of Puget Sound's tonier waterfront communities, anchored in maritime lore and with a picture-frame
view of Mount Rainier. It makes a fun overnight stop for
boaters, or an automobile day trip that can feature exploration, education, and enjoyable ways to spend your money.

WALKING, SHOPPING, DINING

From Pioneer Way and Harborview Drive, it's a two-mile
round-trip walk to the harbor's north end along sidewalks
dotted with shops and heritage markers. (Among the
place's history: it got its name after Wilkes Expedition
explorers running a gig, a small boat, discovered the harbor's thread-the-needle narrow entrance in 1841.)

A well-preserved early-twentieth-century net shed
built by four Croatian-immigrant siblings is the centerpiece of **SKANSIE BROTHERS PARK**, commemorating the
town's fishing heritage. Here you can launch paddle-craft,
play in a fountain, or shop at a farmers market.

Visit **GIG HARBOR BOATSHOP** in the historic Eddon
Boatyard (birthplace of the Thunderbird sailboat) to see
what boatwrights are building. Enjoy fish-and-chips on
the deck of the beloved **TIDES TAVERN** (twenty-one and
older), where they offer dockside service.

BOATING

Moor your vessel; rent a kayak, rowboat, or electric
launch; or ride with a local guide on an authentic
Venetian gondola.

MARITIME MUSEUM

At the **HARBOR HISTORY MUSEUM** (admission fee), watch
ongoing restoration of the sixty-five-foot fishing vessel
Shenandoah.

2 POINT DEFIANCE PARK

On the Water: Dalco Passage, the Narrows
On the Globe: 47.3018°N, 122.5156°W

One of America's great city parks is in . . . Tacoma.
Established as a park in 1888, this 760-acre peninsula
is surrounded by dramatic prospects of saltwater, the
Tacoma Narrows Bridge, and mountains—it's less than
fifty miles from Rainier—that never fail to please.

LEFT Historic Skansie Brothers Netshed is the centerpiece of a public
park where visitors can launch paddle-craft on Gig Harbor.
OPPOSITE Mount Rainier peeks around treetops above broad, pebbly Owen Beach
at Point Defiance Park in Tacoma.

FOREST TIME

Explore five hundred acres of old-growth forest, rare on modern Puget Sound, including the gigantic **MOUNTAINEER TREE,** named for the Tacoma Branch of The Mountaineers. Arborists estimate the Douglas-fir, more than two hundred feet tall, was a seedling when Shakespeare was born.

ZOO AND AQUARIUM

POINT DEFIANCE ZOO & AQUARIUM is one of the Northwest's notable animal parks, including the innovative **PACIFIC SEAS AQUARIUM,** added to the existing aquarium complex in 2018. Admission fee.

SCENIC DRIVE, CYCLE TOUR

The park's one-way **FIVE MILE DRIVE** is among the best driving and biking tours on Puget Sound's shores. Restricted to nonmotorized use during set times daily; check online for hours.

LIVING HISTORY

FORT NISQUALLY LIVING HISTORY MUSEUM replicates an 1833 Puget Sound fort, rebuilt with two of the original buildings. Docents in period clothing demonstrate crafts. Special events include candlelight tours and Queen Victoria's birthday. Admission fee.

BEACH TIME

OWEN BEACH, with picnic shelters and grills, overlooks Vashon Island.

HIKES

About fourteen miles of trails cater to hikers. The 3.6-mile **INSIDE LOOP TRAIL** explores deep into the forest. A 0.8-mile waterfront promenade is ADA accessible.

GARDENS

Impeccable gardens feature roses, dahlias, rhododendrons, and more.

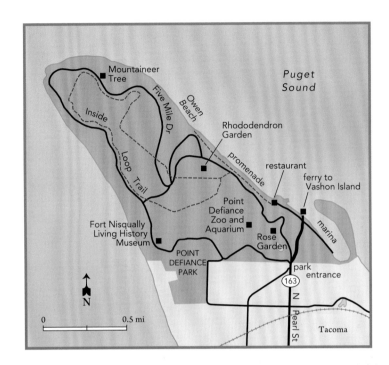

3 PENROSE POINT STATE PARK

On the Water: Mayo Cove, Carr Inlet
On the Globe: 47.2535°N, 122.7484°W

In August, look for dark-blue huckleberries along 2.5 miles of mostly flat trails in **PENROSE POINT STATE PARK** on Pierce County's rural Key Peninsula. Come to car camp (crowds are rare, even in summer) or tie your boat to a mooring buoy in the south cove for in-your-face Mount Rainier views.

CAMPING

The wooded campground has eighty-four sites, including a Cascadia Marine Trail site.

SHELLFISH HARVESTING

State fisheries agents have planted oysters and Manila clams on some park beaches. Harvesting is open seasonally for people with licenses.

NEARBY ATTRACTION

Next door, summer visitors can get ice cream or a burger at the 1930s-era **LAKEBAY MARINA RESORT**, a one-time Mosquito Fleet terminal. Built on high pilings over Mayo Cove's inkwell-size inner bay, it carries the ambiance of days gone by.

4 BILLY FRANK JR. NISQUALLY NATIONAL WILDLIFE REFUGE

On the Water: Nisqually Reach, McAllister Creek, Nisqually River
On the Globe: 47.0726°N, 122.7131°W

While most of Washington's major estuaries have been filled, dredged, or developed, this sprawling preserve where the glacier-fed Nisqually River meets Puget Sound offers one of the most accessible—in every sense of the word—opportunities to observe how freshwater and saltwater interact in a healthy natural setting: (A) it has miles of wheelchair-friendly boardwalk and trails; (B) it's easy to get to, just off Interstate 5; (C) along every path, informative panels tell about the refuge's natural history and more than three hundred species of wildlife; and (D) the small entry fee won't strain a pocketbook.

Also distinguishing the site: In 2009, dike removal reconnected 762 acres with the tides of Puget Sound. In 2015, Congress renamed the refuge in honor of tribal fisheries activist Billy Frank Jr.

WALKS, BIRDING

Four miles of paths traverse freshwater marshes, riparian forest, and saltwater sloughs. A star attraction is the **NISQUALLY ESTUARY BOARDWALK** that ventures a mile into grassy salt marsh. Join a guided birding walk at 8:00 a.m. Wednesdays, year-round.

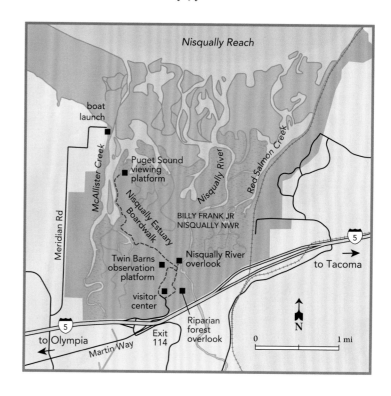

Visitors near the end of the mile-long Nisqually Estuary Boardwalk.

PHOTOGRAPHY

The refuge is a nature-photographer's heaven, promising close encounters with wading herons, soaring hawks, and many migratory species.

HUNTING

Tideflats are open to waterfowl hunting by boat during state hunting seasons.

5 KENNEDY CREEK

On the Water: Kennedy Creek, Totten Inlet
On the Globe: 47.0916°N, 123.0952°W

Take an autumn walk on the **KENNEDY CREEK SALMON TRAIL** to see chum salmon spawning—typically twenty thousand to forty thousand annually. Nature lovers flock to this far reach of Puget Sound, between Olympia and Shelton, on November weekends when docents with the South Puget Sound Salmon Enhancement Group (SPSSEG) host viewings of the returning fish on land owned by Taylor Shellfish Company. The trail is usually only open to the public in November; check the SPSSEG website.

Stroll beneath mossy maples along the half mile of trail, most of it ADA accessible, for a close look at fish flopping through shallows as they search for just the right place to lay and fertilize eggs—a total of thirty to sixty *million* in this stream. Alongside are carcasses of fish that have already spawned and died, part of the cycle of life in Puget Sound.

To get there from US Highway 101, turn west at milepost 357 onto Old Olympic Highway. Go 0.7 mile to a gravel road signed "Kennedy Creek." Continue 0.75 mile to a signed parking area.

FOOD EVENT

Check online for the dates of the annual fundraiser **CHUM, CHOWDER & CHOCOLATE**, when vendors offer seafood and cocoa at the trailhead. Proceeds help maintain the trail.

HOOD CANAL

1 DOSEWALLIPS STATE PARK

On the Water: Dosewallips River, Hood Canal
On the Globe: 47.6854°N, 122.9003°W

A 1,064-acre waterfront park along US 101 by the town of Brinnon offers a taste of rainforest camping and a soul-nourishing walk through an estuary where a glacier-fed river meets a natural saltwater fjord (not an artificial waterway as the "canal" name implies).

CAMPING

More than 120 campsites are open year-round (with limited water in winter), some in a meadow and others beneath mossy maples and cedars, along with cabins and platform tents.

Heading out to fish a slough in the estuary at Dosewallips State Park on Hood Canal

SHELLFISH GATHERING

Washington Department of Fish and Wildlife designates this "an excellent beach" for harvesting oysters and Manila littleneck clams (license required).

WALKS

Five miles of trails include wooded loops and the **NORTH TIDAL AREA TRAIL**, where you can climb a viewing tower to see afternoon light bring out the sage and ochre hues of estuary grasses as sandpipers flit about.

WILDLIFE

A resident herd of Roosevelt elk sometimes wanders the campground.

NEARBY ATTRACTIONS

Visit Brinnon's seven-acre **WHITNEY GARDENS** (donations accepted), specializing in rhododendrons. Just south of the park entrance, the **GEODUCK** is a classic roadhouse where you might share the estuary view with road-tripping families or highway-touring Harley riders.

2 THELER WETLANDS

On the Water: Hood Canal, Union River estuary
On the Globe: 47.4382°N, 122.8362°W

You might call this the birth canal of Hood Canal. At the far end, where the **UNION RIVER ESTUARY** feeds freshwater to saltwater, you'll find this 139-acre preserve in Belfair. ADA accessible, this interpretive trail—much of it wooden boardwalk—navigates marshes where you can watch barn swallows perform aerobatics on summer breezes.

Local philanthropist Sam Theler willed the preserve to the North Mason School District in 1968, an arrangement that has subsequently created financial challenges for the district. The state Department of Fish and Wildlife, which manages adjacent lands, is in line to take over the site.

NATURE WALKS, PHOTOGRAPHY

Bring a camera along trails that explore varying habitat, such as the **ALDER-CEDAR SWAMP TRAIL** through a virtual tunnel of mossy alders. The **SOUTH TIDAL MARSH TRAIL** emerges from woods to a 0.3-mile pier stretching through reeds and mudflats to where the river meets the canal.

Educational buildings offer exhibits, including a whale skeleton.

BIRDING

Besides swallows, watch for dabblers (northern pintails, American wigeons) and divers (ruddy ducks, horned grebes).

LEFT Visitors walk the boardwalk on the South Tidal Marsh Trail, where the Union River feeds Hood Canal at Theler Wetlands Preserve near Belfair.
RIGHT Green sea anemones, surfgrass, and mussels populate a tide pool at Salt Creek Recreation Area on the Olympic Peninsula.

STRAIT OF JUAN DE FUCA

1 SALT CREEK RECREATION AREA

On the Water: Strait of Juan de Fuca, Crescent Bay, Salt Creek
On the Globe: 48.1604°N, 123.6992°W

Just west of Port Angeles, Clallam County's **SALT CREEK RECREATION AREA** is legendary for its tide pools. Colleges from across the continent bring students here to study the marine life.

TIDE-POOLING, DIVING

Schedule your tide-pooling visit during extreme low tides for the best viewing. Multiple stairways lead down to rocks.

Tide pools east of the campground can be best for spotting otters, octopuses, and sea stars. On the west end is the aptly named **TONGUE POINT**, a rocky appendage with acres of tide pools that host everything from crabs to sea snails.

This area is among the best shore-based scuba locales in Washington, with rockfish, nudibranchs, sea pens, and more.

CAMPING

A sunny hillside popular with RVers offers vistas of passing ships and Victoria's lights, while a wooded bluff overlooking Tongue Point's crashing waves is cozier for tenters.

BEACH TIME, BIRDING, HISTORY, HIKING

At the base of a sea stack, stroll the sandy beach of **CRESCENT BAY** and listen for the whistle of nesting black oystercatchers. Upland trails allow exploration of historical **CAMP HAYDEN**, a World War II site. Mountain bikers and hikers may access the state's adjoining **STRIPED PEAK RECREATION AREA**.

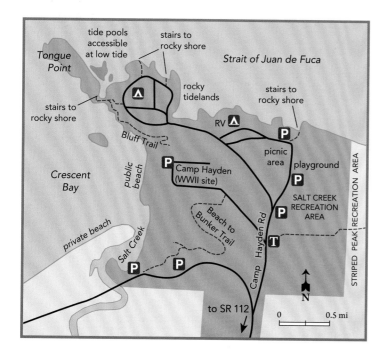

At the mouth of the undammed Elwha River, a renewed flow of sediments has formed a substantial new beach on the Strait of Juan de Fuca. The wild beach is easily accessed by the public with a five-minute walk.

2 MOUTH OF THE ELWHA RIVER

On the Water: Elwha River, Freshwater Bay, Strait of Juan de Fuca
On the Globe: 48.1435°N, 123.5665°W

The world's largest dam-removal project returned free flow to the Olympic Peninsula's **ELWHA RIVER** in 2012, restoring the river's potential for salmon spawning. It also allowed sediments to flow downstream once again, evidenced by the newly forming beach where the river emerges at the Strait of Juan de Fuca.

WALK, BEACH TIME, BIRDING

From State Route 112 west of Port Angeles, go north on Place Road for 1.9 miles to Elwha Dike Road (a sign points right to Elwha River access). Park at the road's end and walk five minutes on the dike—a wheelchair could probably navigate it—to find a sandy beach that has

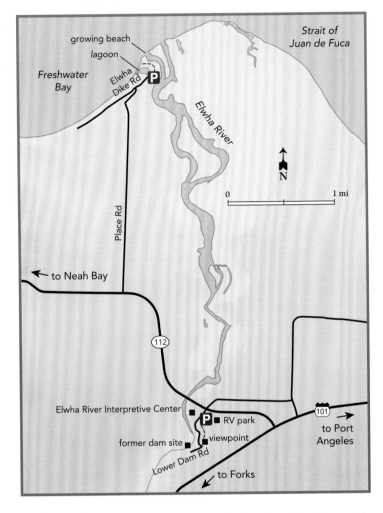

Back at SR 112, go east 1.4 miles to Lower Dam Road and follow signs to the unstaffed, open-air **ELWHA RIVER INTERPRETIVE CENTER** to learn more about the dam and its removal. From a nearby signed parking lot adjoining the Elwha Dam RV Park (slogan: "The Best RV Park by a Dam Site"), a viewpoint overlooking the old dam site is reached in a fifteen-minute hike through woods.

3 DUNGENESS SPIT

On the Water: Strait of Juan de Fuca, Dungeness Bay
On the Globe: 48.1413°N, 123.1905°W

Near Sequim, take an epic beach walk to the lighthouse at the end of Dungeness Spit, one of the world's longest sand spits, in **DUNGENESS NATIONAL WILDLIFE REFUGE**.

HIKING, BIRDING, LIGHTHOUSE TOUR

As much as any mountain trek, this hike takes preparation, because (A) if you go at high tide, your round trip will be ten miles of (much slower, more taxing) driftwood hopping rather than open-sand hiking. Time your outing for a low-tide cycle. (B) you're exposed to a wide expanse of open saltwater, and there's little to stop tempests blowing in from the Pacific. Got a perfect sunny day? Once you hit the beach there's not a shade tree in sight, so pack water, sunscreen, and a brimmed hat.

But the payoff is big: an intimate encounter with the saltwater freeway used by vessels of every size and shape (and, occasionally, whales) as they enter and leave Puget Sound. Watch for nesting Caspian and arctic terns.

At the spit's end, a changing band of lighthouse keepers (who pay to stay) offer free tours of the functional, sixty-three-foot-high lighthouse at **NEW DUNGENESS LIGHT STATION**, which, despite its name, dates to 1857. Did you stay hydrated? No worries, there's a public restroom.

grown dramatically since the river's unleashing. It's a wild, edge-of-the-world place where the earth is rebuilding.

Driftwood shelters sometimes dot the windblown landscape, perfect for kite flying. Look north to see the mountains on **VANCOUVER ISLAND** or south to **HURRICANE RIDGE**.

In fall and winter, watch for roosting Thayer's gulls at this stop on Audubon's **GREAT WASHINGTON STATE BIRDING TRAIL**.

Dungeness Spit reaches out into the Strait of Juan de Fuca like a long arm cozying up to a lover.

ACCESSIBLE START

From the refuge parking lot, the first half mile of the trail leading to Dungeness Spit is paved and wheelchair accessible to a viewpoint. Admission fee for all hikers.

BOAT ACCESS

Seasonal boat access is allowed in **DUNGENESS BAY** and **DUNGENESS HARBOR**, inland of the spit. Boaters may land near the lighthouse by advance reservation. Launch near neighboring **CLINE SPIT**.

CAMPING, FARM STANDS

Camp at adjacent **DUNGENESS RECREATION AREA**, with trails open to hikers, bikers, and equestrians. For your campfire dinner, pick up produce from nearby **NASH'S ORGANIC PRODUCE FARM STORE** (open year-round) or a number of seasonal Dungeness Valley farm stands.

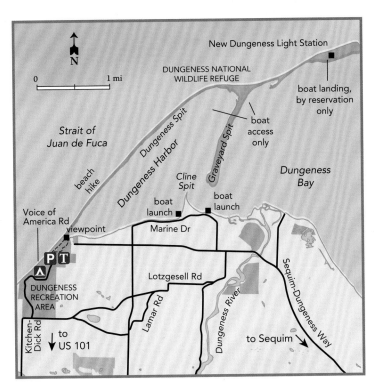

NORTH SOUND

1 BELLINGHAM BAYFRONT

On the Water: Salish Sea, Bellingham Bay
On the Globe: 48.7254°N, 122.5050°W

Watch for the classic schooner *Zodiac* or the Alaska Marine Highway ferry, both based on beautiful Bellingham Bay, from the **SOUTH BAY TRAIL**, an easy walk that includes long stretches over saltwater (**TAYLOR DOCK**, which once supported industrial structures) and traces the route of a defunct interurban railway. The 2.3-mile trail bisects **BOULEVARD PARK** and connects **DOWNTOWN BELLINGHAM** with the historic **FAIRHAVEN** district. Portions of the trail are wheelchair-accessible pavement—the rest is gravel.

NEARBY ATTRACTIONS

At the downtown end of the trail is Bellingham's **SATURDAY MARKET** at Railroad Avenue and East Maple Street. At the Fairhaven end is plenty of shopping and dining, along with **FAIRHAVEN VILLAGE GREEN**, site of a summer farmers market. Bellingham's burgeoning **CRAFT BREWING** industry is within easy walking distance of the trail. Pick up a Tap Trail map, showing local brewpubs, at a visitor information center.

2 OYSTER DOME

On the Water: Samish Bay
On the Globe: 48.6096°N, 122.4264°W

Take an invigorating hike atop the **CHUCKANUT MOUNTAINS**, the only subset of the Cascade Range to reach saltwater, for an eagle's-eye view of the San Juan Islands. Named for the local shellfishing industry, 2,025-foot-high **OYSTER DOME** is accessible most of the year.

There are two trailheads: One, with parking challenges, starts from Chuckanut Drive (State Route 11); the other starts from Samish Overlook (Discover Pass required), accessed by a network of dirt roads from Interstate 5. The latter makes for a (shorter) five-mile round-trip hike.

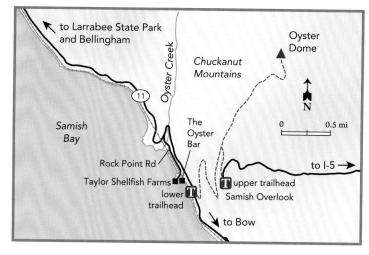

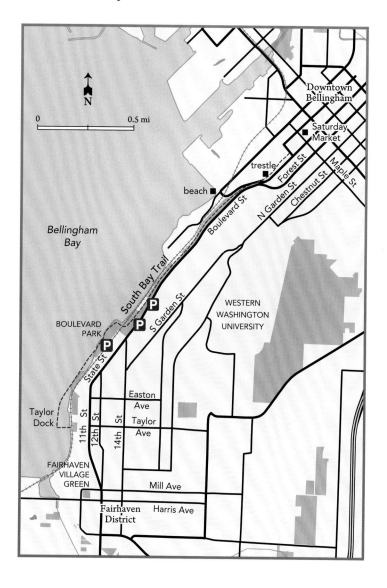

NEARBY ATTRACTIONS

A drive along winding CHUCKANUT DRIVE is worthwhile, with options to stop at LARRABEE STATE PARK and Bellingham's FAIRHAVEN HISTORIC DISTRICT. Pay homage to the local shellfish with a post-hike stop at TAYLOR SHELLFISH FARMS' Samish Bay outpost (2182 Chuckanut Drive) to barbecue your own oysters (grills provided). Or book dinner at THE OYSTER BAR (2578 Chuckanut Drive), a fine-dining fixture since 1946.

3 STUART ISLAND MARINE STATE PARK

On the Water: Prevost Harbor, Reid Harbor
On the Globe: 48.6764°N, 123.1992°W

There are plenty of places to watch for orcas in the San Juans—San Juan Island's Lime Kiln Point State Park is a favorite—but few involve more adventure than TURN POINT on off-the-grid STUART ISLAND at the archipelago's northwest corner. Arrive by sea kayak, sailboat, or yacht to STUART ISLAND MARINE STATE PARK, straddling two protected harbors with docks and mooring buoys. Find campgrounds for paddlers, trails, and little-driven gravel roads to landmarks rich in island history.

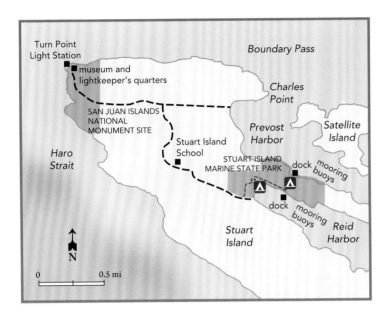

SCHOOL VISIT

STUART ISLAND SCHOOL, founded in 1897, closed due to a lack of students in 2013 but remains an interesting destination. In the schoolyard is a tiny unstaffed museum and an old library, where over the years student-created postcard artwork was sold to raise funds. Nearby, a local family has long sold island-themed T-shirts from an outdoor chest, all on the honor system.

LIGHTHOUSE

From Reid Harbor, walk three miles to 1893-vintage **TURN POINT LIGHT STATION**, part of **SAN JUAN ISLANDS NATIONAL MONUMENT**. Established in 2013 by President Barack Obama, this preserve is home to some of the best wild nuggets of this chain of more than 450 islands, rocks, and reefs. Volunteers staff a museum and offer tours of the restored lightkeeper's quarters. An orca superpod—all three Southern Resident pods swimming together—has been known to take more than thirty minutes to round this kelp-cradled point. Beyond, all you see is Canada.

4 MORAN STATE PARK

On the Water: Rosario Strait
On the Globe: 48.6577°N, 122.8625°W

This 5,424-acre wonderland of unspoiled lakes, hills, and forest on Orcas Island is another showpiece of Washington's state parks. A nineteenth-century Seattle mayor, Robert Moran, who built the nearby mansion at what's now Rosario Resort, donated much of the park. The peak experience, if you will, is atop 2,409-foot **MOUNT CONSTITUTION**, the San Juan Islands' loftiest point. From a stone lookout built by the Depression-era Civilian Conservation Corps and modeled after twelfth-century Caucasus Mountains watchtowers, you'll look almost into the crevasses of snowy Mount Baker and gasp at the jigsaw-like spectacle below of saltwater passages, rocky islands, laden oil tankers, and wind-heeled sailboats.

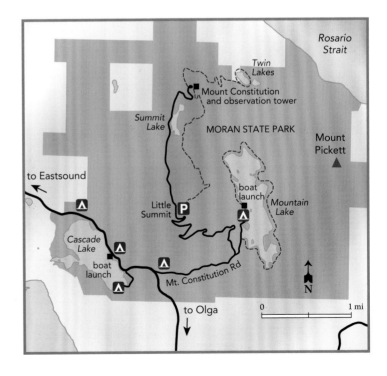

CAMPING

Choose from 151 campsites, many lakefront. A private vendor offers "glamping."

HIKING

Trek thirty-eight miles of trails, circling lakes or climbing Mount Constitution (also accessible by car).

BIKES, HORSES

Cyclists may use eleven miles of trails year-round, plus another twenty-five miles in the off-season (when you can "shoot the mountain" by riding downhill from the top). Designated trails are open to equestrians.

BOATING, FISHING

Nonmotorized boating is allowed on five lakes, with launch ramps and rentals on **CASCADE** and **MOUNTAIN LAKES**. The state stocks Cascade Lake with trout (fishing license required).

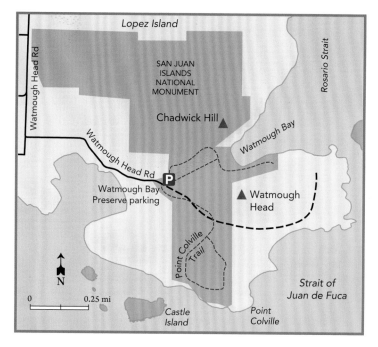

Kayakers cross Prevost Harbor at Stuart Island in the San Juans.

5 POINT COLVILLE

On the Water: Strait of Juan de Fuca, Rosario Strait
On the Globe: 48.4218°N, 122.8121°W

Bike aboard a ferry to cycle-friendly **LOPEZ ISLAND**, where you can hike this easy 2.2-mile loop trail to one of the San Juan Islands' lesser-known corners. You'll whistle through your teeth at the panorama of saltwater, mountains, and sky at **POINT COLVILLE**, one of the more accessible of the scattered holdings of the 1,000-acre **SAN JUAN ISLANDS NATIONAL MONUMENT**.

BEACH TIME, HIKING, BIRDING, PHOTOGRAPHY
Start at nearby **WATMOUGH BAY PRESERVE** (best place to park if you come by car). Here, you'll find a lovely sand-and-pebble beach on a saltwater cleft guarded by 470-foot **CHADWICK HILL**, where bald eagles and turkey vultures soar. Traverse one of Lopez's rare old forests to Point Colville, named for a mid-nineteenth century governor of the Hudson's Bay Company.

Emerge from quiet fir-and-cedar woods to lichen-crusted rocky balds, where you'll enjoy head-turning views of the Strait of Juan de Fuca, the Olympic Mountains, and Whidbey and Fidalgo Islands. Near to shore, aptly named **CASTLE ISLAND** hosts scarlet-footed pigeon guillemots and (rumor has it) the occasional tufted puffin.

Follow the loop trail counterclockwise for the easiest introduction—the footing gets more precarious as you go. Binoculars will help you spy the arching **DECEPTION PASS BRIDGE**, eight miles across Rosario Strait.

A tugboat threads between Colville Island, left, and Castle Island as a hiker eats lunch on a rocky perch at Point Colville on Lopez Island.

A nest in a western redcedar protects the eggs of an American robin. Creatures of all types, from humans to birds to fish, depend on the environment for shelter and sustenance.

Source Notes

OUR PUGET SOUND

34   "The Salish Sea in both nations includes about 10,500 square miles of sea surface area," SeaDoc Society, *Salish Sea Facts*, accessed October 2018. www.seadocsociety.org/about-the-salish-sea.

34   "Its 4,600 miles of shoreline includes 419 islands," SeaDoc Society, *Salish Sea Facts*, accessed October 2018. www.seadocsociety.org/about-the-salish-sea.

34   "more than 68,000 square miles on both sides of the international border," Shaw Centre for the Salish Sea, accessed October 2018. www.salishseacentre.org/#story.

45   "US government agencies declared 2014–2018 to be collectively the warmest yesrs," NASA, accessed April 2019. www.nasa.gov.

45   "However, in some locations, he explains, Hood Canal circulation can be more stagnant," Dr. Parker MacCready email to authors, February 2019.

47   "Oceanographic processes such as freshwater inflows and wind-driven surface currents," SeaDoc Society, *Salish Sea Facts*, accessed October 2018. www.seadocsociety.org/about-the-salish-sea.

EXTRAORDINARY NATURE

55   "some of the most productive habitats," World Wildlife Fund, *Wetlands*, accessed October 2018. www.worldwildlife.org/habitats/wetlands.

57   "The twenty-two-acre oasis provides shelter and food for over 225 species," Puget Sound Bird Fest, accessed July 2018. pugetsoundbirdfest.org/46-birdfest/303-edmonds-marsh.

57   "In King County, Washington's most densely populated region," *Encyclopedia of Puget Sound*, "King County Wetland Habitat," accessed July 2018. www.eopugetsound.org/articles/king-county-wetland-habitat.

58   "Many of our Pacific salmon and trout species are anadromous," King County Environmental Program, accessed July 2018. www.kingcounty.gov/services/environment/animals-and-plants/biodiversity/defining-biodiversity/species-of-interest/freshwater-fish.aspx.

60   "80 percent of tidal marshes and river estuaries in the Sound were diked and drained," Timothy Quinn, Washington Department of Fish and Wildlife, in a paper presented at a science workshop on Puget Sound shorelines.

63   "The Salish Sea of British Columbia and Washington State has a coastline," SeaDoc Society, *Salish Sea Facts*, accessed July 2018. www.seadocsociety.org/about-the-salish-sea.

65   "more than 27 percent of Puget Sound nearshore habitat is armored," Richard Strickland, *Puget Sound Fact Book,* 2015.

65   "the state Department of Fish and Wildlife and the US Army Corps of Engineers," Puget Sound Nearshore Ecosystem Restoration Project, accessed April 2019, www.pugetsoundnearshore.org.

65   "Octopuses are so brainy that some psychologists," Lea Winerman, *Monitor on Psychology*, American Psychological Association, June 2008, vol. 39, no. 6: page 28.

69   "There are many more world-record sea creatures," SeaDoc Society, *Salish Sea Record Holders*, accessed October 2018. www.seadocsociety.org/salish-sea-biggest-oldest.

72   "take up nutrients and minerals coming down the rivers," Puget Sound Restoration Fund ecologist Brian Allen, email message to author, July 23, 2018.

72   "with the help of sunlight, grow into massive structures," Christopher Dunagan, *Encyclopedia of Puget Sound*, posted May 1, 2018.

72   "The Center for Biological Diversity in 2005 recognized," The Center for Biological Diversity, news release, October 6, 2005.

72   "In the Salish Sea marine environment alone, the SeaDoc Society," *Salish Sea Facts*, SeaDoc Society, accessed August 2018. www.seadocsociety.org/about-the-salish-sea.

THE HUMAN CONNECTION

94   "it soon found itself trading for salmon," Wikipedia article, *Fort Langley*, accessed October 2018. en.wikipedia.org/wiki/Fort_Langley

98   "this area was a favorite shellfish gathering site for many Salish tribes," City of Olympia history, accessed October 2018. olympiawa.gov/community/about-olympia/history-of-olympia-washington.aspx.

101   "As early as the 1890s, a few years after statehood," *History of Fish Hatcheries*, Northwest Power and Conservation Council, accessed July 2018. www.nwcouncil.org/reports/columbia-river-history/hatcheries.

123   "The Department of Ecology launched a broad multiyear smelter plume cleanup," *Tacoma Smelter Cleanup Project*, accessed July 2018. www.ecology.wa.gov/Spills-Cleanup/Contamination-cleanup/Cleanup-sites/Toxic-cleanup-sites/Tacoma-smelter.

123 "In 1980, the toxic effects of human activities in and near the Sound took on new urgency," Richard Strickland, *Encyclopedia of Puget Sound*, originally published July 2013, accessed July 2018. www.eopugetsound.org/articles/toxics-research-changed-puget-sound-history.

126 "the number of species of concern in the Salish Sea nearly doubled between 2002 and 2013," Joe Gaydos and Jacqlynn Zier, *Puget Sound Fact Book*, 2015: page 70.

126 "Researchers Jacqlynn Zier and Joe Gaydos say the growing number of species of concern," paper presented at Proceedings of the 2016 Salish Sea Ecosystem Conference, April 13–15, 2016, Vancouver, BC.

129 "In 2000, Commissioner of Public Lands Jennifer Belcher," Robert McClure, *Seattle Post-Intelligencer*, "State Acts to Protect Marine Life in Several Areas of Puget Sound," September 26, 2003.

129 "these special areas conserve and enhance," Washington State Department of Natural Resources, Aquatic Reserves website, www.dnr.wa.gov/managed-lands/aquatic-reserves. Accessed April 2019.

135 "In 2015, more than 3,000 feet of old armoring were removed from the Sound," Christopher Dunagan, *Encyclopedia of Puget Sound,* accessed October 2018. www.pugetsoundinstitute.org/2015/08/could-shoreline-armoring-finally-be-declining-in-puget-sound.

149 "nearly seventy killer whales were captured and taken," G. J. Wiles, *Washington State Status Report for the Killer Whale*, 2004.

150 "constantly exposed to pollution sources from industries, automobiles, trucks, and other sources," Duwamish River Cleanup Coalition website, http://duwamishcleanup.org/community-health/clean-air. Accessed April 2019.

153 "the Thea Foss and Wheeler-Osgood waterways sparkle with new life today." City of Tacoma, *Thea Foss Waterway Cleanup*, accessed July 2018. www.cityoftacoma.org/government/city_departments/environmentalservices/surface_water/restoration_and_monitoring/thea_foss_waterway_cleanup.

References

Bainbridge Island Land Trust. *Stand for the Land*. Accessed July 2018. www.bi-landtrust.org.

Baurick, Tristan. "Challenges Remain as Port Gamble Bay Cleanup Progresses." *Kitsap Sun*. January 23, 2016. http://archive.kitsapsun.com /news/local/challenges-remain-as-port-gamble-bay-cleanup-progresses -29dd7f15-53e5-6cbf-e053-0100007f08ab-366329941.html.

Capitol Land Trust. *Our Mission*. Accessed July 2018. capitollandtrust.org /who-we-are/our-mission.

Center for Biological Diversity. "Study Finds Hundreds of Imperiled Species in Puget Sound." News release on October 6, 2005. www.biologicaldiversity.org/news/press_releases/puget10-6-05.html.

City of Tacoma. *Thea Foss Waterway Cleanup*, Accessed July 2018. www.cityoftacoma.org/government/city_departments /environmentalservices/surface_water/restoration_and_monitoring /thea_foss_waterway_cleanup.

Dodge, John. "Students Excavate 700-Year-Old Camp." *The Olympian*, reprinted in the *Herald*. Everett, Washington, July 22, 2009. www.heraldnet.com/news/recently-reviewed-restaurants-17.

Edmonds Marsh. "Puget Sound Bird Fest." Accessed July 2018. pugetsoundbirdfest.org/46-birdfest/303-edmonds-marsh.

Encyclopedia of Puget Sound, s.v. "Kelp Continues Steady Decline in Puget Sound." By Christopher Dunagan. Accessed May 1, 2018, www.eopugetsound.org/magazine/ssec2018/kelp.

Encyclopedia of Puget Sound, s.v. "Hitting a Wall: Can We Fix Puget Sound's Beaches?" By Christopher Dunagan. Posted October 17, 2016. www.eopugetsound.org/magazine/fix-beaches.

Encyclopedia of Puget Sound, s.v. "Toxics Research That Changed Puget Sound History." Accessed July 2018. www.eopugetsound.org/articles /toxics-research-changed-puget-sound-history.

Encyclopedia of Puget Sound, s.v. "King County Wetland Habitat." Accessed July 2018. www.eopugetsound.org/articles/king-county-wetland-habitat.

Gaydos, Joe. "Species." In *Puget Sound Fact Book*. 2015: pages 70–79.

Gresh, Ted, Jim Lichatowich, and Peter Schoonmaker. "An Estimation of Historic and Current Levels of Salmon Production in the Northeast Pacific Ecosystem." Originally published in the journal of the *American Fisheries Society*, January 2000. Summarized January 9, 2011, at this site: https ://doi.org/10.1577/1548-8446(2000)025<0015:AEOHAC>2.0.CO;2. Accessed April 2019.

HistoryLink, s.v. "Washington State Forest Protection Laws and Practices." By David Wilma. Last modified February 26, 2003. Accessed July 2018. www.historylink.org/File/5299.

Junejo, Samir, and Eric de Place. "What Is the Magnuson Amendment?" Sightline Institute. Last modified April 27, 2016. Accessed July 2018. www.sightline.org/2016/04/27/what-is-the-magnuson-amendment.

King County Environmental Program. *Freshwater Fish in King County*. Accessed July 2018. www.kingcounty.gov/services/environment.

Low Dissolved Oxygen Levels in Hood Canal. Washington Sea Grant Program report, 2004. University of Washington Board of Regents.

MacCready, Parker. "Physical Environment." In *Puget Sound Fact Book*. 2015: pages 16–20.

Mapes, Lynda. "Elwha: Roaring Back to Life." *Seattle Times*. February 13, 2016. http://projects.seattletimes.com/2016/elwha.

———. "Scientists Now Link Massive Starfish Die-Off, Warming Ocean." *Seattle Times*. February 21, 2016.

Northwest Power and Conservation Council. *History of Fish Hatcheries*. Accessed July 2018. www.nwcouncil.org/reports/columbia-river-history /hatcheries.

Puget Sound Fact Book. Version 3.1. Special Edition for the *Encyclopedia of Puget Sound*. University of Washington Puget Sound Institute, 2015.

Quinn, Timothy. "An Environmental and Historical Overview of the Puget Sound Ecosystem." Paper from Puget Sound Shorelines and the Impacts of Armoring—Proceedings of a State of the Science Workshop, May 2009.

SeaDoc Society. *Salish Sea Facts*. Accessed August 2018. www.seadocsociety.org/about-the-salish-sea.

Shaw Centre for the Salish Sea. Accessed October 2018. www.salishseacentre.org.

Strickland, Richard. "Nearshore Environments." In *Puget Sound Fact Book*. 2015: pages 59–64.

Van Pelt, Robert. *Identifying Mature and Old Forests in Western Washington*. Washington Department of Natural Resources. Olympia, Washington. 2007.

Washington State Department of Natural Resources. *Changing Our Water Ways: Trends in Washington's Water Systems*. Olympia, Washington. 2000.

Washington State Department of Ecology. *Tacoma Smelter Plume Cleanup*. Accessed July 2018. www.ecology.wa.gov/Spills-Cleanup/Contamination -cleanup/Cleanup-sites/Toxic-cleanup-sites/Tacoma-smelter.

Wiles, G. J. *Washington State Status Report for the Killer Whale*. Washington Department of Fish and Wildlife. Olympia, Washington. 2004: pages 38–39.

Winerman, Lea. "An Invertebrate with Flair." American Psychological Association. *Monitor on Psychology*, vol. 39, no. 6 (June 2008): page 28.

World Wildlife Fund. *Wetland Habitats*. Accessed July 2018. www.worldwildlife.org/habitats/wetlands.

Help Protect Puget Sound

The future of Puget Sound and the Salish Sea depends on nonprofit organizations, government agencies, and programs. To learn about even more groups, visit www.wearepugetsound.org.

ADOPT-A-STREAM FOUNDATION in Everett, www.streamkeeper.org: Teaches people how to become stewards of their watersheds

AUDUBON WASHINGTON in Seattle, https://wa.audubon.org: State field office of National Audubon Society inspires diverse audiences to conserve natural ecosystems and build healthy communities for people, birds, and other wildlife

BAINBRIDGE ISLAND LAND TRUST, www.bi-landtrust.org: Dedicated to preserving and stewarding the diverse natural environment of Bainbridge for the benefit of all

BEACH WATCHERS in Snohomish County, https://extension.wsu.edu/snohomish/beachwatchers-2: Volunteers dedicated to protecting the Salish Sea through education, research, and stewardship

CAPITOL LAND TRUST in Lacey, https://capitollandtrust.org: Furthers collaborative and strategic conservation of southwest Washington's essential natural areas and working lands

CITIZENS FOR A HEALTHY BAY in Tacoma, www.healthybay.org: Focuses on improving the health of Commencement Bay

DEFENDERS OF WILDLIFE IN THE NORTHWEST in Seattle, https://defenders.org/northwest/defenders-northwest: Dedicated to protecting all native animals and plants in their native communities

DUWAMISH RIVER CLEANUP COALITION in Seattle, http://duwamishcleanup.org: Ensures the Duwamish River cleanup benefits the community, fish, wildlife, and human health

FORTERRA in Seattle and Tacoma, https://forterra.org: Statewide local land trust that secures land for a sustainable future

FRIENDS OF THE EARTH in Washington, DC, and Berkeley, CA, https://foe.org: Organizes to build long-term political power and campaigns to change the rules of our economic and political systems that create injustice and destroy nature

FRIENDS OF THE SAN JUANS in Friday Harbor, https://sanjuans.org: Uses public-private partnerships, applied science, legal advocacy, and community-based initiatives to protect the land, water, and sea

FRONT AND CENTERED in Seattle, https://frontandcentered.org: Statewide coalition of organizations and groups rooted in communities of color and people with lower incomes

FUTUREWISE in Seattle and Spokane, http://futurewise.org: Works to prevent sprawl in order to protect Washington State's resources and make its urban areas livable for and available to all

GOT GREEN in Seattle, https://gotgreenseattle.org: Waging visionary campaigns at the intersection of racial, economic, gender and climate justice that engage in direct action, incite community participation, and foster leadership development for directly impacted communities

KING CONSERVATION DISTRICT in Renton, https://kingcd.org: Promotes sustainable use of natural resources by educating landowners, schools, scientists, consultants, and agencies

KITSAP WATERSHED STEWARDSHIP PROGRAM in Kitsap County, https://extension.wsu.edu/kitsap/nrs/water-stewards: Classes through WSU Extension, including Stream Stewards, Beach Naturalists, and Salmon Docents

LONG LIVE THE KINGS in Seattle, https://lltk.org: Restores wild salmon and steelhead and supports sustainable fishing in the Pacific Northwest

THE NATURE CONSERVANCY IN WASHINGTON in Seattle (and four other locations), www.washingtonnature.org: Conserves the land and waters on which all life depends

NORTHWEST INDIAN FISHERIES COMMISSION in Olympia, https://nwifc.org: A natural resources management support service organization for twenty Indian treaty tribes in Western Washington

ORCA SALMON ALLIANCE, www.orcasalmonalliance.org: Educates the public about the threats facing Southern Resident orcas and chinook salmon and acts to eliminate those threats

PACIFIC EDUCATION INSTITUTE, https://pacificeducationinstitute.org: Achieves systemic change by helping educators embed FieldSTEM model in classrooms, so students become scientifically literate

PCC FARMLAND TRUST in Seattle, www.pccfarmlandtrust.org: Works to protect and steward threatened farmland in Washington

PUGET SOUNDKEEPER ALLIANCE in Seattle, https://pugetsound keeper.org: Helps set strong policies, enforces environmental regulations, engages citizens and businesses in cleanups, and involves the public in local water pollution issues

PUGET SOUND PARTNERSHIP in Tacoma, www.psp.wa.gov: State agency leading the region's collective efforts to restore and protect Puget Sound

PUGET SOUND RESTORATION FUND on Bainbridge Island, https ://restorationfund.org: Works to restore marine habitat, water quality, and native species in Puget Sound through in-the-water projects

PUGET SOUND SAGE in Seattle, www.pugetsoundsage.org: Combines research, innovative public policy, and organizing to ensure all people have an affordable place to live, a good job, clean environment, and access to public transportation

RE SOURCES FOR SUSTAINABLE COMMUNITIES in Bellingham, www.re-sources.org: Promotes sustainable communities and protects the health of northwestern Washington's people and ecosystems through the application of science, education, advocacy, and action

SALMON DEFENSE in Olympia, https://salmondefense.org: Increases public awareness and education and supports legal action to turn the tide on salmon habitat degradation

SEADOC SOCIETY on Orcas Island, www.seadocsociety .org: Conducts and sponsors vital scientific research in the Salish Sea to forge common understandings and design region-wide solutions

SEATTLE AQUARIUM, www.seattleaquarium.org: Inspires conservation of our marine environment; through beach naturalist program, local citizens volunteer to learn about and share knowledge of shorelines with beachgoers around the city

SEWARD PARK AUDUBON CENTER in Seattle, https://sewardpark .audubon.org: Protects birds and the places they need by helping a diverse mix of young people and adults cultivate wonder and develop an insatiable curiosity about the natural world through environmental sciences, outdoor exploration, and play

SIERRA CLUB WASHINGTON STATE CHAPTER, with local groups across the state, www.sierraclub.org/washington: Enjoys, explores, and protects the planet through habitat restoration and lobbying

SOUND ACTION on Vashon Island, https://soundaction.org: Works to protect vital nearshore habitat and species

SOUND EXPERIENCE based in Port Townsend, www.soundexp.org: Sails the historic schooner *Adventuress* to educate people about Puget Sound

SOUND WATER STEWARDS in Island County, https://sound waterstewards.org: Trained volunteers working in and around the county for a healthy, sustainable Puget Sound environment through education, community outreach, stewardship, and citizen science

STEWARDSHIP PARTNERS in Seattle, www.stewardshippartners.org: Creates people-based solutions that engage Puget Sound communities as caretakers of the land and water that sustain us

STREAM TEAMS in Thurston County, www.streamteam.info: Protects and enhances local water resources, associated habitats, and wildlife through citizen education and action; in Bellevue: Gathers information about the city's streams, lakes, and wetlands and helps improve fish and wildlife habitat

SUSTAINABILITY AMBASSADORS in King County, www.sustain abilityambassadors.org: A professional development program for student, teacher, and community leaders committed to educating for sustainability by aligning classroom rigor with community relevance

350.ORG, https://350.org: Uses online campaigns, grassroots organizing, and mass public actions to oppose new coal, oil, and gas projects; take money out of companies that are heating up the planet; and build 100-percent clean energy solutions that work for all

TILTH ALLIANCE in Seattle, www.seattletilth.org: Building an ecologically sound, economically viable, and socially equitable food system

12,000 RAIN GARDENS IN PUGET SOUND, www.12000raingardens. org: Cooperative effort led by Stewardship Partners and WSU Extension to promote rain gardens to address stormwater runoff

WASHINGTON ASSOCIATION OF LAND TRUSTS in Seattle, https:// walandtrusts.org: Uniting Washington land trusts for our land and our future

WASHINGTON SEA GRANT at University of Washington in Seattle, https://wsg.washington.edu: Helps people and marine life thrive by supplying research, technical expertise, and educational activities that support responsible use and conservation of ocean and coastal systems

WOODLAND PARK ZOO in Seattle, www.zoo.org: Dedicated to saving wildlife through more than thirty field projects, and inspiring everyone to make conservation a priority in their lives

About Washington Environmental Council

Since 1967, Washington Environmental Council has advocated across our state to solve Washington's most critical environmental challenges. WEC builds coalitions, mobilizes the public, engages decision makers, and takes legal action to enact and enforce environmental protections and ensure a healthy, sustainable future for all Washingtonians. In 2012, WEC was honored to expand our Puget Sound advocacy efforts by taking on People For Puget Sound's work. All of this work has resulted in foundational protections like the State Environmental Policy Act and the Shoreline Management Act. WEC has also helped Washington take big leaps at the ballot box. For instance, the Model Toxics Control Act, approved by voters in 1988, has cleaned up thousands of polluted sites across the state. When we stand together we can protect, restore, and sustain our environment *for all*.

Today, communities around Puget Sound and across the state face a variety of growing threats like toxics in polluted runoff to rivers, lakes, and marine waters, as well as declines in iconic species like salmon and Southern Resident orcas. Fossil fuel interests still eye the state as a possible hub to ship oil, coal, and fracked gas to markets across the Pacific Ocean. New development, increasingly dangerous fires, and shortsighted clear-cuts threaten forests. Climate change already impacts our communities, our health, and our environment every day. But as this book reveals, these challenges also present opportunities. We have what it takes to thrive, not in spite of our prosperity but because living a full, happy life demands that we protect the home we all share.

Addressing these complicated problems will require a new level of engagement. Crafting solutions will take the expertise of our scientific community, policy professionals, and community and tribal leaders. More than anything, making progress requires people power. When we create a groundswell of public support that demands action, elected officials are inspired—and held accountable—to act.

In short, we must build a movement centered on our connected common values. Shifting to a clean energy economy will help clean up Puget Sound. Thriving salmon runs require forests that filter runoff and keep rivers cool and clean. Shifting away from fossil fuels must include a just transition for communities who have depended on those industries for decades. Solutions have to recognize the long history of inequitable investments and policies that left far too many—particularly people of color and tribal communities—without healthy, thriving places to call home. Acting with that knowledge, we must create a community that is healthy and accessible for everyone.

Over the past five decades, WEC has helped solve some of our state's toughest environmental challenges. The next fifty years will require a new level of commitment and cooperation. We can and must create a healthier thriving home—one that sustains us all.

For more information about WEC and to get involved in the future of forests, climate, clean energy, waterways, and Puget Sound, please visit wecprotects.org.

Photographer Credits

Many photographers contributed to this project to help it showcase the breadth of the creatures and plants that live in and along the shores of Puget Sound, as well as those farther afield in the surrounding landscape whose health is intricately intertwined with the health of the Sound. The credits below include all the photos featured in these pages. Photographers whose work is featured on the front and back covers are credited on the copyright page.

AMY GULICK: pages 52, 112 (top), 121, 138, 173

ART WOLFE: pages 4–5, 42–43, 118 (bottom), 136

BRANDON COLE: pages 1, 20, 23, 49, 66, 68, 69, 73, 77, 78–79, 79 (right), 82, 109, 146, 156, 224

BRETT BAUNTON: pages 41, 53, 141

BRIAN J. CANTWELL: pages 176, 179, 181, 182, 183, 184, 185, 186, 188, 189, 190, 193, 194, 195, 196, 198, 199, 201, 202, 203, 204, 206, 210, 211

BRIAN WALSH: pages 10, 13, 25, 26, 28, 31, 32, 34, 35, 36, 38–39, 40, 44, 46, 48, 54, 58–59, 61, 62, 64 (upper right), 67, 74, 84 (bottom), 86, 87, 91, 92, 97, 103 (top and bottom), 107, 112 (bottom), 113, 115, 116, 118 (top), 120, 122, 125, 127, 130–131 (right), 133, 139, 142, 143, 145, 150

DREW COLLINS: pages 64 (lower left), 70, 81 (right)

GERRIT VYN: pages 50, 51

GLENN NELSON: pages 16, 39 (right), 130 (left), 162

HARLEY SOLTES: pages 14–15

JOEL ROGERS: pages 83, 134, 165

JOHN SCURLOCK: page 29

LAURA JAMES: page 135

LESLIE DORN: page 88

NATALIE FOBES: pages 60, 106, 148

NATIONAL ARCHIVES: page 100 (left), photo no. 12013261

THE NORTHWEST INDIAN FISHERIES COMMISSION: pages 95, 100 (right), 129

PAUL BANNICK: page 17

PAUL SOUDERS: pages 2, 15 (right), 27

ROB CASEY: pages 153, 158

SEATTLE TIMES, STEVE RINGMAN: pages 75, 154, 169 (under NMFS permit 21114)

SOUND EXPERIENCE, ELIZABETH BECKER: page 84 (top)

STEPH ABEGG: pages 56–57

STEVEN KAZLOWSKI: pages 30, 105, 159, 212

SUSAN MACLAREN, STONE SOUP GARDENS: page 124 (top)

TOM REESE: pages 8, 18, 19, 63, 72, 80–81, 85, 114, 119 (top and bottom), 147, 151 (top and bottom), 167, 175

UNIVERSITY OF WASHINGTON LIBRARIES, SPECIAL COLLECTIONS: pages 99 (neg. no. UW 6882), 117 (neg. no. A. Curtis 26368)

WASHINGTON ENVIRONMENTAL COUNCIL: page 171

WASHINGTON STATE HISTORICAL SOCIETY, TACOMA: pages 98 (no. 1911.5.4); page 102, top (no. 2010.185.47609); page 102, bottom (no. 2010.185.47611)

WOODLAND PARK ZOO, JEREMY DWYER-LINDGREN: page 144

ZSOFIA PASZTOR: page 124 (bottom)

In Appreciation

Thank you to the many donors, including individuals, businesses, and conservation partners, whose generosity helped bring this book to life. To learn more about how you can contribute to the ongoing efforts to save Puget Sound, visit BraidedRiver.org.

ORCA CHAMPION ($10,000)

 KETA Legacy Foundation

SALMON STREAMKEEPERS ($5,000)

 Salmon Defense

 Washington Sea Grant

Woodland Park Zoo

Maggie Walker

Martha Kongsgaard and Peter Goldman

Sally and Warren Jewell

SEA STARS ($1,000)

Anna Roberts and Brandon Roberts
Don and Marci Heck
Gary Rygmyr and Jennifer Warburton
Jennifer Steele and Jonathan Hoekstra
Puget Sound Restoration Fund
Stephan Kleine and Gloria Van Dusen
Stephanie Solien

SALISH STEWARDS ($500)

Argosy Cruises
Brian J. Cantwell
Brianne L. Vanderlinden
Eric and Dana Hooper
Forterra
Helen and Arnie Cherullo
In loving memory of my sister
   Elizabeth Balle
Zoe, the sweetest dog ever

Jens Molbak
John E. Spring family
Karen and Rick Dinicola
Kate Janeway
Katie Geraghty and Tom Ostrom
Marek Karbarz
Maya Cailean Mullaney
Mindy Roberts and Jim Gawel
Pam Sheets and Frank Bosl

Richard B. Levenson
Roger Mellem
Ron and Eva Sher
Scott and Joyce Reynolds
Seattle Aquarium
Sheri and Jeff Tonn
Sophia Roche
Tom Vogl

GEODUCK GROUNDSWELL ($100)

Alan Budwill
Alex Sidles
Alison Crabb
Amber Carrigan
Anonymous
Aoife Frost
Audrey, Nathan, and Dell Royston
B. Glosten
Barbara J. Sprecher
Brock Evans
Brynne Koscianski
Cascadia Climate Action
Cathy Silvey and Dick Wood
Chapman J. Root II
Charlotte Watts
Chris Townsend and Daniel Desmarais
Christopher Peñuelas
Chuck Neudorf
Dan Carmichael and Cynthia Whitaker
Dave Griswold

David Brown and Christina Rockrise
David Claar and Patti Polinsky
Ed Chamberlain
Elizabeth M. Watson
Evy Dudey and Mark Glidden
Gianna Cannataro and Gabe Aeschliman
Gretchen Glaub
In memory of Helen Engle
Hendrickson Temkin grandchildren
Isabel Davis
John Scurlock
J Team
James Bernard
James Syck
Jim Burke and April Gerlock
In memory of Jim Leavitt
John Ohlson
John Sharp
Jonathan Heller
Julie Myer and Kevin Hornback

Kara, Jeff, Kaelyn, and Bryer Stone
Kate Rogers and Tom W. Clark
Ken Lans
Kevin and Marty Schafer
Lace Thornberg
Leslie Boies
Liz Banse
Malieka Robinson
In memory of Mark S. Cable
Martina and Michael Kozar
Melissa Brumer and Ben Kossick
Melissa Mager and Rick Butler
Melody Allen
Monica Fisk
Naki Stevens
The Northwest Indian Fisheries
   Commission
In honor of Owen Humbert
Pam and Eric Linxweiler
Paula K. Berman

The Peterson family
Ramesh Chitra Aishwarya and
   Karishma Mandyam
RE SOURCES for
   Sustainable Communities
Rights of the Salish Sea, crsji.org
In honor of Roald Bradley Severtson and
   Liz Gallagher
Salmon Bay Paddle
Sound Experience
Stewardship Partners, in honor of
   Patti Southard
Sue Labrie
In honor of Susan Kennedy and
   Eric Hall
Tonia and Jay Goyal
Tyler Dunning
Virginia Felton and Jeff Hancock
Wade McNaul family
In honor of Wavey Shreffler
Waypoint Outdoor

SPECIAL THANKS TO OUR MEDIA PARTNER

 YES! Media

About the Authors

CLOVER LOCKARD

DAVID L. WORKMAN is a Washington State writer and editor. David was a journalist at several newspapers before entering public service as communications and education director for several state agencies in Washington and serving as executive editor of state-published books and websites on natural resources, environment, social and health services, and technology. A former board director of the Pacific Education Institute, David is the author of *Letter from Alabama: The Inspiring True Story of Strangers Who Saved a Child and Changed a Family Forever* and *An Author Tells All: Surprises and Revelations from Publishing My Story*.

BRIAN WALSH is an environmental planner and nature photographer who has spent thirty years exploring the coastal lowlands and mountains of the Pacific Northwest with his camera. He studied black-and-white photography at Prescott College and The Evergreen State College. Brian teaches photography in Olympia, where he lives with his wife and son. His environmental career spans three decades, including policy positions at the Washington Department of Ecology, the Northwest Power and Conservation Council, the Washington Department of Fish and Wildlife, the Puget Sound Partnership, and the Washington Department of Health.

LEONARD FORSMAN has served as tribal chairman of the Suquamish Tribe since 2005 and is president of the Affiliated Tribes of Northwest Indians. His interests include cultural preservation, sustainable economic development, and habitat protection. A graduate of the University of Washington and Goucher College, Leonard grew up in Suquamish on the Port Madison Indian Reservation and lives there with his wife, Jana Rice.

MINDY ROBERTS leads the People For Puget Sound program at the Washington Environmental Council, advocating for clean water, healthy habitat, and renewed leadership to recover and protect Puget Sound. With degrees from University of California at Berkeley, MIT/Woods Hole Oceanographic Institution, and the University of Washington, Mindy is an environmental engineer with thirty years' experience working at the intersection of natural resources and human needs. She is an avid climber and kayaker who enjoys exploring the mountains and waters of the Puget Sound region.

Seattle native BRIAN J. CANTWELL retired in 2018 as *Seattle Times* travel and outdoors editor. After living on a sailboat on the Columbia River and Puget Sound for more than twenty-five years, he and his wife, Barbara, share a cabin with their two cats in the San Juan Islands.

MARTHA KONGSGAARD was born and raised in Napa, California, to a family of jurists, grape growers, and cattle ranchers. Kongsgaard, a lawyer, married Peter Goldman in 1988 and collaborated with him to found the Kongsgaard-Goldman Foundation, which has invested in not-for-profit environmental, social justice, and arts organizations in the Pacific Northwest and Alaska. Martha serves her community in countless ways through numerous leadership roles, including immediate past chair and founding member of the Leadership Council of the Puget Sound Partnership, and chair of the Marine Resource Advisory Council for Governor Jay Inslee. She currently chairs the campaign to build the new Seattle Aquarium's Ocean Pavilion, the heart of the new "Waterfront for All" reconnecting Seattle with the Salish Sea—and one ocean. Martha and Peter live in West Seattle across the street from the nation's largest estuary, Puget Sound, in the house where they raised their three sons.

BRAIDED RIVER

BRAIDED RIVER, the conservation imprint of Mountaineers Books, combines photography and writing to bring a fresh perspective to key environmental issues facing western North America's wildest places. Our books reach beyond the printed page as we take these distinctive voices and vision to a wider audience through lectures, exhibits, and multimedia events. Our goal is to build public support for wilderness preservation campaigns, and inspire public action. This work is made possible through the book sales and contributions made to Braided River, a 501(c)(3) nonprofit organization. Please visit BraidedRiver.org for more information on events, exhibits, speakers, and how to contribute to this work.

Braided River books may be purchased for corporate, educational, or other promotional sales. For special discounts and information, contact our sales department at 800.553.4453 or mbooks@mountaineersbooks.org.

THE MOUNTAINEERS, founded in 1906, is a nonprofit outdoor activity and conservation organization, whose mission is "to explore, study, preserve, and enjoy the natural beauty of the outdoors . . . " Mountaineers Books supports this mission by publishing travel and natural history guides, instructional texts, and works on conservation and history.

Send or call for our catalog of more than 800 outdoor titles:
Mountaineers Books
1001 SW Klickitat Way, Suite 201
Seattle, WA 98134
800.553.4453
www.mountaineersbooks.org

Manufactured in China on FSC®-certified paper, using soy-based ink.

MIX
Paper from responsible sources
FSC® C008047
www.fsc.org

For more information, visit www.wearepugetsound.org.

Publisher: Helen Cherullo
Project Editor: Laura Shauger
Developmental Editor: Ellen Wheat
Copyeditor: Laura Lancaster
Cover and Book Designer: Kate Basart/Union Pageworks
Cartographer: Erin Greb
Photo Editors: Brian Walsh and Helen Cherullo
Scientific Advisor: Eric Scigliano
Tribal Reviewer: Sally Brownfield, Squaxin Island Tribe

Front cover, first row (left to right): Breaching orca (photo by Brandon Cole); a volunteer learns about her local watershed (photo by Brian Walsh); sockeye salmon (photo by Brandon Cole); *second row (left to right):* connecting through an underwater window at the Seattle Aquarium (photo by Paul Souders); ochre sea star (photo by Brian Walsh); Steller sea lion (photo by Drew Collins); *third row (left to right):* tribal regalia at the Paddle to Nisqually celebration in 2016 (photo by Brian Walsh); sea kayaker in Skagit Bay (photo by Joel Rogers); *bottom row (left to right):* working on the Seattle Mariners T-Mobile Park (photo by Natalie Fobes); lion's mane jellyfish (photo by Drew Collins); musician Riley Mulherkar at Alki Beach in Seattle (photo by Natalie Fobes)

Back cover: Sunset near Cypress Island (photo by Brett Baunton)

Page 1: Decorated warbonnets can be found under ledges, in cracks in rocks, or inside empty barnacles. *Page 2:* A young girl waves to a scuba diver through the underwater windows at the Seattle Aquarium. *Pages 4–5:* Harbor seals are the most commonly seen marine mammals in the Salish Sea. *Last page:* Bull kelp is buoyed up in the water by air-filled bladders called pneumatocysts.

Library of Congress Cataloging-in-Publication Data record available at https://lccn.loc.gov/2019003507